The
Problem of Authority
in
America

The Problem of Authority in America

EDITED BY

John P. Diggins

AND

Mark E. Kann

Temple University Press

Philadelphia

Library of Congress Cataloging in Publication Data

Main entry under title:

The Problem of authority in America.

    Includes bibliographical references.
    Contents: Authority in America—"The three
faces of authority" / by John P. Diggins—"The
idea of the state in America" / by Sheldon Wolin—
"Consent and authority in America" / by Mark E.
Kann—[etc.[
    1. Authority—Addresses, essays, lectures.
    2. Authority—Psychological aspects—Addresses,
essays, lectures.   I. Diggins, John P.
II. Kann, Mark E.
HM271.P7   303.3′6   81-8869

    ISBN 0-87722-220-7   AACR2

To Sam and Ann Kann, Kenneth and Robert Kann,
who have taught me how to find dignity in the midst of crisis

To Gerald T. White,
Mentor, Colleague, Friend

Contributors

WILLIAM ARROWSMITH, Professor of Classics and Humanities at Johns Hopkins University, is author of *The Satyricon of Petronius, The Birds of Aristophanes,* and other works on classical literature. As a Rockefeller Fellow, he is currently engaged in a study of the Italian film director Michaelangelo Antonioni.

JESSICA BENJAMIN, a Psychotherapist and Fellow of the Institute for the Humanities, New York University, has written articles on the family and authority in such journals as *Telos, New German Critique,* and *MS.* She is presently writing a book on the psychology of domination.

JOHN PATRICK DIGGINS, Professor of History, University of California, Irvine, has written *Up from Communism, The Bard of Savagery,* and other studies in American intellectual history. His major research at present involves a book on "The Autumn of Authority: Dilemmas of Liberal Social Thought in America, 1875–1975."

RUSSELL JACOBY is a recent Guggenheim Fellow working on an intellectual biography of Otto Fenichel. He is author of *Social Amnesia* and *Dialect of Defeat: Contours of Western Marxism.*

MARK KANN teaches political theory at the University of Southern California. Author of *Thinking about Poltiics* and other studies in political theory, his current research centers on political authority and power in America.

ALFRED KAZIN, Distinguished Professor of English at the Graduate Center, City University of New York, is author of numerous studies of modern literature, as well as his own biographical memoirs, including *On Native Grounds* and *Starting Out in the Thirties.* He is presently completing a book on nineteenth- and early twentieth-century American novelists and poets.

PHILIP RIEFF, Distinguished Professor of Sociology at University of Pennsylvania, has written *The Mind of The Moralist* and *Triumph of the Thera-*

peutic: Uses of Faith after Freud. He is now working on a cultural analysis of the idea of authority in the past and present.

JOHN H. SCHAAR, Professor of Politics at the University of California, Santa Cruz, is author of *Escape from Authority, Legitimacy in the Modern State,* and other studies in modern social theory. He is presently engaged in a series of studies on authority in American political thought.

SHELDON WOLIN teaches political theory at Princeton University and is Chairman of its Program in Political Philosophy. Author of *Politics and Vision* and editor of *democracy,* he is writing a book on western political thought from classical antiquity to the present.

Contents

Acknowledgments

The essays in this book were originally presented at the Authority and the Crisis of Legitimacy Conference in Los Angeles, March 20–22, 1980. Ronald Gottesman, director of the Center for the Humanities at the University of Southern California, was the driving force behind this conference. Financial support came from the Rockefeller Foundation and from the Center for the Study of the American Experience, Annenberg School of Communications, USC. The editors would also like to thank the following conference participants who offered commentary on the papers: Judith Stiehm, Warren Bennis, David Malone, Jay Martin, Barbara Laslett, Mark Poster, Ronald Berman, Vincent Farenga, Philip Gay, Joel Colton, and Richard Lowenthal. We are especially grateful to Mark Poster for authoring the introduction to the "Psychology and Authority" section. Finally, we acknowledge a large debt of gratitude to Sharon Morris of the USC Center for the Humanities; her assistance from the planning stages of the conference to the completion of this volume has been invaluable.

The
Problem of Authority
in
America

Authority in America:
The Crisis of Legitimacy

Authority is a word on everyone's lips today. The young attack it and the old demand respect for it. Parents have lost it and policemen enforce it. Experts claim it and artists spurn it, while scholars seek it and lawyers cite it. Philosophers reconcile it with liberty and theologians demonstrate its compatibility with conscience. Bureaucrats pretend they have it and politicians wish they did. Everybody agrees that there is less of it than there used to be. It seems that the matter stands now as a certain Mr. Wildman thought it stood in 1648: "Authority hath been broken to pieces."

This passage, from John H. Schaar's "Legitimacy in the Modern State,"[1] speaks volumes on the crisis of authority that has bewildered Americans for the past decade. The longer the situation continues, the more one wonders whether the "pieces" can ever be put back together again. Is there anything in our history and culture that will help us understand the full implications of this lingering predicament? Today scholars in various disciplines are addressing themselves to the problem with a sudden sense of urgency. The situation is not a little ironic. For authority has become a central concern of intellectuals themselves, the very group that has done so much to call it into question. Indeed, one might say that the relation of intellectuals to authority is the same as the relation of coal miners to the canary in the mine shaft—it becomes important only when its voice falters and stops.

The voice of authority has faltered today, and intellectuals are more worried than usual about its periodic silence. Traditional conservatives like Robert Nisbet, once cast out of the mainstream, now warn of a "twilight of authority" without sounding reactionary. American liberals have always distrusted authority. Yet, like Samuel P. Huntington, they now wish to strengthen it by having Americans place greater trust in their leaders while making fewer demands on them. American radicals once wrote off authority as simply another aspect of bourgeois hegemony. Now left intellectuals like Christopher Lasch and Richard Sennett wonder aloud whether particular forms of authority might enhance rather than inhibit the struggle for human liberation. Even the distinguished former radical Daniel Bell, who now defines himself as a conservative in culture, a liberal in politics, and a radical in economics, sees the necessity of reconsidering authority even if it means asking intellectuals to suspend disbelief in order to return to the sacred. All agree, somehow, that the faltering of authority is a problem.

When we turn to American history to understand and to answer the problem of authority, we may understand why Lincoln felt the need to "disenthrall" himself from the past. Politically, America was born in an act of resistance to constituted authority, and since the eighteenth century, America has been pervaded by a liberal culture that conceived history as the story of liberty in flight from authority. This tendency was manifest in a Protestantism that stressed individual conscience at the expense of institutional authority, a nascent capitalism that declared the individual producer and consumer sovereign and thereby diminished the authority of public good, and an expansive environment more likely to nurture restlessness than to encourage disciplined obedience to authority. By the mid-nineteenth century, authority existed everywhere in America only because, as Tocqueville noted, it could be located nowhere save in the "tyranny" of public opinion, not in formal political ideas or institutions, but in the norms and values of mass society, in what people think others think. This socialization and democratization of authority, a theme that links together such disparate thinkers as Jefferson, Whitman, and John Dewey, was the logical outcome of a liberal ideology that had set out to inculcate the values of democracy, not those of authority, and democracy itself had as its "mission" the repudiation of the Old World and the exaltation of America as a nation uniquely free to choose its own destiny. In choosing the future over the past, the American people became, in the telling description of D. H. Lawrence, "runaways from authority." Americans were "born free," Tocqueville observed, with no conscious association to traditional European institutions of authority such as church and state. The only real authority that ought to exist in America, wrote Emerson, would be found in the ideal of individualism, the authority of the "divine" self. "Trust thyself!"

A measure of how far we have descended from the heights of nineteenth-century Emersonian optimism may be seen in the decline of trust in trust itself. Today more and more Americans are full of doubt and distrust because they have seemingly lost faith in many of the contemporary institutions that shape their lives. Hence, politicians are met with the cynicism of the citizenry, among whom are the parents who encounter the defiance of their own children, who in turn are the bored students who answer their teachers with a yawn. There seems to be a growing disbelief in the validity of older creeds and values that had buoyed previous generations of Americans. What accounts for today's doubts and fears? One possibility is the widening disillusionment following a series of shocking events that seem to have left America vulnerable: a debilitating war in Vietnam, the Watergate scandals and other revelations of national corruption, new fears about America's dependency on foreign oil and the exhaustion of our own resources, rage about the captivity of American hostages in Iran, an uncontrollable arms race, and rampant inflation. These are some of the frustrations that lead Americans to look to some source of authority for an answer to current problems. The deeper frustration may result from the absence of a political figure who can inspire a worried people, a movement or party that can organize their interests and concerns, and, above all, an idea that can penetrate to the heart of the complex problems besetting the country. In this respect the present crisis of authority derives from the ironic fact that Americans find themselves living in a country without a meaningful idea of authority. How then can there be a crisis about an idea whose time has yet to come?

The question suggests that at the heart of Schaar's illuminating passage exists a paradox. While almost all Americans claim the need for a coherent sense of authority, and while many would agree that there is less of it than there used to be, few Americans are willing to submit to authority. Nowhere is this reluctance more apparent than in the political domain, where the authority of the office of the president of the United States, as a symbol of leadership and trust, has deteriorated to its lowest level in more than half a century. To overcome the alienation of the people from their government, President Carter organized a Camp David "summit" in the summer of 1978. There he called together some of the country's leading academic intellectuals to help the White House staff explore the reasons for the "national malaise." Carter's aides also read their works, which included *The Cultural Contradictions of Capitalism,* by Daniel Bell of Harvard University, *Human Conditions for a Good Society,* by Robert A. Bellah of the University of California, Berkeley, and *The Culture of Narcissism,* by Christopher Lasch of the University of Rochester. They also studied Tocqueville's *Democracy in America,* that great classic that, balancing aristocratic prejudices against democratic passions, attempts to explain why America lacks the established old-world institutions—church, crown, nobility, and the like—necessary to perpetuate the traditional values of authority. It is not without significance that those invited to Camp David have themselves been wrestling with the problem of authority in the modern age: Bell has explored the fate of the Protestant ethic in view of the precarious legitimacy of industrial society; Bellah has been trying to establish the basis for "civil religion" in America; and Lasch has alerted the public to the implications of the loss of patriarchal authority for the future of the family.

The Camp David meeting may seem as unique as it is curious, yet it has many antecedents. It was hardly the first time in Western intellectual history that a ruler, whether prince or president, turned to the intellectual community for advice involving not so much the formulation of policy as the legitimation of authority. For authority, among other things, is an intellectual issue that asks the intellectual not only to describe behavior but to prescribe the reasons for right conduct: ought we to obey, and on what grounds does society or the state command our allegiance?

"Obedience?" The very word stinks in the nostrils of many an American writer. "Resist much, obey little"—Whitman. Yet the problem of authority as the problem of obedience has been approached from a variety of perspectives by past and present thinkers. Plato saw obedience to authority as willful submission informed by the wisdom in both the mind and the polis; St. Augustine saw it as faith inspired by hope; Hobbes as fear trembling with doubt; Rousseau as liberty prescribed by the will of all expressed by the assembled people; Locke as prudence determined by property and the life-preserving interests of the majority; Burke as tradition governed by the habit of settled beliefs; Freud as need driven by anxiety; Marx as labor alienated from value; Tocqueville as loneliness in flight from solitude; Lincoln as duty guided by the covenant of nationhood; Melville as tragedy necessitated by the reconciliation of discipline and democracy; Henry Adams as belief liberated from doubt; Walter Lippmann as knowledge liberated from desire; and Hannah Arendt as action founded on memory, the very seat of authority. This list is extended over the centuries to indicate not only that authority is a constant preoccupation of the intellectual but that it could not exist without the intellectual. For authority, unlike power, requires justification; and in the course of history it is the intellectual who fulfills this crucial role, either by rejecting the world of power, as did Rousseau and Marx, or by defending it, as did Burke and Hobbes, or by balancing power with authority, as did Locke and Lippmann. Today it remains no less true that the theoretical intellect may legitimate the power of any given political and social order by turning it into authority by the use of reason, and what the intellect has made it may also destroy. Authority, then, represents the intellectual expression of power, and the problem of authority remains the problem of the men and women of ideas, of those who find the reasons for granting or denying legitimacy to the existing state, society, and culture.

A number of problems confront anyone who attempts to face squarely the issue of authority. We must try, for example, to become defenders of authority without becoming apologists for power, and we must do so in full knowledge of an insight that Machiavelli discovered in politics and Hegel incorporated into philosophy and history—that truth resides in power. We must also distinguish between the ways in which authority loses its legitima-

cy, perhaps the task of the historian, and the proposals by which it ı
regained, perhaps the challenge of the moral philosopher. We m
addition, acknowledge the tensions and ironies in the problem and fɛ
possibility that authority may not be entirely compatible with liberty and
democracy or with science and skepticism. There is also the matter of
disciplines. Is authority a philosophical problem requiring a theory of
obligation, or an empirical question based upon a behavioral understanding
of the causes for domination and submission? Insofar as this anthology
draws upon the disciplines of history, political theory, literature, and
psychology, one may well wonder which discipline can provide the best
knowledge not only for penetrating the problems of authority but for offering solutions to them. Finally, insofar as the contributors to the anthology
are all scholars and intellectuals, we need to consider their relation to the
audience they feel compelled to teach and enlighten. While intellectuals ask
that authority have its reasons so that obedience to it allows man to live by
principles rather than surrender to power, the people may very well be
content to live by the gut conviction that power is all and that therefore
authority, any authority, deserves automatic respect. Do the people know
intuitively something that the intellectual must face: that authority cannot
stand the examination of reason? Or do intellectuals know something that
we must all face: that any authority that cannot explain and justify itself
remains nothing more than power without meaning?

This anthology is divided into three sections. Part One, "Politics and Authority," deals with the various expressions of authority in America as reflected in the writings of early theologians and political thinkers and also
with the more recent issue of authority as it pertains to the idea of the state
and to the politics of social control. Part Two, "Literature and Authority,"
explores the meanings of authority in the writings of the novelist William
Faulkner and of the poets Ezra Pound and T. S. Eliot. Part Three, "Psychology and Authority," addresses itself to the alleged decline of the family and
to the theoretical implications for authority in Freudian psychology, modern
anthropology, and classical literature.

It should be noted that authority has always been a problem in American
history primarily because the founding fathers were deeply ambivalent about
the location of sovereignty in the federal constitution. The very word
"sovereignty," the fount from which all legitimate power flows, was located
neither in the state nor in the people. Indeed, it would not be inaccurate to
say, as it had been said by both the eighteenth-century Antifederalist John
Taylor and the twentieth-century political philosopher Hannah Arendt, that
the principle of sovereignty was abolished in the Constitution on the grounds
that "sovereign power was destructive" of the rights of self-government.[2]
This meant that America never really had a concept of the state as a corpo-

rate entity that embraced more than the sum of its part. In the nineteenth century, writers like Emerson could applaud this political vacuum because of their conviction that with the appearance of men of wise and true character "the state expires." Yet those interested in the question of authority, statesmen like Daniel Webster, Rufus Choate, and Abraham Lincoln, believed that America could not survive unless the people possessed a spirit of reverence toward their political institutions. It was one of their noblest duties, Senator Choate told a group of young lawyers in 1845, to "keep the true idea of the State alive and germinant in the American mind." Although such a task would serve "to keep alive the sacred sentiments of obedience and reverence and justice," Choate realized, as do the contributors to Part One, that the idea of the state had no precise meaning in America:

> Its boundary lines, its constituent numbers, its physical, social, and constitutional identity, its polity, its law, its continuance for ages, its dissolution, all these seem to be held in the nature of so many open questions . . . it might also seem to be growing to be our national humor to hold ourselves free at every instant, to be and do just what we please, go where we please, stay as long as we please and no longer; and that the State itself were held to be no more than an encampment of tents on the great prairies, pitched at sun-down, and struck to the sharp crack of the rifle the next morning.[3]

If America lacked a clear idea of the state that would instill respect for the authority of politics, so too did it lack the depth of a meaningful culture that would instill respect for the authority of art and knowledge. Such was the conclusion arrived at by many American writers, especially three of the "lost generation" who are examined in Part Two. The fame of Faulkner, Pound, and Eliot rests upon an alienation from the very established order that they sought to probe, or perhaps more accurately, a disorder and chaos where the moral idea of authority is implied by its very absence. While Pound made the mistake of confusing power with authority, translating the idea of an action into the action of an idea, Faulkner and Eliot, each in his own way, tried to uphold specific values that would invest power with the meaning that makes the inevitability of unequal human relations just and rightful.

No less than literary intellectuals and political theorists do psychologists, intellectual historians, and cultural critics take seriously the question of authority, especially as it pertains to the character structure and moral fiber of a nation. This is the concern of the contributors to Part Three. While they take their point of departure from Freud's writings, the contributors offer differing approaches to the family as the basis of socialization and the transmission of values. Is there really a crisis in the family as the basic unit of society; and, if so, does the revolt against traditional patriarchal authority—an authority once rooted in the oedipal instinct—suggest a revolt against authority in general or a revolt against the lack of a genuine authority, against the lack of credible parental moral standards that reveals a deeper longing for authority?

Three themes seem to run through the following essays: the American government lacks the authority to lead; American culture lacks a consensus on the values that would give coherence to the social order; and the American family, one of the last bastions of authority, is in danger of giving way to relationships seemingly more instrumental than affective. Ultimately, all the authors are concerned about values, about moral qualities that elevate human conduct. Values are essential not only to the solution of society's problems but also to the solution of authority itself. For it is only out of a sense of values that people are ready to accept sacrifices, and no society can endure if at least some of its people are not willing to undertake sacrifices for it. Whether or not such values must partake of the "sacred," values enable people to submit themselves to authority. What then might these values be?

Notes

1. John H. Schaar, "Legitimacy in the Modern State," in *Power and Community: Dissenting Essays in Political Science,* ed. Philip Green and Sanford Levinson (New York, 1970), p. 276.

2. John Taylor, *Constitution Construed and Constitutions Vindicated* (Richmond, 1820), p. 37; Hannah Arendt, *On Revolution* (New York, 1963), pp. 139–215.

3. Rufus Choate, "The Position and Functions of the American Bar, An Element of Conservatism in the State: Address Delivered Before the Law School in Cambridge, July 3, 1845," quoted in Jean V. Matthews, *Rufus Choate: The Law and Civic Virtue* (Philadelphia, 1980), p. 87.

PART ONE

Politics and Authority

The state of political authority in America directly influences authority relations in culture and society. When most Americans consider the political system to be legitimate, political stability and public quiescence prevail. Citizens may disagree with some or even many political decisions but will recognize them as binding and deserving of compliance if they recognize the government's right to issue them. We may grumble about our taxes, but we generally pay them. In this atmosphere, political authorities can invest their own legitimacy in the cultural norms and social institutions at the foundation of politics and cue the American people to be thankful for them. Skepticism of political authority, however, has the opposite effect. When Americans distrust their government and question the right of political officials to make binding decisions, they simultaneously raise a more general question about authority: Does any "authority" exist that obligates individuals to voluntarily obey it? If we question the president's authority, for example, should we not also question the authority of religious leaders, corporate executives, experts and intellectuals, teachers, and even parents?

And when we begin to question cultural and social authority, our skepticism will usually spill back into the political arena. Americans who accept the received truths of the past and the social institutions of the present are not apt to make especially controversial claims on government. They may ask for a little more or a little less of what government already provides, or they may compose a "silent majority" that tacitly consents to the political system. However, Americans who question their parents' values and the conventional social roles around them may seek new sources of authority, thereby generating tremendous conflict. Catholic parents who believe abortion is tantamount to murder may beget an agnostic daughter who believes that abortion is an acceptable option for women, who have the right to control their own bodies; a hierarchically organized college may find itself with a student body believing that it has a right to determine its own curriculum. In many instances, such conflicts surface in the political arena, and the government is expected to resolve them. If the government cannot satisfy both parties, tries to compromise and satisfies neither party, or refuses to deal with the issue, the government itself is likely to become an object of public distrust.

Have we entered "the twilight of authority," as sociologist Robert Nisbet calls it,[1] in which we cannot agree about the basis or nature of political authority? American conservatives believe that the government has too much authority; liberals hope to strike a new balance between political authority and individual rights; radicals wish the government had enough authority to contain corporate domination but not enough authority to inhibit participatory democracy. Political scientist Theodore Lowi suggests that American political leaders no longer wield authority "with the resoluteness of men certain of the legitimacy of their positions,"[2] and public opinion polls indicate that many Americans no longer believe that those positions have much legitimacy. Few Americans take for granted the authority of the political system while many Americans feel compelled to justify or criticize it; and most Americans cannot agree on a reasoned basis for it.

How might we explain this current "crisis" of political authority? The three essays in Part One agree on the significance of two factors. First, the question of political authority involves the role of intellectuals in political life. Political power requires no justification; it is mainly a matter of the resources a government can garner to enforce its will. Political authority, however, is power justified by the values and reasons that command citizens' voluntary compliance. As John Diggins suggests in the introductory essay, intellectuals are the protagonists who promote the values and reasons that mediate political authority and citizen consent. Sheldon Wolin considers the significance both of the Founders' "new science of politics" and of modern political scientists' complicity in justifying the American political system. Mark Kann focuses on the ways in which political officials claim to represent the values and expertise that will win public support for their policies. Each author in Part One sees the labor of intellectuals as a crucial factor affecting people's perceptions of the political system's legitimacy.

Second, these authors agree that Americans' current distrust of authority is not particularly new; any understanding of political authority requires a historic' perspective comprehensive enough to include the founding of the nation. In the decade before 1776, Americans engaged in a major debate over the authority of the corrupted British Constitution. Between the signing of the Declaration of Independence and the framing of the U.S. Constitution, Americans questioned and sometimes contested the authority of individual states, constitutions, governors, and legislatures. Tremendous intellectual ferment was accompanied by moblike electioneering and radical pamphleteering, extralegal conventions and illegal conventions, popular demands for "actual" rather than "virtual" representation, and occasional rebellions. The "people out-of-doors," according to historian Gordon Wood,[3] used words and actions to challenge attempts to reconstitute political authority. Fearful that the democratic impulse would bring on anarchy, scholar-politicians like John Adams, James Madison, and Alexander Hamilton helped to found a single, federal government though they continued to debate the appropriate basis for political authority. Their historical debates set the framework for discussing authority that modern Americans would inherit.

The ironies involved in "inventing America," to use journalist Garry Wills's phrase,[4] lend themselves to numerous interpretations. While Diggins, Wolin, and Kann agree on the significance of the early architects, each author attributes a different meaning to the Founders' blueprints for political authority. Diggins argues that the Founders' debates occupy the center position in the "three faces of authority" in American intellectual history. The Puritans based authority on abstract spiritual values; the Founders deprived the political system of authority, for they feared that particular factions might harness that authority to the detriment of liberty; and soon thereafter, the vacuum in political authority was filled by the diffuse, but democratic, authority of society as a whole. Today, political authority is primarily vested in an American society lacking the spiritual or governmental guidance that might help it solve its mounting problems.

No one face of authority has won an abiding or dominant place in America. Instead, Diggins suggests, Americans are bound together by a fragile agreement on individualism that is continually tested by their value differences, or as political theorist Wilson Carey McWilliams indicates, "There may be an American creed, but it is a compendium of convictions hardly consistent with one another."[5] Disagreement has its price. Diggins recalls John Adams's fear that the absence of common values inhibits the development of authoritative leadership and Tocqueville's warning that society's authority may become manifest in an "omnipotent majority" that destroys everything in its pathway. Diggins concludes that political authority today is a function of the shifting tides of public opinion; American government in itself has no authority.

For Sheldon Wolin, the evolution of the "idea of the state in America" suggests that the absence of political authority results not in the democratic omnipotence of public opinion but in the public's undemocratic dependence. Wolin views the Founders as the first modern liberals to design an antidemocratic political system. Fearful of majority rule, they diffused political authority by instituting a mechanistic set of checks and balances. They then provided a steady stream of legitimacy for this system by adapting John Locke's "thin theory of legitimacy": people consent to government through periodic elections but are distanced from it by having no systematic means of effective participation in political discourse, decision-making, or administration. The result was a political system powerful enough to protect private property but one without the authority or democratic means to challenge propertied interests. In short, the absence of political authority in America insulates social elites from public accountability.

Wolin's mapping of liberal ideas of political authority routes him through Madisonianism and pluralism to the 1930s, when the thin theory of legitimacy was absorbed into the welfare state. It was then that American government developed into a vast bureaucratic beast that complemented the private sector of the economy. Since then, Wolin argues, the true crisis of American politics has not been one of authority per se but of people's lack of autonomy. Americans have become "social infantrymen," a surplus population managed by bureaucratic elites, suffering major casualties in the name of their own welfare and reaping few tangible benefits. Whereas Diggins ultimately locates political authority in society as a whole, Wolin suggests that elites are America's current sovereigns and the American people are their subjects.

Have Americans been accomplices in their own subordination to elites? Mark Kann's essay on "consent and authority in America" suggests that Americans have consistently consented to the authority of political elites, but the price of their consent has become more dear and its benefits to elites less clear. In early America, consent was based on a shared view of natural law limits on government and was manifested in general acquiescence to governmental authority. While the Founders accepted this tradition, they also introduced two new elements. First, they added a utilitarian element that suggested that government may have some responsibility in assuring general prosperity; second, they introduced the notion that consent, rather than simple acquiescence, might be manifest in voting. In the nineteenth century, the utilitarian element grew stronger, and government expanded to play a more active part in American social life; numerous social groups demanded and won fuller voting rights and more extensive forms of participation as manifestations of their consent. By our time, Kann suggests, government has become extremely centralized and powerful to meet the mixed demands of Americans, but its authority is imperiled by a people unhappy with governmental services and with its own inability to control political power through more direct forms of participation. As a result, American government is more powerful but less authoritative than ever.

Like Diggins, Kann believes that political authority is contingent on the consent of American society; like Wolin, he believes that bureaucratic government is accessible to propertied elites but generally inaccessible to most Americans. But Kann argues that the consequence is neither social authority nor social dependence. On the one hand, Americans do continue to consent to the authority of their governors. On the other hand, they do not invest their consent with moral meaning; consent has become an expedient measure that signifies public compliance but not moral obligation to political elites. Americans are accomplices in their subordination to elites, but their complicity is limited by their own understanding of it.

Taken together, the three essays in Part One suggest that political authority in America is a problem today because its relative absence limits Americans' ability to solve basic dilemmas, renders them dependent on forces seemingly beyond their control, and signifies the ineffectiveness of their political voices. The essays also raise a number of questions essential to any treatment of authority: To what extent does political authority rest on cultural truths and social norms? What costs are involved in the absence of political authority? How is political authority related to social institutions like the family, the schools, or private property? Diggins, Wolin, and Kann touch on all of these questions; Parts Two and Three directly focus on them.

Notes

1. Robert Nisbet, *The Twilight of Authority* (New York: Oxford University Press, 1975), esp. pp. v–vii.

2. Theodore J. Lowi, *The End of Liberalism* (New York: Norton, 1969), p. 288.

3. Gordon S. Wood, *The Creation of the American Republic, 1776–1787* (New York: Norton, 1969), pp. 319–328.

4. Garry Wills, *Inventing America* (New York: Vintage, 1979), esp. pp. xiii–xxvi.

5. Wilson Carey McWilliams, *The Idea of Fraternity in America* (Berkeley: University of California Press, 1973), p. 107.

1

The Three Faces of Authority in American History

John P. Diggins

(*conclusion*)

When thinking about authority one is also thinking about power, and thinking about each phenomenon is precisely that—an act of thinking, meditating, reflecting, that is to say, a mental exercise, something that keeps the intellectual off the streets if not out of trouble. *and as*

What is the relationship between authority and power, and why is the intellectual so crucial to that relationship? I should like to begin this essay by suggesting one possible way of looking at the relationship of all three phenomena and then by discussing in more detail three ways in which past thinkers in American history have approached the problem of authority. No doubt the following definitions may be disputed, for the obvious is not so easy to define. But perhaps these opening remarks will help us begin thinking about authority as a multidimensional problem involving more than one historical perspective. *declare as*

At its most fundamental level, power is the exercise of force to produce desired effects, and authority is what power becomes when it is voluntarily accepted by those who experience it.[1] Authority is rightful power, power justified by reason. Crudely put, one might say that power depends on coercion, authority on consent. How power comes to be accepted or rejected is the process by which it is legitimated or deauthorized, and this role is most frequently assumed by the intellectual, who speaks truth to power to see if power can answer with reason rather than with force. This process, we should remember, takes place not only behind "the iron curtain." Even in the open society the legitimacy of the state is challenged, indeed, because it can be without reprisal. Thus, in the early twentieth century, the historian Charles Beard challenged the legitimacy of both the Constitution and the Supreme Court, depicting them as undemocratic institutions conceived and ratified without the popular consent of the people, while the political philosopher Walter Lippmann attempted to demonstrate why the contemporary American citizen lacked the knowledge and rationality to render such consent. Whether the intellectual questions the right of the government to rule or the ability of the citizen to be ruled, it is the intellectual who mediates between the state and its subjects, or more prosaically, the president and his people. We were not surprised when President Carter called to his Camp David "summit" some of the leading academic intellectuals to help the country resolve the "national malaise" that came to be called "the crisis of authority." Some intellectuals were now being asked to help restore confidence in a culture and "system" to which other intellectuals, or perhaps even the same intellectuals earlier in their careers, had denied legitimacy. To try to restore legitimacy to a particular institution or social order is not in itself a necessarily illegitimate enterprise for the intellectual, the alleged "treason" of mind in the service of power. But how can it be done?

In a symposium on "Religion and the Intellectuals" that appeared in the *Partisan Review* in 1950, most American writers—James Agee being the emphatic exception—answered no to the question: "Assuming that in the past religions nourished certain vital human values, can these values now be maintained without a widespread belief in the supernatural?" The trouble with the formulation of the problem, as Hannah Arendt pointed out, is that "one cannot really escape the question of truth and therefore cannot treat the whole matter as though God had been the notion of some especially clever pragmatist who knew what it is good for." The suggestion that religion ought to be organized as "an institution only because one likes to have a culture" struck Arendt as absurd, indeed as "rather funny."[2]

The suggestion that is currently being made by some social scientists that authority be "respected," that it be trusted and obeyed, is also not a little absurd. To refrain from questioning what one is being asked to believe or do would certainly make the acceptance of authority an easier proposition on the part of those who are being asked to accept it. And no doubt those who exercise authority would be relieved of offering reasons why they should be obeyed. The idea that authority does not require the elaboration of its reasons, that it does therefore allow us to "escape the question of truth," may be tempting to those who desire to study the patterns of behavior as opposed to the discourses of mind, and perhaps this is why social scientists favor such a functionalist approach. But this approach seems itself to function only to the extent that society remains stable and the intellectual silent, which is to say that the approach resolves the problem of authority by denying its existence. Yet the problem will not go away precisely because unexamined authority will be unable not only to command the reflective mind but to defend itself when that mind becomes critical of existing systems of power and social relations. As Philip Rieff has warned, "Authority untaught is the condition in which a culture commits suicide."[3]

Granted the claim that authority deserves automatic respect is a dangerous illusion, how is authority taught? Let us examine how this question was addressed during three different episodes in American intellectual history.

The Idea of Spiritual Authority

Among the many rich legacies of New England Puritanism was its profound sense of authority, a spiritual heritage from which America's political culture chose to become disinherited. When we examine two of the central documents of American Puritanism, John Winthrop's "A Model of Christian Charity" (1630) and his "Speech to the General Court" (1645), we are immediately struck by two considerations: that for the Puritans authority was essentially spiritual in nature, based on divine revelation comprehensible to human reason, and that it was inextricably bound up with a deep sense of community. These documents provide perhaps the first statement in American thought on authority based on transcendent religious imperatives. Winthrop's rhetoric is suffused with the imagery of binding, tying, knitting. The power of love and grace will enable man to realize "the two rules whereby we are able to walke towards another: Justice and Mercy." God has structured a hierarchical social order, "some highe and eminent in power and dignities; others meane and in subjeccion," so that "every man might have need of others, and from hence they might all be knitt more nearly together in the Bond of brotherly affeccion." To call upon imperfect man to perfect society is to ask the impossible, and thus Winthrop's social philosophy must begin and end with the sense of duty and the force of obligation. Justice and mercy are "rules" to be obeyed; the "laws" of nature and of grace must be followed; the Gospel "commands" us to love our neighbors and even our enemies. These moral prescriptions are necessary because man is in his "natural state" only capable of a kind of freedom that is "common with beast and other creatures." True "civil liberty" is thus experienced when persons willfully enter the moral covenant between God and man and the political covenant among men themselves. This liberty, which enables regenerate men to do "that only which is good, just, and honest," is the purpose of true government and the "proper end and object of authority."[4]

Although the Puritan notion of authority involved the renunciation of "natural" liberty, and although it expressed itself in terms of commands, Winthrop nonetheless is spiritualizing the concept of both authority and liberty, for he is appealing to men's minds, not their bodies, to ideas rather than to interests, and he is hopeful that men could be brought to assent not by coercion but by conviction. Rather than curtailing liberty, Winthrop is offering men the ability to choose, and to be able to choose is to consider reasons for or against a given proposal. Only a system of authority based on voluntary submission could make possible the post-Calvinist synthesis of freedom and necessity. In this respect Winthrop can be seen as trying to curb the need for the advent of temporal or political authority, which usually enters social consciousness as an external compulsion when the individual senses the discrepancy between what he desires and what society permits.

By appealing to man's informed spiritual conscience, Winthrop could treat authority not only as a form of necessity that conferred dignity on the person who accepted it but as a form of freedom that liberates man from his natural condition. The whole foundation of Puritan political theory rested on theological convictions, on beliefs that must not be challenged. Yet the beauty of moral persuasiveness in the Puritan concept of authority is such that it not only elevates authority to the status of a normative ideal but convinces us that authority is possible only within a community. The cohesion of community is achieved by moral obligations that impel man to transcend his selfish nature, and thus the locus of authority is spiritual in that it is not made by man but lies in a source beyond and above man himself.

If the genesis of authority is ultimately God's will and is realized only in an intimate community of shared values, what happens to authority when God disappears as an agency and moral community collapses as a reality? This was the question that the Founding Fathers had to face.

The Authority of Political Institutions

When Jefferson declared that "all authority belongs to the people,"[5] he was reiterating the Lockean precepts that pervaded America's political culture in the eighteenth century. Yet as the framers of the Constitution realized, to state the problem in these terms is by no means to resolve it. If authority "belongs" to everyone in general, it belongs to no one in particular, and neither the state nor the citizen can exclusively claim that which by definition must be shared. Perhaps we should not look to the philosopher of freedom for answers to the riddle of authority. Indeed, Jefferson desired what Winthrop dreaded: the spacious American environment would make men less dependent upon one another. Embodying ultimate authority in the will of the people was a bold and radical act on Jefferson's part, for henceforth the masses themselves could not alienate what was theirs by right of nature. But in democratizing the problem of authority Jefferson succeeded only in unburdening himself of it.

The framers agreed with Jefferson that human society could not be held together through a common acceptance of a theory or a principle. Considerably less confident in the people themselves, however, the framers were even more convinced that power could not be restrained by beliefs, the traditional domain of moral sentiment. To Madison the need for government reflected man's fallen state, and in that crippled condition man would be incapable of responding to ideas that appealed to reason or conscience. John Adams agreed. "I have been long settled in my opinion," Adams wrote Jefferson, "that neither Philosophy, nor Religion, nor Morality, nor Wisdom, nor Intellect, will ever govern nations or parties, against their Vanity, Pride, Resentment or Revenge, or their Avarice or Ambition. Nothing but

Force and Power and Strength can restrain them." Convinced that morality and religion could no longer supply the basis for authority, Adams concluded that "power must be opposed to power, force to force, strength to strength, interest to interest, as well as reason to reason, eloquence to eloquence, and passion to passion."[6] The framer's solution to human imperfectibility and social divisiveness ("factions") was to substitute external controls for inner compulsions in order to disperse power through the institutional means of "checks and balances," what Arthur O. Lovejoy has aptly called "the method of counterpoise."[7]

Did this method resolve the problem of authority? Some political scientists have argued that the framing of the Constitution itself indicated the Founders realized the need for establishing a more centralized authority, and subsequently respect for authority developed out of obedience to the laws of the new nation.[8] Sociologists have also maintained that the early republic's success in economic development, in the evolution of political parties, and in the forging of national unity provided the means by which the American system of government was "legitimized," a process aided by the role of President Washington as a "charismatic leader" and authority figure.[9] Such interpretations suggest too much social science—always a bad sign. As advocates of the "new science of politics," the authors of *The Federalist* saw their role as providing the theories that would stabilize the vicissitudes of power without having to establish the virtues of authority. The Founders demonstrated by their very vocabulary that they were less interested in the promises of good authority than in the perils of bad institutions, less concerned about the metaphysics of obligation than the "machinery of government" and the "geometry" of power. At best, the framers aimed at establishing what Max Weber would call "rational-legal authority," popular acceptance of systems of rules and submission to those in power on the basis of an "impersonal bond," not to leaders and their ideals, but to the functional "duty of office."[10] The framers succeeded brilliantly in the new enterprise of institutionalizing authority in the agencies of government. But I think it would not be too inaccurate—or unfair—to suggest that the framers were more concerned about controlling power than explaining authority. Their whole enterprise rested on the assumption that the only ideas or institutions that men will obey are those that express their interests. Insofar as the idea of "interests" presupposes the wants that exist within men's desires, the framers asked of men only that they know their interests and obey them. Thus the Preamble to the Constitution enumerates the purposes of the new government; namely, "to establish justice, insure domestic tranquility, provide for the common defense, promote the general welfare, and secure the blessings of liberty to ourselves and our posterity." These goals would evolve from the citizens' rendering compliance to the Constitution, and the framers did not need to explain why citizens ought to strive to seek such goals since they were inherent within the nature of man. Hence the dilemma: if citizens have no duty to obey a government that reflects their nature, how can authority be taught?

Not, it seems in *The Federalist*, through political means. When comparing that document to Winthrop's sermons, we miss the Christian language of love and affection. Government was not to be an agency of moral education; on the contrary, the framers avoided considering the problem of how to train a public to accept the authority of the good, true, or beautiful. Subjection to the a priori realities of the good, just, and honest, the antecedent verities that are supposedly self-justifying by virtue of their moral essence and spiritual persuasion, is no longer the proper end of government. Unwilling to rest authority upon positive conceptions of duty and the ethical life, or even upon the "sacred" and "undeniable" truths that are "self-evident" in the Declaration of Independence, the framers drew back from defining and asserting ideal aims that have as their purpose the attempt to shape and direct society in accordance with "higher" ends. Accepting man as he is, they defined politics as little more than the pursuit of private interests, and they hoped that social order would emerge from the countervailing balance of these interests not because of the presence of virtuous leaders or obligatory norms but because of the smooth functioning of impersonal devices and mechanical contrivances. In this system, which depended more upon the perpetuation of good machinery than upon the reappearance of good men and ideas, where did authority ultimately lie? Who would teach the self-governed how to govern themselves?

The term "authority" derives, in its original Latin meaning, from the word *auctoritas* and the verb *augere,* to "augment," and hence it implies, among other things, the capacity of a power to enlarge itself, grow, expand, initiate action, inspire belief, command allegiance, and authorize the rightness of things. It is that capacity that *The Federalist* denies to the people. The framers believed that authority, although deriving from the people, could not be expressed directly through them because the masses of citizens were not only incapable of safeguarding their own liberties but were too divided to bring forth the general good and to engage in the necessary unity of common action that could exercise sovereign authority in one body. Thus Madison openly advocated a "republican principle" of government wherein members of the majority must be made incapable of acting together effectively. Hamilton's solution was to invest "the majesty of national authority" in the independent judiciary, which would mediate between the people and their representatives by assuming the function of interpreting law. Thus, while the framers were reluctant to endow the legislative branch with authority, Hamilton sought to grant it to the Supreme Court primarily because it had, in his words, "neither Force nor Will" and was therefore the "weakest" of the three departments of government.[11] Through this ingenious arrangement the framers managed to separate power from authority, popular will from judicial wisdom, but they also restricted authority to the role of judging law rather than making it. Authority could now speak but it could not act or "augment"; it could passively review matters pertaining to the letter of the Constitution but it could not, theoretically at least, shape the values and customs of the nation by defining the good life, the just state, and the moral society. Political authority had lost its power to authorize.

The Socialization of Authority

One writer who would see clearly that authority in America could no longer be found in political institutions was, of course, Alexis de Tocqueville. "In no country in the world are the pronouncements of the law more categorical than in America," Tocqueville noted in *Democracy in America,* "and in no other country is the right to enforce it divided among so many hands." Americans are scarcely conscious of their government because it lacks effective, centralized power. In America "authority exists, but one does not know where to find its representative."[12] Authority could not be found in the old-world institutions that never sunk roots in the New World: crown, aristocracy, established church, centralized state. Where, then, could the source of authority be located in democratic America? For Tocqueville the answer lay in the coercive power of public opinion and the brooding presence of the majority—quiet, invisible forms of "tyranny" that led to one of the deepest ironies in American life: the illusion of individual freedom and the reality of social repression. In America authority became little more than what people thought that other people thought. It was seated in opinion, not knowledge.

Tocqueville's conviction that the nature of society explains the nature of the state gave America an extrapolitical focus where the issue of authority no longer revolves around the forms of government. Tocqueville's genius lies in providing America with a discourse on society almost completely emancipated from the traditional categories of political philosophy. "What is meant by a 'republic' in the United States is the slow and quiet action of society upon itself."[13] But what Tocqueville perceived—that the leveling processes of democracy could lead to despotism and that "individualism" weakened a social order that could never be greater than the sum of its parts—proved too alien for most contemporary Americans to grasp. We shall later return to a closer look at Tocqueville's analysis of the problem of authority in America. First—the fate of *Democracy in America* in nineteenth-century America.[14]

That Tocqueville's analysis should receive so little approval in America should not surprise us, for the French theorist was writing against three tendencies in American life that made authority a thing of the past: a Protestant culture that stressed the preeminence of individual conscience over institutional or doctrinal authority; a capitalist economy that placed at the center of social life the sovereignty of the individual producer and consumer and juxtaposed the claims of private interests to the authority of the public good; and a spacious natural environment that could scarcely encourage discipline, order, and other normative values that might nurture a restless people into accepting the constraints of authority. The Transcendentalists, it might be noted, were also struggling against these tendencies, for the structural traits of democratic society could be as threatening to freedom as to authority. Consider Thoreau and Tocqueville, an unlikely pair, to be sure. Although the one might have pondered the meaning of the Ganges and the other the Bastille, both could agree that in America society had become everything and the individual nothing. In the writings of both critics, society took on the character of a reified force that not only stood over and above the individual but possessed the power to transform human character. And the more free the individual felt himself to be, the more isolated and lonely he actually became until he craved to forsake his solitude in order to surrender his self to the new invisible authority of society itself. Thus as authority drifted from the once-conscious individual to the collective stupor of mass society, the whole idea of natural rights, the assumption of individual autonomy and freedom characteristic of eighteenth-century thought, was collapsing in the face of nineteenth-century social realities. "The idea of rights inherent in certain individuals is rapidly disappearing from the minds of men," wrote Tocqueville. "The idea of the omnipotence and sole authority of society at large rises to fill its place." Thoreau summed up in four words what Tocqueville described in two volumes: "Society paws at me."[15]

When one compares the fears and complaints of Tocqueville and Thoreau to the convictions of modern sociologists, we find ourselves in two different worlds. The sociologist sees the principles of order and integration in the very forces that the poet finds menacing. The real "socialization of authority" took place in the late nineteenth century, and in America it is possible to trace its origins and development to two sources: the rise of sociology as a discipline of study and the rise of pragmatism as a philosophy of knowledge.

Sociology did much to reorient traditional thinking about the nature of the social order, for it could now be asserted that society should be understood in its own terms, not necessarily by the impressions of those who participate in it, but perhaps by the more profound causes that remain unperceived by its members. Consciousness could then be explained by social life rather than life being explained by the conscious individual, and the causal explanation of human behavior could be found in social forces external to the individual. Similarly, pragmatic philosophers denied the primacy of the individual ego and thereby challenged the notion that the self is a Cartesian presupposition of consciousness. From this new perspective, man could no longer postulate an original individual consciousness, society could no longer be seen simply as the object of mind's contemplation, and the "majesty of authority" could no longer claim the capacity to compel the mind. Indeed, in the writings of most pragmatists authority ceased to be a subject worthy of philosophical consideration. Charles S. Peirce likened "the method of authority" to the doctrines of medieval Catholicism.[16] John Dewey also believed that authority was synonymous with the Christian and Greek notion of universal and antecedent truth, and thus the search for authority in immutable ideas amounted to a false and almost childish quest for certainty and security.[17] In pragmatic philosophy, and in much of modern philosophy in general, the concept of authority was transformed in much the same way as the concept of truth itself. Neither truth nor authority could any longer be considered as something given to or disclosed to consciousness; instead, they were produced by the human mind, and the mind itself is a product of social interaction.

The sociological implications of this new epistemology were carried out in the work of Charles Cooley and especially George Herbert Mead. Elsewhere I have commented on their work in relation to the problem of authority and have tried to relate it to the "structural functionalism" of Talcott Parsons.[18] Although Parsons hails from a different generation and draws upon European thinkers, the writings of the functionalist as well as the interactionist have the same effect of externalizing authority by presupposing the social nature of consciousness. Indeed, Cooley, Mead, and Parsons all came from devout religious backgrounds, and it may be no coincidence that they tend to invest society itself with redemptive spiritual significance. Having found their "calling" in their chosen academic discipline, all three could find the answer to an earlier crisis of religious authority in the very operations of society that give meaning and value to life. Investing all meaning and value in society, society itself becomes reified since it is now seen as a structure of roles, not of people being "pawed" at by forces alien to their nature, and authority inheres in the functional relation of positions, not in the individual or in institutions or principles that transcend the individual or in any particular source that can be distinguished from the undifferentiated whole. Authority, then, has no content and meaning superior or anterior to society, and it cannot command the self because the self belongs to "others."

Mésalliance: Authority and the Intellectuals

Can intellectual history shed some light on the present concern with authority that occupies statesmen and social philosophers today? How would authority be taught on the basis of the three perspectives discussed above? If we approach authority as involving an ethic of obligation, the grounds on which we should comply with an institution or give allegiance to an idea or person, we are offered three options. The Puritans asked man to obey God's will, however inscrutable it would be to fathom; the Founding Fathers expected man to obey his own pursuits, the irrational "passions" and "interests" that could be rationally controlled by political means; and modern sociologists predicted that man would continue to obey the "generalized other," the roles and functions that man assumes as an agent who acts in response to the actions of those around himself. Perhaps the most curious feature of these three types of authority is that none has won an enduring place in American thought and culture.

The Puritan concept of authority not only failed to survive the rebellion of its own children but continued to suffer a bad name at the hands of the debunkers of the early twentieth century. For all the brilliant efforts of Kenneth Murdock and Perry Miller, they could not put back together what Van Wyck Brooks and Vernon L. Parrington had torn asunder. As Puritanism became identified with authoritarianism, authority as a challenging moral proposition, the ethic of "inwardness" and the imperative of the "good, just, and honest," all but disappeared from historical consciousness. H. L. Mencken wrote the epitaph when he defined Puritanism as the tyranny of superstition and repression, the fear that someone, somewhere, sometime might be happy.

The institutionalized form of political authority, first theoretically developed by Madison, later rediscovered by Charles Beard and Arthur Bentley, and ultimately raised to the status of "pluralism" by heirs like Robert Dahl and David Truman, also appears to have had an unsteady career. Pre-World War I social philosophers like Lippmann and Herbert Croly rebelled against the notion of politics as a "machine process," and earlier Woodrow Wilson had criticized congressional government for having forsaken the duty to lead, educate, and enlighten the public as it became lost in a ceaseless "dance of legislation."[19] Today the "behavioral persuasion" in political science fails to persuade those who believe that history and politics must involve something more than quantifying the actual and treating the given as the norm. Indeed, if there is a crisis of authority today, it may well be that interest-group behavior can obey only the logic of its own behavior: more means more.

Even less favorable in intellectual circles is the third type of authority, the socialization of mind and the instrumentalization of knowledge by sociologists and philosophers at the turn of the century. Formerly, intellectual historians were inclined to believe that American writers of the early twentieth century found a sense of liberation in the ideas of Dewey and Mead as they enthusiastically adopted pragmatism as a weapon of reform. The Greenwich Village rebels, however, rejected many of the liberal assumptions about consciousness and society,[20] and by the time of the "Lost Generation," almost every major premise of sociology and pragmatism had been repudiated by the leading literary intellectuals. "Primary group" associations hardly seemed nuturing to Sinclair Lewis, Sherwood Anderson, and other novelists in flight from small-town life; and as for the family, the presumed source of warm, healthy emotional growth, one merely has to survey the drama of the twenties, from Eugene O'Neill to Sidney Howard, to discover what that sticky primary unit does to children, women, and manhood. The kind of consensual authority that sociological theory developed at the turn of the century never had deep roots in American cultural history. Indeed, from Jefferson to the Transcendentalists, from Mark Twain to John Dos Passos, the integrity of the self against the pressures of society seemed all that remained to define one's moral character. To writers, the socialization of authority and its accompanying loss of authentic selfhood is not liberating but alienating. "I know myself, but that is all," concluded F. Scott Fitzgerald in *This Side of Paradise*, only to come to the realization in *The Crack-Up* that he did not know himself, that indeed he had no self and had lost his identity without knowing it as the glamour of social relations and role-playing totally absorbed him. Sociologists might cheerfully deny the ontological status of the self, but it took a novelist to actually experience the metaphysical dread of that proposition.

The "Lost Generation," perhaps the most thoroughly alienated generation in American intellectual history, rejected conventional religion, interest politics, and modern sociology as sources of authority. The perspective of that group of writers deserves the attention of anyone wrestling with the contemporary "crisis" of authority. They seem to have recognized that a mere description of the movement of power or the mechanisms of social interaction does not answer the larger questions of truth, value, and meaning. Dewey's proposal that life be viewed as a "social experiment" does not so much resolve such questions as postpone them. T. S. Eliot, who sensed the need for authority and tradition to enable man to confront the anxieties of alienated existence, might have said of Dewey what Santayana said of James—he offers us courage when we hunger for wisdom:

> The endless cycle of idea and action,
> Endless invention, endless experiment,

Brings knowledge of motion, but not of stillness;
Knowledge of speech but not of silence;
Knowledge of words, and ignorance of the Word.
All our knowledge brings us nearer to our ignorance,
All our ignorance brings us nearer to death,
But nearness to death no nearer to God.
Where is the life we have lost in living?
Where is the wisdom we have lost in knowledge?
Where is the knowledge we have lost in information?
The cycles of Heaven in twenty centuries
Bring us farther from God and nearer to the Dust.[21]

Where is the wisdom of authority that has been lost in knowledge of democracy? We need to return to Tocqueville and then to John Adams.

Tocqueville and the House of Adams

In *Democracy in America* Tocqueville put his finger on a problem the Founding Fathers believed they had successfully resolved through political institutions: the relationship among liberty, authority, and power. The framers believed that human liberty best flourishes to the extent that the individual retains his independence and pursues his self-interests apart from the state in a diverse society of competing interests and factions, and the federal constitution was to have made possible this version of modern pluralism. Tocqueville, however, seemed to be updating the older French criticisms of the American Constitution by drawing attention to the fact that America was not a differentiated society, and thus he dismissed the proposition of a balanced government that would counterpoise factions against one another as a "chimera." Tocqueville saw in American individualism not so much the virtues of pluralism as the perils of an amorphous society, a society of uniformed sameness in which the individual loses his strength of character and independence. Insofar as liberal individualism asserted the sovereignty of the individual over himself, it liberated man only by abrogating all authority of custom and tradition. Yet authority does not simply disappear. In a democratic culture the more power is weakened the more its sphere is widened until society itself becomes the seat of both power and authority. Similarly, the more the conditions of equality increase, the more people desire to be like each other; and the more they strive to emulate existing mores and customs, the less capable they are of practicing a civic virtue that requires personal involvement in political affairs concerning the commonweal. Thus, in contrast to the Founders' conviction that liberty would be sustained by the activities of self-directed individuals in a competitive society, Tocqueville believed that the private "pursuit of happiness" would weaken the social body, undermine liberty, and eventually consolidate power and authority in the sovereign state. To be sure, Tocqueville specified certain American institutions that could prevent democracy from evolving into despotism— namely law, religion, commerce, and local voluntary associations. But he also saw the possibility that the solitary individual, cut off from all previous historical associations of family and community, might unconsciously allow the centralization of power to develop, therefore losing his liberty without being aware of it. "The idea of a single power directing all citizens slips naturally into their consciousness without their, so to say, giving the matter a thought."[22] A democratic society offers no guarantee that a democratic people cannot lose their own authority as a natural right, the political right of a people to consent to the exercise of power over themselves. If the Founders showed Americans how power could be won from the forces of politics, Tocqueville showed how authority could be lost to the forces of society.

Although Tocqueville and the Founders differed in many respects, *Democracy in America* and *The Federalist* may be profitably compared with the question of authority in mind. For one thing, both the French writer and the framers of the Constitution agreed that authority in America would not be sustained by virtue or by any moral idea that appealed to reason or conscience. "The Americans are not a virtuous people, and nevertheless they are free," wrote Tocqueville in response to Montesquieu's argument that virtue was essential to the existence of republics. The Founders, seeing man as a creature of self-interests and self-love, also had little faith in virtue, which Tocqueville had defined as "the moral power which an individual exercises over himself." "To expect self-denial from men," wrote John Adams, "when they have a majority in their favor, and consequently power to gratify themselves, is to disbelieve all history and universal experience; it is to disbelieve Revelation and the Word of God, which informs us, the heart is deceitful above all things and desperately wicked."[23] In *The Federalist* one also finds little hope for the self-mastery of egoism (or perhaps "narcissism"), the inner ethical strength that enables man to resist the temptation to oppress others and to know right from wrong. On the contrary, Madison structured the American government on the premise of man as aggressor. If left unrestrained by external checks, any individual or group of individuals will tyrannize others. To deflect this inexorable tendency, Madison believed that the motives, interests, and passions of dominant majorities must be "broken" by a well-ordered constitution so that popular democracy would be frustrated at every turn. Thus Tocqueville's fear of the "tyranny of the majority" had an earlier expression in Madison's fear of the tyranny of majority factions, and Madison's recognition that "all governments rest on opinion" foreshadowed Tocqueville's discovery that "public opinion" derived from the "omnipotent" majority, an "authority" to which all democratic citizens must submit. Somehow authority had slipped away from the Founders of the Republic.

Convinced that democracy and authority must not be regarded as synonymous, the framers were also convinced that authority should not be identical to society. They rejected Thomas Paine's argument that society was the source of legitimate authority and government of repressive power. Paine's belief that society is produced by our "wants" and government by our "wickedness" led to his notorious conclusion that the state is basically a historical aberration and moral embarrassment—"the badge of lost innocence." Ironically, the Founders could agree with Paine's conclusion only because they rejected his premise about man's natural sociability. "Why has government been instituted at all?" asked Hamilton. "Because the passions of men will not conform to the dictates of reason and justice without constraint." Possessed of a darker, Calvinist vision of human nature, the framers could scarcely emphasize the distinction between society and the state in order to uphold the autonomy and independence of society from political authority. Nor could they use government to forge political unity out of a social context of diversity. It was precisely because society, even "natural" society, was so divided and faction-ridden that the authority of government had to be imposed on the freedoms of man's natural rights in the state of nature, and that new government had to be so constructed in terms of the divisions of power and the balance of interests as to reflect accurately the divisions of society. Thus, whereas Tocqueville believed that the social would dominate the political, the framers believed that society had to be mastered by a government that somehow could be strong and effective without abusing its powers. And herein lies the dilemma: if a society without government could result in anarchy, a government without authority could result in tyranny. What is to be done? Madison's solution was to legitimate the new government not so much by articulating its authority as by dispersing its powers:

> The great security against a gradual concentration of the several powers in the same department consists in giving to those who administer each department the necessary constitutional means and personal motives to resist encroachments of the others. The provision for defense must in this, as in all other cases, be made commensurate to the danger of attack. Ambition must be made to counteract ambition. The interest of the man must be connected with the constitutional rights of the place. It may be a reflection on human nature that such devices should be necessary to control the abuses of government. But what is government itself but the greatest of all reflections on human nature? If men were angels, no government would be necessary. If angels were to govern men, neither external nor internal controls on government would be necessary. In framing a government which is to be administered by men over men, the great difficulty lies in this: you must first enable government to control the governed; and in the next place oblige it to control itself. A depen-

dence on the people is, no doubt, the primary control on the government; but experience has taught mankind the necessity of auxiliary precautions.[24]

There can be no doubt that the American Constitution is a triumph of political intelligence, and Madison could rightly feel that "experience has taught" man the necessity of controlling power. Yet the wisdom of authority seems to have been lost in the network of "auxiliary precautions." For the Constitution as devised by Madison aimed to prevent the historical goal of authority as envisioned by Locke: the ability of a collectivity of individuals to agree on what is to be done and to take action as a democratic majority. Thus the U.S. Constitution, drafted in response to the inadequacies of the older Articles of Confederation, presented something of a rarity in the history of Western liberal thought: a political system that advocated more centralization of power in the government while opposing more unification of authority in the people.

Contemporary scholars have paid insufficient attention to the tensions between power and authority at the heart of the Constitution. Arthur Schlesinger, Jr., maintains that the Founding Fathers "assumed collaboration with power as the natural order of things"; and Morton White, in questioning Bernard Bailyn's argument that the colonists saw power and liberty as mutually antagonistic, claims that colonial thinkers advocated the positive uses of power as strength and coercion and that, indeed, the American Revolution itself could only be defended on the grounds that the "right" to abolish a government presupposes the ability to do so.[25] Be that as it may, we need to keep in mind that the making of the Revolution and the framing of the Constitution are two profoundly different episodes, for the one called for resisting tyranny to safeguard liberty and the other for controlling democracy to safeguard society. In the first instance the Founders aspired to limit the power of government in England, in the second to create more power in the new federal government in America. In both episodes their thoughts were filled with fears about man's "love of power" and "thirst for domination."[26] This deep pessimism about political power, a British Whig sentiment shared by the Federalists and Antifederalists alike, had profound implications for the problem of political authority in America. On the eve of the Civil War, at the moment when the Republic was threatened with disintegration, Henry Adams reflected on the dilemma with characteristic astuteness:

> The generation that framed the American form of government meant it to be, not only in mechanism but in theory, a contradiction to opinions commonly accepted in Europe. The men who made the Constitution intended to make by its means an issue with antiquity; and they had a clear conception of the issue itself, and of their own purposes in raising

it. These purposes were perhaps chimerical; the hopes then felt were almost certainly delusive. Yet persons who grant the probable failure of the scheme, and expect the recurrence of the great problems in government which were thought to be solved, cannot but look with satisfaction at the history of the Federal Constitution as the most convincing and most interesting experiment ever made in the laboratory of political science, even if it demonstrates the impossibility of success through its means.

The great object of terror and suspicion to the people of the thirteen provinces was *power*; not merely power in the hands of a president or a prince, of one assembly or of several, of many citizens or of few, but of power in the abstract, wherever it existed and under whatever name it was known. "There is and must be," said Blackstone, "in all forms of government, however they began or by what right soever they exist, a supreme, irresistible, absolute, uncontrolled authority, in which the *jura summi imperii*, or the rights of sovereignty, reside"; and Parliament is the place "where that absolute despotic power which must in all governments reside somewhere is entrusted by the Constitution of the British kingdom." Supreme, irresistible authority must exist somewhere in every government—was the European belief; and England solved her problem by entrusting it to a representative assembly to be used according to the best judgment of the nation. America, on the other hand, asserted that the principle was not true; that no such supreme power need exist in a government; that in the American government none such should be allowed to exist, because absolute power in any form was inconsistent with freedom, and that the new government should start from the idea that the public liberties depended upon denying uncontrolled authority in the political system in its parts or its whole.[27]

The Founders could hardly establish the legitimate basis for authority in America. Their conspiratorial fear of power prior to the Revolution led to the conscious fragmentation of authority in the Constitution. Yet it is necessary to mention that the Founders did not conceive themselves as departing from European traditions in every respect, as Adams might lead us to believe. On the contrary, they believed that the mechanisms of checks and balances and division of powers were necessary precisely because America's social structure replicated rather than repudiated that of Europe. Nowhere was this view articulated more passionately than in the post-revolutionary writings of John Adams, the great-grandfather of Henry Adams.

John Adams's *A Defense of the Constitutions of Government of the United States of America* was written in reply to French criticisms of American political thought in the aftermath of the Revolution. One critic, Baron Turgot, had charged Americans with something like plagiarism, claiming that in the various state constitutions, and later in the federal constitution, the English model of government was being imitated. Instead of sovereignty residing in one principle, which Turgot called "the Nation," it seemed to reside everywhere and nowhere in America to the extent that power was divided into several branches of government. In England the Whig theory of dispersing power may have been necessary because England had distinct social classes and a tradition of monarchy and aristocracy. But America? In a republic based on the revolutionary principle of equality there is no need for such divisive institutions as a bicameral legislature or a federation of powers between the states and the central government. In America all authority could be brought under one political body and have its direct expression in a national assembly representing "the people."

Adams's *Defense,* like Madison's *The Federalist,* illustrates again how the problem of authority may elude any solution to the problem of power. Replying to Turgot, Adams argued that the people as "a whole body" simply does not exist as a political entity since it neither gathers, reasons, nor acts together. Moreover, the people cannot be entrusted with all authority and power since it is the people who are their own worst oppressors as long as the many continue to invade the liberties of the few and the few to dominate the lives of the many. Lastly, Adams argued against Turgot's proposal to invest all authority "into one centre, the nation," on the grounds that the "collection" of authority must be derived continually from the voluntary agreement of the people, from those very acts of collective will that constitute authority. In arguing that authority is brought into being by human acts, Adams could scarcely conclude that human activity itself is by definition authoritative. Instead, he distinguished the authority of the people from the sovereignty of the people, their right to authorize political actions through their representatives from their right to undertake such actions on their own. Why was this distinction so important? Political theorists suggest that Adams made the distinction because he, like other eighteenth-century political thinkers, saw that all sovereign authority could not be placed in the hands of the people for the same reason that all power could not be entrusted to a sovereign king or government. "One can declare," writes Charles W. Hendel, "that all authority derives from the people and still not be committed to the alien doctrine that the people themselves act as a sovereign, exercising authority as one body with undivided power, performing all the functions of government. The reason for saying 'alien' is that the smell of absoluteness clung to the notion of sovereignty which had been defined by Bodin, Grotius, and many others in that line, as the power to make laws 'without the consent of those governed,' independently of anybody on earth, either within or without the state, that is, in reality, unlimited power. To substitute the nation for a personal sovereign is not to change the meaning of such sovereign authority."[28]

That the people have the right to "act as a sovereign" would scarcely be an "alien doctrine" to an eighteenth-century Lockean or Jeffersonian. Whose "consent" must the governed seek to govern themselves? It should be noted that Adams justified his attitudes toward authority not so much by reference to European political theories as American social realities. Adams remained convinced, even in the face of European critics like Turgot, that America had monarchial, aristocratic, and democratic tendencies that must be balanced against one another lest the rule of the one man degenerate into tyranny, of the few into oligarchy, and of the many into anarchy. The *Defense* rested on the conviction that American society was divided into "the rich and the poor, the laborious and the idle, the learned and the ignorant"; and even though class distinctions and privileges may not be hereditary in America, they remained as characteristic of the New World as of the Old. Only a balanced constitution could control the irrationalities of men and accommodate the social divisions between the few and the many, neither of which could be entrusted with absolute authority. Adams legitimated the new federal constitution not so much by demonstrating its affinities with European political philosophy as demonstrating its compatibility with America's environment. Government could control society by virtue of accurately reflecting it. But did it?

It may be one of the great ironies of American history that political authority was dispersed, fragmented, and ultimately abolished for reasons that proved to be unfounded. Where the American Adams saw his country as replicating Europe's social structure, the Frenchman Tocqueville saw America as unique, a social order unburdened by the feudal remnants of monarchy and aristocracy and a political culture committed to change, opportunity, and equality. Adams failed to perceive the homogeneity and uniformity that Tocqueville would later describe; and thus he defended a government on the basis that aristocracy would be represented in the upper house of Congress and democracy in the lower, and both these supposedly contending social elements would in turn be mediated by "an independent executive power, the one monarchial element of the society."[29] Small wonder that Louis Hartz has referred to the "Phantom World" of the Federalists and Gordon Wood to "The Relevance and Irrelevance of John Adams."[30] America's most profound political philosopher of the eighteenth century, perhaps of all times, defended a constitution that had no basis in America's social realities, a constitution that could not have survived had there actually existed such sharp value differences between a real aristocracy and democracy. All the checks and balances designed to resolve the problem of power and authority could work only because such class conflicts never developed. "The Founding Fathers," writes Hartz, "devised a scheme to deal with conflict that could only survive in a land of solidarity. The truth is, their conclusions were 'right' only because their premises were wrong."[31]

Adams believed that all authority could not be vested in the people because the divided nature of America's social order precluded such a collective, all-encompassing body; Tocqueville believed that all authority had, in fact, gravitated to the undifferentiated mass of people because in America there existed no distinct classes or established institutions that enjoyed authoritative status. Although Tocqueville's writings disprove Adams's convictions, one suspects that Adams would not have been surprised by the ascendancy of the "tyranny of the majority." Adams could hardly deny the eighteenth-century axiom that all political authority derives from the people, but he could not agree with Locke that the people themselves should rule because the will of the majority constitutes the principle through which society acts. That doctrine served well the purposes of the American Revolution, as the Declaration of Independence made clear. But like Madison and Hamilton, Adams was reluctant to allow the people to be the final expression of authority even though they remain its ultimate source. Thus at the very conception of American government one encounters the perennial dilemma of authority in liberal American society. Adams saw that the English Whig ideology could disperse power in order to control it better; but apparently he did not contemplate what his great-grandson would come to understand: that authority, as opposed to power, cannot be dispersed without being destroyed. The Founding Fathers left America in a post-Lockean limbo, where there remained no source of authority to articulate the nation's basic convictions on important issues. The power of government is justified by a right that it derives from the sovereign consent of the people; yet the sovereign will of the people must not prevail because the masses lack the virtue to translate their collective power into moral authority. Who then possesses such virtue?

Somehow the burden of American history always seems to return to the house of Adams, perhaps because a study of the Adams family itself offers a study of the erosion of the idea of authority in America. To understand the decline of that idea we need to appreciate its original conception. John Adams had once held out hope for a "Republic of Virtue," an American nation in which the squalid but inescapable realities of ambition, avarice, and resentment could be tempered and perhaps tamed by the higher ideals of virtue, benevolence, and duty. But after the Revolution, Adams came to realize that no social class or constituency, neither the "rich, well-born, and able" nor the one, the few, or the many, could be trusted as the guardians of the Republic. He arrived at the somber conclusion that the federalist system embodied in the Constitution could no longer regenerate the ideals that made the Revolution possible. "Virtue" could be found neither in the overweening ambitions of the aristocracy nor in the voracious appetites of the people. Could the Republic endure without a moral foundation? If power had to be dispersed and authority fragmented, what could prevent the restless young country from tearing itself apart? Adams's answer lay in the leadership of the aristocracy that, though short on virtue, still had plenty of "talent." He hoped that an American aristocracy, however potentially dangerous, could be safely "ostracized" by being located in the Senate, where the people and the nation would benefit from its "wisdom" without fearing its "passions." He also believed that the masses would be restrained not only by the effective representation they would enjoy in the lower house but also by the cultural pressures of deference that would lead them to "emulate" the status and ambitions of their betters. Thus while political sovereignty may ultimately rest with the people, social and intellectual authority could possibly descend and permeate a body politic, whose members would aspire to adopt the values and behavior of those above them.

Adams's emphasis on "emulation" as the psychological cement of political order anticipates by more than a century Thorstein Veblen and Antonio Gramsci's analysis of the ruling class' cultural hegemony. Adams attempted to exploit the talent and to control the power of the aristocracy by using the "love of praise" and the "passion for distinction" as a surrogate for reason and virtue.[32] By this strategy he could separate authority from power insofar as the aristocrats in the Senate would be able to counsel but not necessarily to command. Yet Adams's effort to find some sphere for the function of leadership and authority in America proved futile, and not only because America lacked a genuine aristocracy.

The dilemma lay in applying institutional solutions to ethical problems on the assumption that a system of government could accomplish what its citizens could not. John Taylor, a Virginia contemporary of Adams, immediately perceived this dilemma when reading the *Defense*. The balanced American Republic, Taylor observed, rested on the proposition that the principles that govern society are "virtuous" while the individuals who compose it are "vicious."[33] The criticism hardly troubled Adams, for he and the founders deliberately used the vices that had doomed ancient republics (such as rival factions) and incorporated them into the very structure and function of government. While this strategy enabled the framers to avoid the problem of defining the nature of authority, it rested on three precarious assumptions that Adams himself saw as problematic: that no single faction could be allowed to control the state, that natural social and cultural leaders, men of talent and energy, would filtrate upward to positions of political leadership, and that the human tendency to emulate superiors would possibly assure that society could be sustained by some measure of deference and moral authority. These assumptions contained their own problems and paradoxes. What motive or force would assure that each branch of government would check one another and that factions could be controlled by means of external restraints alone?[34] Why would people incapable of virtue and wisdom be capable of choosing virtuous and wise leaders? How could a workable mechanical whole be constructed out of defective human parts? Just as the Puritans had preached that man would be saved not by but to virtue, Adams believed that a balanced government could not be made by virtue but that virtue would flow from it. Ultimately, good government would grow out of the actions of those who are not necessarily good men. As in theology, so in political theory—we rub our eyes!

John Adams's great-grandson was born into a world in which many of the Founders' hopeful assumptions had been shattered. By the middle of the nineteenth century new forms of economic power had become alienated from the older legitimate sources of political authority as corporate wealth came to influence, if not dominate, the state. Henry Adams could look on the Constitution almost with amusement as he observed its "delusive" and "chimerical" premises and assumptions. The last great figure in a family that included two presidents and a foreign ambassador, Adams was the first of his dynasty to sense the gloomy end of the bright heritage of Enlightenment political thought on which his ancestors rested their hopes for the American Republic. Adams recognized that with the passing of the heroic ideals of the Revolution and the advent of the liberal realities incorporated into the Constitution, government would only be able to function as a mediator of conflict rather than as an authority of the good, the just, and the beautiful. The young Adams had to move in a new political universe eclipsed by moral darkness, and he found it necessary to go beyond the Enlightenment, with its tenuous balance of passion and reason, its juxtaposition of countervailing factions, and its network of checks and restraints, to find a basis of authority that would remain impervious to the vicissitudes of interests and power and the corruptions of time and history. In this quest he admirably took up the burdens of his ancestors, and those burdens remain ours.

Notes

1. These definitions represent something of a distillation based on a variety of different sources. For a recent and thorough analysis of the problem, see Steve Lukes, "Power and Authority," in *A History of Sociological Analysis*, ed. Tom Bottomore and Robert Nisbet (New York, 1978), pp. 633–676. See also "Authority," *Proceedings of the Aristotelian Society*, supp. vol. 32 (1958); C. J. Friedrich, ed., *Authority* (Cambridge, Mass., 1958); Sebastian de Grazia, "What Authority Is Not," *American Political Science Review* 53 (1959): 321–331; Hannah Arendt, "What Is Authority?" in *Between Past and Future* (New York, 1961), pp. 91–141; John H. Schaar, "Legitimacy in the Modern State," in *Power and Community: Dissenting Essays in Political Science*, ed. Philip Green and Sanford Levinson (New York, 1970), pp. 276–327. For a valuable bibliography, see Richard T. De George, "Authority: A Bibliogra-

phy," in *Authority: A Philosophical Analysis,* ed. R. Blaine Harris (University, Ala., 1976), pp. 141–170.

2. "Religion and the Intellectuals: A Symposium," *Partisan Review* 17 (1950): 113–116.

3. Philip Rieff, *Fellow Teachers* (New York, 1972), p. 12.

4. Perry Miller and Thomas Johnson, eds., *The Puritans: A Sourcebook of Their Writings* (New York, 1963), I, 194–199, 205–207.

5. "Thomas Jefferson to Spence Roane, June 27, 1821," in *The Writings of Thomas Jefferson,* ed. Alberth E. Bergh, XV (Washington, D.C., 1907), 328.

6. "John Adams to Thomas Jefferson, October 9, 1781," in *The Papers of Thomas Jefferson,* ed. Julian Boyd, XII (Princeton, N.J., 1950), 221.

7. Arthur O. Lovejoy, *Reflections on Human Nature* (Baltimore, 1961), pp. 37–65.

8. David Minar, *Ideas and Politics: The American Experience* (Homewood, Ill., 1964), p. 102.

9. Seymour Martin Lipset, *The First New Nation: The United States in Historical and Comparative Perspective* (New York, 1963), pp. 1–60.

10. H. H. Gerth and C. Wright Mills, eds., *From Max Weber: Essays in Sociology* (New York, 1958), p. 299.

11. *The Federalist,* no. 78.

12. Alexis de Tocqueville, *Democracy in America,* ed. J. P. Mayer (New York, 1969), p. 72.

13. Ibid., p. 395.

14. On the reception of Tocqueville in America, see Yehoshua Arieli, *Individualism and Nationalism in American Ideology* (Baltimore, 1964).

15. Tocqueville, *Democracy in America,* p. 669; Henry D. Thoreau, "Civil Disobedience," in *Walden and Other Writings* (New York, 1962), pp. 84–104.

16. Charles Sanders Peirce, "The Fixation of Belief," in *American Thought: Civil War to World War I,* ed. Perry Miller (New York, 1954), pp. 132–135.

17. John Dewey, *The Quest for Certainty: A Study of the Relation of Knowledge and Action* (New York, 1960).

18. "The Socialization of Authority and the Dilemmas of American Liberalism," *Social Research* 46 (1979): 454–486.

19. Walter Lippmann, *A Preface to Politics* (New York, 1913); Woodrow Wilson, *Congressional Government: A Study in American Politics* (Meridian ed.; New York, 1956).

20. Randolph Bourne's criticisms of Dewey are well known to students of American history; less known are Max Eastman's witty criticisms of pragmatism as an epistemology. See my *Up from Communism: Conservative Odysseys in American Intellectual History* (New York, 1975), pp. 57, 464–465.

21. T. S. Eliot, "Two Choruses from 'The Rock,'" in *The Waste Land and Other Poems* (New York, 1934), p. 81.

22. Tocqueville, *Democracy in America,* p. 668.

23. Tocqueville is quoted in Raymond Aron, *Main Currents in Sociological Thought* (Garden City, N.Y., 1968), I, 258; John Adams, *A Defense of the Constitution of Government of the United States of America* (London, 1787–1788; reprint ed.; New York, 1971), III, 289.

24. *The Federalist,* no. 51.

25. Arthur Schlesinger, Jr., *The Crisis of Confidence* (New York, 1968), p. 46; Morton White, *The Philosophy of the American Revolution* (New York, 1978), pp. 192–195.

26. Bernard Bailyn, *The Ideological Origins of the American Revolution* (Cambridge, Mass., 1967), pp. 94–159.

27. Henry Adams, *The Great Secession Winter of 1860–61 and Other Essays,* ed. George E. Hochfield (New York, 1958), pp. 193–194.

28. Charles W. Hendel, "An Exploration of the Nature of Authority," in *Authority*, ed. Carl J. Friedrich (Cambridge, Mass., 1958), p. 23.

29. "John Adams to Roger Sherman, July 18, 1789," in *The American Enlightenment*, ed. Adrienne Koch (New York, 1965), p. 193.

30. Louis Hartz, *The Liberal Tradition in America: An Interpretation of American Political Thought since the Revolution* (New York, 1955), pp. 78–86; Gordon S. Wood, *The Creation of the American Republic, 1776–1787* (New York, 1969), pp. 567–588.

31. Hartz, *The Liberal Tradition*, p. 86.

32. Lovejoy, *Reflections on Human Nature*, pp. 195–208.

33. Taylor's critiques are cited in Wood, *Creation of the American Republic*, pp. 588–592.

34. On this matter, see Robert A. Dahl, *A Preface to Democratic Theory* (New Haven, 1956), pp. 30–33.

2

The Idea of the State in America

Sheldon Wolin

A few years ago Americans celebrated the bicentennial of their revolutionary and democratic origins. Or, rather, they had that celebration organized for them by the governmental bureaucrats in charge of public culture, the National Foundation of the Humanities, and by the corporate managers of the mass media. The incongruity of entrusting the celebration of a revolution for self-government and freedom to those who manned the instruments for the control and consumption of culture insured that the effort would turn out flat and uninspiring. However, to conclude that it was a failure because the end product was banal would be to miss the point.

If, by some miracle, the Bicentennial had become the beginning, the first step toward national renewal and a contemporary redefinition of the democratic and revolutionary principles of the Declaration of Independence, then Americans might have gained a foothold from which to observe their actual condition. Then they might have been less willing to accept the condition that, for the brief moment of the Nixon presidency, had been exposed in all of its corruption and potential for tyranny. The bicentennial celebration was a studied effort at controlling what the eighteenth-century Federalists would have called "the popular passions." In the post-Vietnam and post-Watergate years it was crucially important to keep the citizens in a subdued mood, to have them feel somewhat depressed while they were being told that the crucial contrast was not between the political condition of America in 1976 and the democratic promise of America in 1776, but between the freedoms enjoyed by Americans and the slavery and brutality experienced, not by black South Africans, but by the inmates of concentration camps in the Soviet Union. The message that Americans were fortunate and ought to feel grateful—it was never made clear to whom—was part of a larger campaign to deflate popular aspirations and expectations and to prepare Americans for a leaner future.

The same message was delivered in a different package by self-styled academic intellectuals and opinion-makers. The message was encoded as "the end of American exceptionalism." Among other things, it taught that the political values associated with democracy—intense participation, close control over elected representatives, and strict limits on the exercise and scope of public power—might have made sense in pastoral America, but in today's complex, tense world they are dangerous. Survival dictates that we reduce the role of the citizen, replace participatory politics with bureaucratic politics, eliminate deliberative forums in favor of organizations that are hierarchical, managerial, and elitist, and declare that in the age of the scientific revolution the technician is the logical successor to political man.

My present concern is with a particular instance of American exceptionalism that went unnoticed in the discussions surrounding the Bicentennial. The main reason for recalling this neglected matter is that it has a special relation to the next bicentennial in 1987. That year will mark the two-hundredth anniversary of the American Constitution. The decision to found a government on the basis of a written constitution and to circumscribe its powers by enumerating and limiting them was a remarkable innovation, a genuine original. Exceptionalism was not confined, however, to what the Constitution affirmed but also to what it denied. The Constitution perpetuated the most basic claim of the revolutionaries that the highest political authority was a limited authority. The colonists had developed this claim in rebuttal to the British assertion that the authority of Parliament was sovereign and that, by definition, sovereign authority could not, in principle, be limited. The revolutionary position was incorporated into the Constitution in an early decision of the Supreme Court, *Chisholm v. Georgia* (1793). The author of the Court's opinion was Justice James Wilson, who had been one of the most influential members of the Philadelphia Convention, which had drafted the original document. "To the Constitution of the United States," Wilson averred, "the term sovereign is totally unknown."[1]

In the history of Western political thought, sovereignty was seen as the decisive attribute that marked the emergence of the modern state. As we shall see shortly, the claim that the state was sovereign was typically a claim that the state possessed absolute authority within its jurisdiction. The American Constitution, in denying that any such authority was lodged in any of its institutions, singly or in combination, appeared to set itself against the doctrine of sovereignty and, along with it, the modern conception of the state. America presented itself to the world as a political society that, while it had several "branches of government," had neither a sovereign state nor the politics associated with absolutism.

The American political tradition has, accordingly, been interpreted as an antistatist tradition that has continued uninterruptedly down to the present.

Throughout most of this century American politics has been carried on with virtually no reference, either by politicians or political scientists, to the existence of "the state" or to a conception of it.² During much of the period and in other parts of the world "the state" was a familiar, even exalted, idea, most notably in Mussolini's Italy, Stalin's Russia, and Hitler's Germany. Not surprisingly, "the state" was frequently used as a term of abuse, a near synonym for "totalitarian dictatorship," and, hence, in the propaganda battles of the thirties and forties, states were the political forms that "they" had, while "we" were a democracy whose organized power was lodged in a "government," a nondescript, unthreatening term that befitted an unmetaphysical people. Our antistatist tradition was contrasted with the Teutonic tradition of Fichte, Hegel, Treitschke, whose determination to sacrifice the individual for the greater glory of the state was so deeply engraved that even when their writings were translated into English, the translators felt compelled to preserve the capital "S" from *Staat*. It should also be noted that from 1930 to 1945, it was commonplace for writers who were championing the cause of democracy and representative government to discover a crucial contrast between democratic and totalitarian attitudes toward "authority." Democratic man was typically described as a cracker-barrel skeptic, disrespectful, wry, and nonconforming. Totalitarian man, on the other hand, was fawning, servile, fearful, and deferential. The contrast was memorialized in *The Authoritarian Personality*, that curious and belated monument to World War II erected by American social scientists working, ironically enough, under the supervision of some of the most renowned "critical theorists" of the Frankfurt School.³

Beginning with the administration of John Kennedy and gathering momentum through the years of the campus upheavals of the sixties, the civil rights movement, ghetto riots, intensifying opposition to the Vietnam War, the abdication of Lyndon Johnson, the defeat in Vietnam, the Watergate scandal, and the eventual resignation of Richard Nixon, a reshuffling of the old contrasts has occurred. New patterns have emerged that suggest a reevaluation is taking shape. Authority and deference, for example, appear in a more positive light, while democracy, antiauthoritarianism, and the political accountability of elected officials are viewed with indifference or are openly criticized. One measure of these developments is that the "state" is no longer a scatological word. It is widely used by political scientists who have even taken to inventing variations, such as "statist paradigm," "state-centric," "state-actors," even—shades of Hegel!—"organic-statism."⁴ The current situation in political science contrasts strikingly with the sentiments expressed by a prominent political scientist in 1953: "Neither the state nor power is a concept that serves to bring together political research."⁵

The thesis I wish to explore is this: the turn toward the state is the expression of a profound crisis in American society, a crisis that is political in nature. It is a crisis of democracy, and it has been built into our political system from its eighteenth-century beginning. I also want to suggest that this crisis is importantly reflected in American political science.

Within political science, the crisis takes the form of a sudden interest in the idea of the state. Political scientists are concerned with the state's effectiveness, that is, its power, and with its legitimacy, that is, with its evaporating support and loyalty. Although this concern leads political scientists to begin with what they perceive to be the weakness of the American state, their inquiries invariably lead them to the discovery that the crisis lies within and is produced by democracy.

The contradiction between the American democracy and the American state is also a crisis within political science. For almost a century, political science has consistently denied the existence of both democracy and the state, claiming that American politics was a unique "process" in which the main actors are interest groups, not "the people," while the main problems of group politics are decided by bargains struck between the groups or their representatives and not determined by the policies of a state standing impartially above the struggle. But, as we shall see, from the beginning of the republic political science *qua* science has defined itself in opposition to democracy. This function was part of its role of providing legitimation for political authority by interpreting the meaning of the collectivity sketched at the Philadelphia Convention and of the form of politics proper to it.

To grasp what is at stake in the current controversies we need to go back to the beginnings of the modern idea of the state, and then to see the extent to which the new constitution incorporated the substance while denying the form of the idea.

The early modern state was conceived to be the expression of the unity of the nation, that new form of collectivity that was beginning to make its presence felt in sixteenth-century Europe. The essence of sovereignty was identified with the authority to make laws, an authority that was declared to be unlimited, save for some hesitations by some traditionally minded legists and theorists about whether the state, in principle, was justified in overriding the dictates of natural and divine law. The formula borrowed from Roman law and applied by sixteenth-century legists and political theorists to the newly centralized states was *Legibus solutus*. The authority of the state was "freed" from legal restraints, and as the source of legislation it was entitled to ignore its own enactments at any given moment. Although state and sovereignty tended to be employed interchangeably, their relationship was of complements rather than of synonyms. The theory of sovereignty was usually cast in formal and juridical terms, as befitted its emphasis upon law-making as the core notion of the state. The formative concern was to establish the state as the final decision-making and rule-making authority.

The modern theory of the state, while incorporating the main tenets of the doctrine of sovereignty, was concentrated on finding the best ways of mobilizing the power and support needed by the sovereign for the effective discharge of his functions. The great builders of the early modern nation-states needed power as well as authority if they were to overcome feudal and ecclesiastical resistance to their centralizing efforts at home and to conduct aggressive military, diplomatic, and commercial policies abroad. The modern state found its theorist in Thomas Hobbes, whose contribution was to base sovereign authority and state power upon consent, thereby giving them the appearance, although not the reality, of a democratic foundation. Hobbes's absolute sovereign was personified in one breath as a "mortal god," but, in another, as depersonalized. "I speak not of the men" who actually exercise power, "but, in the abstract, of the seat of power."[6] By making authority appear abstract rather than personal Hobbes could lessen the apprehensiveness that might be aroused by the amount of power that would be available to the sovereign under the terms of the Hobbesian covenant. For Hobbes proclaimed openly that his purpose was "to advance the civil power,"[7] advance it, we might add, until its power was commensurate with its authority. Accordingly, the covenant, which was to be voluntarily accepted by each individual and on terms that acknowledged the natural equality of all men, would offer the sovereign the power of "every particular man in the commonwealth" to use as much as he deemed necessary "to form the wills of them all, to peace at home, and mutual aid against their enemies abroad."[8]

The most glaring weakness in the Hobbesian formulation was its assumption that the awesome authority and power of the state could be generated and guaranteed in perpetuity by a single act of consent registered in one moment of time. His belief in a minimal requirement of legitimation was connected to his contempt for those who advocated frequent political participation or who reechoed the Aristotelian conception of man as a being naturally destined for political life. Hobbes was among the first to proclaim that man was essentially self-interested, that his power drives could be directed at socially beneficial goals, such as those represented by science, technology, practical arts, and useful learning, and that what the new man essentially demanded of political authority was to be protected, encouraged by subsidies, and allowed to enjoy most of the fruits of his efforts. But, because the Hobbesian vision of a scientifically oriented society required a longer period to prepare Western mankind for its demands and a state that would enjoy a continuous lien on the energies, skills, and resources of the members of society, there was need for a more continuous, institutionalized method of securing legitimacy for the actions of the state, especially for the more unpleasant ones.

This need can be compressed into a formula: the need was for a method of legitimation that would be sufficient to gain the loyalty and support of the citizens but would not be so demanding as to distract them from the private callings by which they gratified themselves and contributed to the sinews of state power. The problem was to secure a steady and continuous flow of legitimacy *from* the people without promoting steady and continuous interference *by* the people. The solution was provided by the political theory of John Locke, worked out in practice in the British House of Commons, and perfected later in the American system of elected legislators and executives. The solution was representative government based upon periodic elections. It was perfectly designed to provide the means for renewing the legitimacy of the governors while protecting the governed against the arbitrariness that is likely to occur when office-holders remain in power for indefinite terms. Above all, elections held at intervals of four or five years, or even two, would not impose a hardship on electors by demanding too much of their time. Locke even went so far as to deny the value of "constant, frequent meetings of the Legislative and long Continuations of their Assemblies," contending that the executive supplied a constant presence ("always to be present"), "whose business it was to watch over the publick good."[9]

Thus Locke succeeded in putting into place most of the pieces in the modern liberal theory and practice of the state. He had improved upon Hobbes, first, by supplementing the original democratic covenant and its single moment of legitimation with the continuous legitimation supplied by periodic elections and representative government, and second, by qualifying the Hobbesian conception of sovereignty, mainly through insisting on the privileged status of the right to private property. Neither of these moves weakened the state. If anything, they increased its potential power by grounding the state more securely in consent, that is, in periodic appeals to "the people."[10] Formulated slightly differently, sovereignty was divided by Locke, who distributed pieces of it to the legislature, executive, and the "people," giving the impression that he had lessened it. In a formal sense he had, but he had also increased the power at the disposal of the state by using representative institutions to promote a sense of popular identification with the authority of the state, thereby enabling the state to claim great powers in the name of the people.

There was one regressive element in Locke's political theory. Unlike Hobbes, who was convinced that politics could be reduced to a science that would produce "absolute truths," Locke made no greater claim for his ideas other than that they were grounded in rational argument and common experience, and, on occasion, even in Holy Scripture. This historical point might be put slightly differently by saying: while Locke's political theory was aimed at the dangers of royal absolutism and Hobbes's science of politics was addressed primarily to a crisis in the political elites of his day, neither theorist fashioned his theory as a weapon against democracy, even though it was during their century that modern democratic ideas were first sketched out. The development of an avowedly antidemocratic science of politics was the contribution of Americans. It was made during the crucial moment when the Americans were on the verge of giving themselves a new political form and when, therefore, their political identity—how they were to see themselves as a political people—was to be fixed.

It is a matter of cold historical fact that the science of politics was present at the creation of the American republic and that it produced the theory that provided the basis for much of our political self-conceptions as well as our formal and systematic study of politics. *The Federalist Papers,* which were written to promote the ratification of the Constitution, were penned mainly by Hamilton, who, more than any single individual, established the importance of executive power, of public bureaucracy, of the union of public policy and economics, and by Madison, who has been called the "Father of the Constitution" for his efforts at the Philadelphia Convention and who was later elected president.

Hamilton, in the ninth article of *The Federalist,* and, above all, Madison, in the fourteenth and thirty-seventh, appeal to the "new science of politics" and to "political science" as authority for the principles that were explicitly aimed at proving that democracy was impractical, undesirable, unnecessary, and dangerous. The intensity of Madison's feelings may be judged by his total rejection of the democratic idea of continuous participation: "Had every Athenian citizen been a Socrates; every Athenian assembly would still have been a mob."[11] The numerous devices written into the original constitution were the praxes of that theory: representative government, indirect elections, staggered terms, separation of powers, checks and balances, and the exploitation of huge space to dissipate the effects of "factions" and prevent a coalesced majority. Equally significant: the Federalists grasped the vital point that while democracy must be devitalized, it must not be eradicated. There had to be a place for a formal principle of legitimation by popular approval, a thin theory of legitimacy that inserted the "people" into the system but took every precaution to keep that presence within narrow bounds. The deepest hope of the Federalists was to distance the people from the actual system, much as the deists of the eighteenth century distanced God from the daily operations of the Newtonian world-system—*vox populi, vox dei,* indeed!—to treat "we the people" as the ultimate source of authority for a constitution that, it was hoped, would serve as the source of legitimation. The Constitution would provide the strong theory of legitimacy, the people the honorific but weak theory. The purpose of the new constitutional structure in Madison's words was: "To secure the public good and private rights against danger of (a majority) and, at the same time, to preserve the spirit and form of popular government."[12]

Although many scholars have long acknowledged that the original constitution was designed to protect property against majority-rule democracy, it is not always appreciated that this project could succeed only by sacrificing the clarity achieved in the early modern idea of the state to the mechanical checks and balances incorporated into the Constitution to prevent the majority from overwhelming the system in all of its branches. Would it be an exaggeration to say that the Federalists traded off the state for a political system that was legitimated by the people but stacked against their rule, that they preferred a weak state, bounded by constitutional limitations, to a strong state that might be captured by the majority? This, in rough outline, was Madison's view. Madison was persuaded of the need for a modern state up to a point. He accepted the need for a strong national government, for centralization of certain functions and powers, but he did not take the next step, as Hamilton did, of envisioning a national destiny shaped by a powerful state that stood above class interests and was administered by a public-spirited elite that was prepared, when urgent occasion warranted, to subordinate private property to public power. Instead of a vision of the state, Madison created a vision of politics, that, for more than two centuries, was accepted as the correct interpretation of American politics. That vision was deeply antidemocratic by design.

Madison's epigones were to call that vision "pluralism": he called it "factionalism." Even though Madison's exposition of it is familiar to most students of American politics, it is worth recalling because it captures perfectly the reasoning that rejects the sovereign state as a consequence of its concern to prevent democracy from ruling. "If a majority be united by a common interest, the rights of the minority will be insecure." The lengths to which Madison was willing to go in dispersing the state to save it from democratization can be judged by the following:

> Whilst all authority in [the federal republic] will be derived from and dependent on the society, the society itself will be broken into so many parts, interests, and classes of citizens, that the rights of individuals, or of the minority, will be in little danger from interested combinations of the majority.[13]

As a consequence of the determination to make it as difficult as possible for majorities to form, a profound incoherence was introduced at the center of the political order. Madisonian politics virtually makes the Hamiltonian state necessary, and yet the Hamiltonian state has *insufficient* legitimacy for doing what Madisonian politics thrusts upon it.

To understand the source of the incoherence, we need to lay aside the

ideological euphemism of "pluralism" and return to the unvarnished original
of Madison's definition of "faction":

> By faction I understand a number of citizens, whether amounting to a
> majority or a minority of the whole, who are united and activated by
> some common impulse of passion, or of interest, adverse to the rights of
> other citizens, or to the permanent and aggregate interests of the
> community.[14]

Before interpreting this passage, it is necessary to complete Madison's line
of thought about factions. He discerned different types of factions, some
organized around religious beliefs, others around political ideas or political
leaders. The most important source of faction, in his eyes, was "the various
and unequal distribution of property." Besides the crude division between
haves and have-nots, "distinct interests" were formed by creditors, debtors,
a "landed interest, a moneyed interest, with many lesser interests." These
were, he asserted, "different classes, actuated by different sentiments and
vices."[15]

It is only part of the truth about the political constitution of Madison's
state that it was designed to protect private property against the majority. It
must be remembered that in addition to its economic significance, property
signified inequality—inequality of capacities and, consequently, of power.
The determination to protect property by constitutional guarantees was
understood to mean the protection, perpetuation, and encouragement of inequality. Here are Madison's words:

> The diversity in the faculties of men, from which the rights of property
> originate, is not less an insuperable obstacle to a uniformity of interests.
> The protection of these faculties is the first object of government. From
> the protection of different and unequal faculties of acquiring property, the
> possession of different degrees and kinds of property immediately results:
> and from the influence of these on the sentiments and views of the
> respective proprietors, ensues a division of society into different interests
> and parties.[16]

The protection of inequality becomes a hazardous business, as European
societies were to discover from 1789 to 1848, if the condition of the unequal
many is hopeless. But hope is a function of expectation and expectations are
a function of opportunities. And this is where Madison's stratagem, of
connecting interests with unoccupied space and hence unexploited opportunities, was so appealing: inequality can be protected and promoted as long
as opportunities encourage the unequal to hope.

But what if the unequal run out of hope? Does the Madisonian state have
an answer to the central question that all Western political societies since the
polis have acknowledged must be answered by any society that makes the

slightest pretense to being political? The question is about justice, and Madison acknowledged its cardinal importance. "Justice," he asserted, "is the end of government. It is the end of civil society."[17] But what is justice beyond what Madison once called "the steady dispensation" according to the laws? The only answer that Madison could muster was that justice was the protection of the weak against the strong. Why the strong should support such a system was explained as a matter of self-interest. The strong could not perforce protect themselves without protecting the weak.[18]

The awkwardness of the answer was directly related to the incoherence in the conception of the state that we noted earlier. Justice cannot be promoted without exerting some control over social and economic interests, as Madison himself pointed out. "The regulation of these various and interfering interests forms the principal task of modern legislation."[19] The difficulty is, as Madison acknowledged, that a free society permits the pursuit of interests and it even opens up its political institutions—by elections, representation, and petitioning (that is, lobbying)—to the influence of interest groups. "The spirit of party and faction," Madison wrote, is involved "in the necessary and ordinary operations of the government." How can there be an appeal to justice when the interested groups "must be themselves the judges" and when "the most powerful must be expected to prevail"?[20]

Although Madison posed the question, he had no answer, only a desperate and contradictory hope that perhaps the democratic system of representation would devolve power upon "a small number of citizens . . . whose wisdom may best discern the true interest of their country, and whose patriotism and love of justice will be least likely to sacrifice it to temporary or partial considerations."

The modern idea of the state in its first American formulation was the work of Hamilton. It was never fully articulated because it had to be expressed through the distorting arrangements of the republican constitution adopted in Philadelphia. But we do get glimpses of it: in the claim that the war powers of the Constitution "ought to exist without limitation" and be "coextensive with all the possible combinations" of unexpected contingencies; or in the even broader assertion that "a government ought to contain in itself every power requisite to the full accomplishment of the objects committed to its care . . . free from every other control, but a regard to the public good and to the sense of the people"; and, finally, that "there ought to be a capacity to provide for future contengencies, as they may happen; and as these are illimitable in their nature, it is impossible safely to limit that capacity."[21] This last formulation, it should be noted, was advanced not in the context of national defense, but of protecting American commerce wherever it might happen to go. To put the matter concisely, the Hamiltonian state was not suppressed but repressed only to return in the interpretation to be given to certain clauses of the Constitution, notably, the commerce clause and the "necessary and proper" clause. These Hamilton quickly exploited when he became secretary of the treasury.

Hamilton's conception of the state was rounded out by the enlarged conception of bureaucracy, which was one of his most original contributions to the American science of politics: "The administration of government, in its largest sense, comprehends all the operations of the body politic, whether legislative, executive, or judiciary."[22]

This sweeping claim was immediately qualified, and Hamilton acknowledged that administration was more conventionally understood as "limited to executive details." But lest that bland phrase mislead, it should be noted that Hamilton included under those details such important functions as the conduct of foreign relations, preparation of financial plans, spending appropriations, "the arrangement of the army and navy," the conduct of war, and "other matters."[23] Thus Hamilton presented a full conception of state power, locating it in the elements furthest removed from popular participation—in the military, the bureaucracy, and the executive, who, it will be remembered, was not elected directly by the voters in the original constitution. But that conception had no basis in legitimacy other than what was supplied in the "thin conception" of Madison's periodic appeals and in the new constitution itself, supplemented, of course, by the elastic interpretation that Chief Justice Marshall obligingly supplied during the early crucial years of the republic.

The Civil War and the constitutional crisis provoked by the challenge to national authority led to a renewed interest in the idea of the state. That revival occurred, predictably, among academic political scientists, some of them highly influential in establishing political science as a field of graduate education. Among them were Woodrow Wilson, John Burgess, and William Archibald Dunning. All were strong unionists; all wrote books about the state; none was democratic in his political outlook; and all were true believers in a scientific political science. It is easy enough to recognize that the strong conceptions of state held by these writers were a response to the trauma of the Civil War.

The revived interest in the state provided the immediate occasion for the new political science of Arthur Bentley. It was precisely the political science of these late-nineteenth-century Germanophiles and their conception of the state that constituted Bentley's starting point and provoked some of his most characteristic outbursts. He characterized their work as "dead political science," the "formal study of the most external characteristics of governing institutions," and their state as a "bloodless abstraction," a "metaphysical spook," the creation of those whose "world has gone crackly and dry."[24]

Bentley is widely credited with having created the theory that came to define mainstream American political science of the twentieth century and to lend it its distinctive character. The theory goes by the name of "interest-group politics" or, more simply, "pluralism." Its basic principle is that politics is essentially a phenomenon of organized "groups," each acting to promote or defend its "interests." "The 'state' itself," Bentley emphasized, "is . . . no factor in our investigation." "When the groups are adequately stated, everything is stated. . . . The complete description will mean the complete science."[25] Bentley did to the people what he did to the state: he dissolved the notion and replaced it by a welter of groups, contending against each other, balancing, forcing compromises, overcoming resistance, a "limitless criss-cross" of forces and counterforces.

The upshot was to destroy the notion of a corporate people and to deprive state action of its most effective justification, that it reflected the "will of the people." Without realizing it, Bentley had created a politics without a legitimating principle. Recall that even the Federalists had insisted on a weak theory of legitimacy. But Bentley went even further and insisted that constitutional law could not be given any privileged status; that while it furnished "rules" of the game, rules, too, owed their formation and continuance to group interests. Thus the legitimating role of the Constitution was also downplayed. Bentley attempted to substitute what we can call "legitimation by fact." Groups and their interests were viewed by Bentley as "life-forms"; he refers to them as "felt facts," "real interests," "raw materials." They are, in short, social reality and what they do in the way of shaping policies, defining institutions, making laws, expressing ideas, and the like, is equally real, and because real, "true." Empirical truth is the new form of legitimacy.

These same notions reappear in the foremost political scientist of my generation, Robert Dahl. In his *A Preface to Democratic Theory*, Dahl attacked the democratic idea both as ideal and as an understanding of the world (that is, as "normative" and "empirical" theory). On the first score, he declared that only a "fanatic" would want to "maximize" "political equality" and "popular sovereignty" at the cost of values of leisure, privacy, consensus, and stability. A theory that cannot give us specific information about "costs" and "gains" is "too incomplete to assist us much in the real world."[26] As an empirical theory, he declared, democracy "tells us nothing about the real world. From it we can predict no behavior whatsoever." He then went on to indicate that only a theory that could tell us about the real world is entitled to render advice: one needs to know, he asserted, a "great variety of empirical facts" about "the real world" before one could decide about the proper political rules for that world.[27] The conditions for "maximizing" democracy depended, he said, upon grasping the meaning of the phrase "in the real world."[28] That Dahl's "real world" is the political scientist's mystification of Hegel's civil society is demonstrated by the political form that

Dahl recommended as both normatively and empirically superior to democratic theory and democracy. Polyarchy is simply interest-group politics updated to diminish democracy further; along the way he casually admits that polyarchy is stacked against the poor and the uneducated.[29] This culminates in a further argument that not only perpetuated Bentley's dismissal of the people and of the status of constitutional law but also restated what I have called the "legitimation by fact." Dahl explicitly argued that the Constitution could no longer be relied upon to provide the checks against democracy that the Federalists had hoped for. A new system had to be sought, one that lay not in the political realm at all, but in "society"; and once again Dahl presents his new constitution as a fact that legitimates a political system by virtue of its being a fact. Polyarchy, he noted, "focuses primarily not on the constitutional prerequisites but on the social prerequisites for a democratic order." The Constitutional Convention designed a constitution not "a society"; in fact, the results have "hindered realistic and precise thinking about the requirements of democracy. Because we are taught to believe in the necessity of constitutional checks and balances, we place little faith in social checks and balances . . . we often ignore the importance of the restraints imposed by social separation of powers. . . . [T]he theory of polyarchy suggests that the first and crucial variables to which political scientists must direct their attention are social and not constitutional."[30]

From approximately 1910 to 1960, American political science appeared to discuss "the state" and "power" by means of another vocabulary. Instead of "the state" the word "government" was used; instead of "power" the phrase "pressure politics." Beginning in the 1950s an interesting language shift occurred. The concept of political "system" was introduced that rapidly gained favor among political scientists and among social scientists in general. Aside from its putative theoretical advantages, "system" had the not inconsiderable merit of appearing to be scientific because scientists were using it, especially in the new exciting fields of cybernetics and communications "theory." Before one could utter the word "feedback," government had disappeared into an elaborate circuitry of serve mechanisms, or nervous systems, and emerged in the unlikely form of an "output." However numerous the variations, the typical usage emphasized the unified, interconnected structure of the system and its potentialities for internal control and external adaptation. In respect to these characteristics, "system" was more than a useful explanatory or heuristic model; it seemed the most appropriate symbolic form to express the meaning of the political world at mid-century, a world increasingly unified by American power and its extraordinary potential for production and destruction made possible by its new "more perfect union" of technology, big science, and corporate capital. The fact that the concept of "system" was used by government planners, corporate executives, management analysts, and engineers meant that, finally, a consensual symbol had emerged that could unify various branches of knowledge and complement the emerging American world-system. In "system" America seemed to have found a collective identity appropriate to the "American Century."

Between the time of these heady visions and the current interest in the idea of the state, much has happened and most of it is depressing to the leadership elites of American politics, economic life, and what a distinguished conservative economist once called "the knowledge industry." Merely to allude to Watergate, Vietnam, OPEC, and stagflation is to furnish the main headings for an inventory of signs indicative of the decline of American power and the erosion of the assumptions that had nourished the vision of a finely tuned American system in control of itself and of the world.

The response of today's neostatists is to argue that there is "an excess of democracy," and it has produced an "ungovernable" society. "Democracy," they allege, "is more of a threat to itself in the United States than it is in either Europe or Japan where there still exist residual inheritances of traditional and aristocratic values."[31] Thus the dilemma is that the state needs legitimacy if it is to be able to govern effectively, but the source of legitimacy is also the cause of the state's weakness. The form of the legitimation crisis is a conflict between the state and democracy.

As an alternative, I would suggest what has happened is that the thin theory of consent, taken over by Madison from Locke, was transformed. Beginning in the 1930s, the electoral conception of legitimation was joined, then overshadowed, by a form of social legitimation. The remains of democracy were mostly absorbed into the theory and practice of social welfare services and benefits. Democracy reemerged as dependence.

The domination of economic life by private corporate organizations and of public life by administrative organizations has introduced and promoted dependence throughout the entire society. At first the effects were masked because there was something for everybody and a great deal for the few. The affluent and educated were absorbed into private bureaucracies and corporations to serve the control function: those lower socially, economically, and culturally became dependents of the welfare state.

Dependence, not the fiscal crisis of the state or the crisis in capital accumulation or the crisis of authority, is the true crisis because it hints at the conception of normality that is beginning to emerge. Dependence signifies the existence, first, of a surplus population that must be managed; and, second, of a type of population that can be, as it were, expanded or contracted, depending upon the requirements of a relatively volatile and somewhat unmanageable economy. Dependent man, the rump remains of democratic man, is a new type of man, the man intended for the new version of a more perfect union: the union of theoretical and applied science, corporate capitalism, and public bureaucracy.

The main characteristic of dependent man is not simply that he lacks autonomy but that he is demoralized and, for that reason, functional. Demoralization stands for living continuously and hopelessly in circumstances where one is assailed endlessly by forces that one cannot understand, much less control, but that others seemingly do know about and do control. Demoralized man has no control over his employment or his retirement; his skills, such as they are, are rapidly obsolete; education is no guarantee of a way out because it no longer can promise upward mobility; his life has no settled rhythm to it: only an intense week of work and a weekend of collapse, periods of protracted layoffs followed by periods of employment.

The pervasiveness of demoralization was most acutely experienced during the Vietnam War. One does not have to be an apologist for the war-makers to realize that when the decision to withdraw was finally made, the demoralization in the country and in the councils of government itself was no small consideration. Equally significant, perhaps more so, was the widespread demoralization of American troops abroad. Insubordination, rebellion, low morale, and high rates of drug use are well documented. These forms of demoralization were profoundly symbolic because of the carriers; the typical serviceman was poor, black, and a foot soldier. That is, he had the lowest skills in an increasingly sophisticated technological force, and he was the most dispensable. He was the military counterpart to the unskilled worker, the welfare dependent. As such he transcends his military status to become, not a member of the so-called "underclass," or the *Lumpenproletariat*, but the superfluous man of technological society. He is only partly described by Marx's famous concept of "the industrial reserve army"; he is better called "the social infantryman."

To be a social infantryman is, like the member of the industrial reserve army, to be at the behest or summons of society, to expand one's numbers or to contract them, depending on the needs of the draft/market. It is, at the same time, to be the enemy of those like you, for you are a competitor with the skilled and seek to depress his wages or status. You are a competitor with the unskilled, for your presence serves to strain the social services the society gives and withdraws at periodic intervals, reminding you in the process that you are a private, that is, capable of being deprived and needful of discipline from above. Above all, you are a social infantryman because the infantry suffers more casualties than any other service. Contemporary society, in its welfare and medical services, recognizes its obligation to infantrymen because this is the first society in human history in which the ruling groups know as a matter of objective knowledge that the current form of economic, social, political, and scientific-technological organization will necessarily produce casualties, as necessarily as wars produce them: super-fluous populations, obsolete skills, industrial disease, environmental damage that will be internalized by the population and urban battlegrounds, such as the South Bronx.

But demoralization is not a nameless condition. Like the God of the Book of Genesis, the powers that have created demoralized man are also the powers that have supplied the categories for interpreting him—categories that enable the powers to reproduce him. Demoralized man comes to us sometimes as alienated man, sometimes as anomic man, sometimes as the authoritarian personality, sometimes as mass man, sometimes as the func-tionally unemployed. All of his names have been given to him by political and social science. Social and political science supply not only the theoreti-cal categories for interpreting demoralized man but also the theoretical *praxis* for shaping and misshaping him. These sciences may survey demoralized man, but their derivatives practice and reproduce him—the derivatives of management psychology, market analysis, industrial relations, private sur-veys of public opinion, the whole range of practical powers that social science theory has created.

In perspective social science theory is performing a crucial role in the crisis of democracy: it is contributing powerfully to what we may call the "delegitimization of democratic man." The classic instance is that creature constructed by social science to replace the "citizen" and known familiarly as "the American voter." Social science discovered that when the voter went to the polls he went as a being who was ignorant, prone to illiberal views, fickle, alienated, and fearful. When he did not go to the polls, he was declared apathetic but functional. As the findings began to cumulate, the irresistible conviction grew that no one in possession of his faculties would dare trust the fate of the republic to so unlovely and unpromising a species as "the American voter."

A state that needs only formal legitimation has reduced the citizen to such a negligible consideration that all the burning issues of political theory—participation, equality, civic virtue, and justice—no longer seem to matter, auguring a new conception of the state. From the time that Western thinkers first began to reflect upon political association, they concluded that such an association had to be grounded in a definite place and in some truth—whether religious, philosophical, or political. But that seems to be changing and the contemporary state seems poised uncertainly between yesterday's vision of a developing, expanding state—whose being was most quintessen-tially revealed by its power, influence, and prestige abroad—and tomor-row's half-understood idea of a state that will have to supervise and manage society in an era of receding expectations and dwindling resources. We stand between a conception of the state, so distended and grotesque as to be without any political content, however formidable its bureaucracy, and a conception of a tightly organized state dedicated to guiding profligate humanity through its seven lean years. But the lean state, too, is politically empty, however prudent its managers.

The end of the state raises the question of our state or condition. The answer is simple and impossible, or so it must seem; it is to reclaim our politicalness. This means not only finding new democratic forms but of recovering an old idea, the idea of Everyman as a morally autonomous agent. The steady discreditation of that idea, which has culminated in the pummeling of its remains in "the American voter" and in the general contempt for popular participation among social and political scientists, has worked to deny what moral autonomy desperately needs—the opportunity, in the literal sense, for moral and political practice. This is what the fundamental point of participation has been: not to effect democracy in some abstract sense, but to perpetuate the idea of moral autonomy and political agency by furnishing the citizen with the opportunity to acquire political experience.

Notes

1. Wilson's remark is, of course, an echo of Lord Coke's dictum that "Magna Carta is such a fellow that he will have no sovereign."

2. A minor qualification would have to be added to this generalization. "The state" has consistently figured in international law and has occasionally been introduced into Supreme Court decisions whenever issues have been raised about the president's authority in the conduct of foreign policy or as commander in chief.

3. For a discussion, see Martin Jay, *The Dialectical Imagination: A History of the Frankfurt School and Institute for Social Research, 1923–1950* (Boston and Toronto, 1973), pp. 238–255.

4. See, for example, Stephen D. Krasner, *Defending the National Interest* (Princeton, 1978), p. 5 ff.; R. Gilpin, *U.S. Power and the Multinational Corporation* (New York, 1975), passim; A. Stepan, *The State and Society* (Princeton, 1978), p. 3 ff.; R. O. Keohane and Joseph S. Nye, Jr., eds, *Transnational Relations and World Politics* (Cambridge, Mass., 1970), passim.

5. David Easton, *The Political System* (New York, 1953), p. 106.

6. Thomas Hobbes, *Leviathan*, Dedicatory Epistle, ed. Michael Oakeshott (Oxford, 1946), p. 2.

7. Ibid.

8. Ibid., pt. II, chap. 17, p. 112.

9. John Locke, *Two Treatises of Government*, II, 156.

10. It is worth noting that Locke employs the term "people" whereas Hobbes rarely does, preferring the word "multitude" with its connotation of inchoateness and inability to concert its "will."

11. *The Federalist*, ed. J. E. Cooke (Middletown, Conn., 1961), no. 55.

12. Ibid., no. 10, p. 61.

13. Ibid., no. 51, p. 351.

14. Ibid., no. 10, p. 57.

15. Ibid., p. 59.

16. Ibid., p. 58.

17. Ibid., no. 51, p. 352.

18. Ibid., pp. 352–353.

19. Ibid., no. 10, p. 59.

20. Ibid., pp. 59, 60.

21. Ibid., no. 23, p. 147, no. 31, p. 195, no. 34, p. 211.

22. Ibid., no. 72, p. 486.

23. Ibid., pp. 486–487.

24. Arthur F. Bentley, *The Process of Government* (Bloomington, Ind., 1949), pp. 199, 263.

25. Ibid., p. 263.

26. Robert Dahl, *A Preface to Democratic Theory* (Chicago, 1956), pp. 50, 51.

27. Ibid., p. 52.

28. Ibid., p. 64.

29. Ibid., p. 81.

30. Ibid., p. 83.

31. Samuel Huntington, "The United States," in *The Crisis of Democracy* (New York, 1975), pp. 113–114.

3

Consent and Authority in America

Mark E. Kann

Political authority in America is not in immediate danger. Governmental officials may not be leading Americans in any particular direction, but they still have the authority to issue decisions that command general public compliance. But for how long? The architects of American political authority are worried that its moral foundation is eroding. Americans increasingly lack confidence in political leadership, and public compliance with official laws and policies is less than enthusiastic. Robert Gilmour and Robert Lamb reflect the findings of many empirical studies in their own conclusion: "There appears to be a latent sense that the government may no longer be *legitimate* in the eyes of the governed."[1] Were this latent sense to become a manifest sense of government illegitimacy, American political authority would rapidly deteriorate—a crisis for its advocates and an opportunity for its adversaries.

Is this latent legitimacy crisis simply another episode in Americans' persistent effort to escape from all forms of authority? I think not. It may represent a more fundamental weakness that is only now becoming apparent. From the beginning of nationhood, American political authority has been founded on the doctrine of consent: first, government's authority is derived from representative processes that allow for public participation, and, second, such participation obligates the public to follow government's leadership and to obey its directives. Within the context of early America, this was an effective legitimation device. But as American government became more centralized and distant from public participation, the effectiveness of consent as a legitimation device steadily diminished. Americans began to associate their consent not with individual liberty and autonomy but with social control over their everyday lives. But rather than withdraw their consent, Americans increasingly perceive it as a temporary expedient rather than as an affirmation of political authority. My thesis is that political authority today is still founded on "consent," but it is a consent with little moral significance attached to it.

The Escape from Authority

Americans have always had major reservations about authority. The Puritans and other early Americans sought freedom from the authority of the Anglican and Catholic churches of the Old World. The Founders declared their independence from the authority of British government. And many of the nation's early entrepreneurs demanded an end to government mercantilist authority over their economic opportunities. America's developing culture of radical individualism guaranteed that future generations would question ascriptive and even achieved authority in all realms of social life. Periodically, such questioning would manifest itself in significant protest movements, ranging from Shays' Rebellion or the Civil War to the more contemporary civil rights movement, antiwar disobedience, feminist protest, and ecological discontent. Each protest, however, generated enough of a backlash in support of political authority to sustain it with relatively little damage.

Samuel P. Huntington suggests that today's latent legitimacy crisis is mainly one more manifestation of Americans' periodic assault on political authority. This assault began in the 1960s:

> The essence of the democratic surge in the 1960s was a general challenge to existing systems of authority, public and private. In one form or another, this challenge manifest itself in the family, the university, business, public and private associations, politics, the governmental bureaucracy, and the military services. People no longer felt the same compulsion to obey those whom they had previously considered superior to themselves in age, rank, status, expertise, character, or talents.[2]

For Huntington, the 1960s was another one of those decades when individuals placed their own particularistic and immediate interests above those of political authority; they then used democratic processes in ways that undermined authority. The decade of radical individualism might have run its course, and backlash calls for "law and order" indicated it was exhausting itself. But the political scandals and economic crises of the 1970s exacerbated the problem of authority and prolonged the distrust of it. Somehow, in Huntington's view, a new balance between individualism and political authority must be struck.

Huntington's prescription is for Americans to moderate their demands on government and to exhibit greater trust in their political leaders.[3] With less public pressure constraining them, leaders will have the breathing space necessary to employ their expertise to help solve pressing public problems. Finally, the relative successes of leaders in problem-solving will constitute definitive evidence that public trust is merited. What Huntington does not consider is why Americans should trust that their leaders will be honest, effective, or responsive. A new basis for such confidence is needed.

Alexis de Tocqueville was sensitive to this issue. He too wished to balance individualism and political authority, for he feared that, too often,

> democracy . . . has been abandoned to its wild instincts, and it has grown up like those children who have no parental guidance, who receive their education in the public streets, and who are acquainted only with the vices and wretchedness of society.[4]

Tocqueville believed that the democratic spirit of individualism must be tamed, not simply by calling for trust in leaders, but by leaders exhibiting the qualities inherent in good parenting. Leaders must nurture public values and visions of national accomplishment in order to restrain individual selfishness. Otherwise, individuals will demand "freedom from" authority without recognizing that a common authority can provide them the "freedom to" accomplish consensual goals.[5] Leaders must also exemplify and teach public responsibility that includes the idea that mature citizens who participate in politics are obligated to obey political authority.[6] Tocqueville's guide to political parenting suggests, in short, that leaders must periodically renew national *consensus* and reestablish the responsible *consent* of the governed each generation. And this is precisely what great leaders like Lincoln, Wilson, and Roosevelt tried to do during some of the most difficult moments in American history.

Nonetheless, where past American leaders have succeeded, present American leaders are consistently failing. In the article "Our Leadership Crisis: America's Real Malaise," Henry Steele Commager argues that our current generation of leaders lacks the national vision that might moderate radical individualism:

> One of the most obvious explanations of the failure of leadership in our time is that so few of our leaders—and our potential leaders—seem to have any road map. It is hard to lead when you yourself are in a labyrinth.[7]

Furthermore, Huntington is himself aware that the idea of responsible consent is something less than popular today. People do not obey the law because it is the result of representative and electoral processes in which they have participated; instead, "law-abiding behavior . . . depended upon what was in the laws."[8] And this is only a step away from the idea that people ought to obey the laws only when they find them consistent with their own interests.[9]

Why have American political leaders failed in their quest to solidify authority by renewing consensus and consent? Commager blames the current generation of leadership and Huntington the current generation of Americans, but neither argument is wholly convincing. I believe that Marxist analysts are moving in the right direction: the social context of American politics has shifted.[10] Important changes in the international capitalist sphere are now surfacing in the political arena. National consensus is impossible when class interests clearly conflict; consent of the governed loses its moral content when government is perceived as a tool of multinational corporations rather than as a neutral arbiter in the pluralist arena or as a representative of the majority. The problem with the Marxist explanation is that it does not go far enough into the political arena itself. It is conceivable that political leaders can renew consensus and consent even when economic contradictions are most manifest. This was what happened in the 1930s when the Roosevelt administration sustained political authority by nurturing a consensual vision of a "new deal" and by reinvigorating the moral content of consent by offering workers new forms of political participation through legislation like the Wagner Act. Let me suggest that a fuller understanding of the inability of American political leaders to engage in political parenting today must include an analysis of the strengths and weaknesses of "the doctrine of consent" as a legitimation device within changing political contexts.

Consent and Legitimacy

The most important justification for political authority in American history has been the doctrine of consent. Joseph Tussman asserts:

> Consent has not always been regarded as a necessary basis for the claim to political authority, but for the last three hundred years every other basis has been so badly shaken that there is hardly a government which does not claim, however fraudulently, to rest upon it.[11]

Tussman's assertion is especially warranted in the American case. The notion of consent was embedded in an American political culture founded on Protestant norms of "consenting" to a covenant with God, political ideals of "consenting" to a social contract, and capitalist practices of "consenting" to contractual relations in the marketplace.[12] Political common sense in America was intertwined with the idea that individuals are born free and equal and owe their allegiance to authority only on the basis of their own voluntary choice. The earliest factions in American politics adopted this common sense, labelled it fairness, and invested it with interpretive meanings appropriate to their own interests. To have done otherwise would have been tantamount to declaring themselves supporters of tyranny.

As a systematic doctrine rooted in seventeenth- and eighteenth-century thought, consent has three basic tenets that appear in almost all variants.

The first tenet is "believing skepticism."[13] The doctrine of consent is usually based on a set of absolute beliefs in divine natural law or secular justice.[14] These beliefs provide meaning to human life, norms for human relationships, and values, goals, and visions that transcend individuality. Inherent in the doctrine of consent is a consensus on the ends of political life. However, the doctrine of consent is also based on a substantial dose of skepticism that sinful, irrational, or fallible humans can actually discern political ends or be guided by them in their everyday political lives. The road to political salvation is always an uncertain one.[15]

The second tenet is that no group or individual has a monopoly on political righteousness; men are born free and equal, and ultimately each individual is responsible for making political choices in the realm of uncertainty. Most variants of consent assert that individuals have a natural right to make political choices as well as to values like life and property.[16] As such, when individuals suffer from Hobbesian wars, Lockean inconveniences, or Rousseauvian selfishness, they have the right, voluntarily, to erect a common political authority to adjudicate their disputes and protect their rights. Political society derives its authority from individuals' consent, and political authority is bounded by individuals' natural rights.

The third tenet is the glue that binds the first two tenets into a justification for political obedience: by consenting to political authority, the individual takes on a moral obligation to obey it. Tussman reminds us that

> the consent of the governed, upon which we insist, is consent to be governed. If it is a voluntary act, it is nevertheless an act of voluntary subordination.[17]

The meaning of consent, whether expressed through oaths, political participation, or tacit acquiescence, is a promise to obey established political authority and to suffer voluntarily the consequences for one's own disobedience. The underlying assumption, of course, is that an individual will subordinate himself voluntarily only if he expects to find political authority more beneficial than not.

Since the seventeenth century, it has never been easy to persuade most individuals that voluntary subordination is beneficial. Many individuals have preferred to seek God or justice outside of the political realm despite risks and inconveniences. Many other individuals have taken a Thoreauvian attitude, feeling that their rights were more secure when ignoring or disobeying political authority. And still others have felt it expedient to obey political authority when it enhanced their material opportunities but inexpedient to obey it when it seemed to deny opportunities.[18] Protestant conscience and marketplace freedom were always available to justify a challenge to political authority. The significance of the consent doctrine as a legitimation device is highlighted by the fact that it has been extremely effective in spite of the modern tendency toward radical individualism.

John Locke implicitly suggested that only the threat of extraordinary human crises would adequately motivate individuals to enter into political society voluntarily. Locke himself lived within a historical context where major changes highlighted three such crises. The first was a religious crisis suffered by Protestants living in the shadow of Catholicism; the temptation to sin was especially great in these circumstances. The second crisis was a political one; as the feudal state was being transformed into the modern state, the likelihood of human conflict becoming violent confrontation was quite real. The economic crisis was third; the early stages of capitalism generated great hopes for some classes but tremendous fear among the lower classes that traditional means of subsistence were being displaced.[19] In essence, Locke argued that a political authority based on consent rather than paternalism would ease the worst effects of these crises by supporting religious tolerance, extending political rights, and nurturing economic growth. Locke's argument provided significant groups of people good reasons for believing that a government based on consent would subordinate them less than previous governments and provide them greater opportunities for satisfying individual desires; political authority based on consent would maximize individual freedom and autonomy.

The motivational value of these crises is long lasting. They are crises that can be considered permanent parts of human existence; only their worst effects are subject to human intervention. Protestants believe that individuals are "naturally" tempted to sin; liberals usually assume that individuals are "perpetually" in conflict with one another over scarce values; and those who affirm capitalism generally believe that individuals must "inevitably" suffer the pains of labor to provide subsistence for themselves and their families. Even during times when people seem appropriately religious, peaceful, and prosperous, the architects of political authority need only remind them that sin, violence, and impoverishment always stalk the corridors of political disorder. Consensus and consent must be renewed lest these crises strike with greater force than ever. Of course, some individuals may ignore this reminder and set themselves against political authority. But they can easily be labelled sinners, criminals, and anarchists and considered evidence of the continued threat of these crises. The prophecy of permanent crises becomes a self-fulfilling one.

Under the right conditions, leaders can use this crisis atmosphere to renew national consensus and responsible consent time and again. As long as there is a public consensus that sin, violence, and impoverishment are real threats, leaders can transform perceptions of crises into powerful visions of accomplishment: people may all be tempted by sin, but Christians are specially chosen to undertake the pilgrimage to salvation; conflict may be the human lot, but a system of impartial law can peacefully and fairly resolve most conflicts; economic want may be a constant threat, but Americans can achieve unprecedented prosperity. Murray Edelman provides a way of understanding how perceptions of crises can be transformed into visions:

> Many problems that impoverish or ruin millions of lives are not perceived as crises because we attach labels and "explanations" to them that portray them as natural and inevitable. . . . We see poverty, crime, sickness, emotional disturbance, carnage on the highways, and similar disasters as chronic social "problems" rather than as crises.[20]

Once people perceive these crises as permanent, the crises disappear as immediate objects of thought and action; they are taken for granted as part of the human condition. However, the crises do generate "problems" that leaders can use as the foundation for their national visions of nearly problem-free futures. To the extent that the public sees these problems as real ones not amenable to individual solutions, individuals are likely to give their consent to political authority.

Furthermore, if leaders are chosen through representative processes in relatively decentralized settings, they do not necessarily need to realize their visions or actually solve problems to maintain their legitimacy. When leaders and constituents agree on the nature of the visions and problems, when leaders are convincingly chosen through representational processes, and when individuals have easy access to their leaders, the blame for failures can readily be shifted from leadership to the community. First, leaders can persuasively claim that their failures are the community's failures; they were only doing as directed. Second, they might claim that their failures are due to constituents' unwillingness to give leaders adequate support or to exercise their freedoms responsibly. Those who continue their sinful, violent, or lazy ways have only themselves to blame. Furthermore, if leaders are trusted members of the community, they can persuasively argue either that failures are important steps toward success (for example, recessions are the basis for economic growth) or that failures reevoke the specter of crises and require greater unity than ever (for example, failures in diplomacy result in a threat of war calling for community support). In this case, "the messenger who brings the bad news" is not shot but rather is rewarded with a badge of strengthened legitimacy.

Once a system of political authority based on consensus and consent is established, it tends to perpetuate itself. Perceptions of crises, visions of accomplishment, promises of problem-solving, the nurturance of individual blame for failures, and the renewed evocation of crises will be reproduced in public institutions and reinforced through acculturation and socialization.

Even if some segments of the population have "objective" reasons for rebelling against political authority, their subjective subordination will insulate leaders for some time. The doctrine of consent is a potent device that leaders can use to secure and reinforce their political hegemony. On this point, many modern liberals and Marxists are in agreement.[21]

Consent and Contextual Change

The structure of the consent doctrine has changed little since Locke penned his *Second Treatise*. Its major tenets continue to be believing skepticism, individualism, and voluntary subordination motivated by the specter of crises.[22] However, the utility of consent as a legitimation device is only partially contingent on its content. It is also a function of the political context in which the doctrine is used. This context has changed dramatically since Locke's time. While many changes in the political context may be traced back to the evolution of capitalism, I believe they are themselves of enough significance to merit our attention. In particular, I will suggest that a political culture of mixed beliefs and much skepticism, a political system of centralized power and individual impotence, and a world system in which crises are everyday affairs constitute a political context that radically undermines the potency of consent as a persuasive foundation for political authority.

When common beliefs are highly abstract and transcendental, as in natural law, political leaders have many options for developing national visions and for claiming visionary accomplishments. Almost any act can be interpreted as a positive step toward establishing or administering common goals. It is virtually impossible for citizens to verify or falsify such interpretations, but it is reassuring to hear them.[23] However, when common beliefs become more concrete, leaders' options shrink. The principle of the greatest happiness suggests that individuals can measure leaders' achievements in terms of their own personal feelings. And when utilitarianism becomes increasingly materialistic, people can gauge leadership success or failure in terms of dollars: Has the general standard of living risen, and is there a chicken in every pot? Where leaders can be held accountable in such concrete ways, the greatest weight of their authority lies in the realm of human uncertainty where corruption and ineptitude can be suspected if not charged.

Leaders can avoid these suspicions in two ways. First, they can clearly make good on their promises, in this instance, seeing to it that standards of living rise and pots are filled. But if they are too successful and general prosperity prevails, they may eliminate the major basis for their authority.[24] People who have known only prosperity may not take seriously warnings of impending poverty. Second, leaders who fail to make good on material promises must promote secondary explanations for continued poverty. A functional theory of inequality (that is, everyone ultimately benefits from disparities of wealth) and a theory of equal opportunities (that is, everyone may potentially increase his wealth through his own efforts) may help elicit the consent of the poor, who, according to this wisdom, have only themselves to blame for their condition.[25] These theories may be persuasive if most people perceive upward mobility as a possibility for themselves and their children.[26] The most difficult circumstances for leaders hoping to renew public consent would be when some citizens have achieved great prosperity (and call for new limits on political authority) while others perceive little hope of upward mobility (and call for greater authoritative action in their behalf).[27] Where leadership is based on promises of material prosperity and society is divided into haves and have-nots, it is likely that the consensus of belief will begin to deteriorate perceptibly.

Some individuals may return to spiritual beliefs, others to new variants of utility, and still others to social equality as the primary basis for political vision and action. To satisfy these groups simultaneously, political leaders would have to develop a fairly intricate public relations effort to portray their goals and values in ways that appear consistent with the mixed beliefs of the majority.[28] In a logical sense, this may be impossible if beliefs are not only mixed but contradictory (for example, functional inequality versus social equality). In this context, political leaders may try to maintain their legitimacy by spinning a web of lies, exercising modes of doublethink, and practicing a symbolic politics. However, this opens them to the dangers of self-deception, public scandal, and an ensuing credibility gap.[29]

These outcomes could be avoided if leaders shed the mantle of absolute belief and political vision altogether. They could base their authority, instead, on their ability to guarantee individuals the right to pursue their own values and goals.[30] Yet, this is precisely the same situation that Commager labels a "leadership crisis." Without a generally attractive road map to the future, leaders can do little to moderate radical individualism. When belief wholly gives way to skepticism, individuals are likely to obey government when they find it personally beneficial and to disobey when they think they can get away with it. Their confidence in leadership will be instrumental at best.

If political leaders are forced by circumstances to rely heavily on their role as representatives and guarantors of individual choices, perhaps they could use the individualism inherent in consent to deflect social dissatisfaction from themselves. They may claim that their acts merely reflect the political choices of the citizens they represent and that individuals have not used their choices wisely and have only themselves to blame. This approach to maintaining legitimacy might work in a participatory community where people do feel that leaders represent them,[31] or in a relatively egalitarian community where leaders can actually represent the common aspirations of constituents.[32] However, it is not likely to be an effective tactic where political power is centralized and society is riddled with inequalities.

In centralized political systems, individuals have little concrete evidence that their participation influences the nature of political authority, the selection of politicians who fill positions of authority, or the decisions issued by them. The sheer distance that separates leaders from constituents is likely to nurture mutual suspicions, even during good times. Leaders may feel that the public does not understand the complexity of important problems, and constituents may feel that their leaders are not responsive to public demands. Mutual alienation is especially apt to surface when leaders appear to give preference to visible powerful groups (like oil companies) at the public's expense (at the filling station).[33] Political authority will increasingly be perceived as an instrument of social elites and of social control over the public.

Leaders must somehow reestablish in the public mind links between central political authority and individual choice. One way for them to do this would be to suggest institutional reforms: streamline the federal bureaucracy and make it more accessible to public scrutiny or establish programs of "maximum feasible participation" to allow individuals greater involvement in local administration. If people initially accept local administration as a significant arena and participate in it, their complicity in political authority reopens the door to self-blame. When problems occur, they will be forced to ask themselves and to answer to others whether they have participated fully and effectively enough.[34] Nonetheless, the door to self-blame is not likely to remain open very long. Once involved in local politics, these maximum feasible participants may learn that central leadership still is not responsive to local concerns, that local administrators have little political leverage, and that particular social groups consistently win the lion's share of governmental benefits.[35] These participants may get co-opted; but they also may use their new positions as bases for challenging central leadership and for organizing protests.[36] Ultimately, extending consent processes to include new avenues of local participation may accelerate rather than alleviate central leadership's legitimacy problems.

Central leadership does have an option. It may try to justify the distance between political authority and individual choice as being in the individual's interest. Arguing for the prerogatives of efficiency, special expertise, and professionalism, leaders could claim that even greater centralization of authority is necessary in order to solve nationwide problems.[37] Leaders could then appoint expert commissions, create new central public agencies, package comprehensive legislation, and even delegate some authority to private groups of professionals.[38] Each action may be greeted by public applause if the public perceives that leadership is finally taking the initiative and required steps for dealing effectively with individual demands. This option too, however, carries with it the seeds of self-destruction.

Which problems require expertise the most? Without a basic consensus of beliefs, all problems are potentially pressing ones for some groups. Political officials will feel pressures to assume responsibilities for harnessing expertise in all areas of social life, the effect being to politicize social issues while depoliticizing society. This development may generate new sources of public displeasure and suspicion. Groups may feel displeased if their particular issues are not prominent enough on the experts' agenda, if expert solutions are not adequate, or if attempted solutions cause new problems. Fearing such displeasure, leaders may practice a cautious incrementalism that might lead people to suspect that no real attempt is being made to meet their demands.[39] Not insignificant is the expense of harnessing all this expertise. And tax increases may result in fiscal stress and taxpayer distress.[40] Moreover, a central leadership that assumes so much responsibility cannot easily deflect blame for failure from itself. The claim that citizens have participated in the political process and must accept the consequences of that process is not likely to be persuasive in this context. Herein lies one source of Huntington's fear that Americans today dissociate their participation from their obligation to obey outcomes.

When all else fails, leaders may try to avoid a manifest legitimacy crisis by reevoking the permanent crises of humankind. This tactic has a demonstrated history of success. For example, the crisis of World War I proved to be a major asset to Western capitalist leaders threatened by powerful radical movements.[41] Nevertheless, in a changing historical context, *which* crisis to reevoke may become problematical. The crisis of original sin means little in predominantly secular societies; the crisis of human violence may appear to be an opportunity to revolutionary groups and their supporters; and the crisis of subsistence may possess little motivational value for many members of affluent societies.[42] Consequently, leaders may have to raise the specter of new crises that potentially speak to the hopes and fears of diverse groups of individuals. The logic here points to the evocation of larger and more numerous crises and, at some point, a law of diminishing returns is apt to set in: with so many crises, each new one is less haunting than the last. Even newer and larger crises must be evoked, if not actively promoted, to sustain imperiled political authority.

Political leadership here would be tantamount to crisis management aimed at keeping afloat the ship of state by preventing or retarding the growth of even more ominous crises.[43] Leaders' ability to nurture visions of collective accomplishment, to solve problems, or to encourage self-blame among constitutents all but disappears when they can only call on the public to protect past gains against future catastrophes. Can such crisis managers inspire public trust and confidence? To the extent they solve some problems, their achievement will be paled by expectations of new crises ahead. If leaders fail to solve significant problems, citizens may continue to comply with their directives if they perceive no alternatives. Yet, in a legitimacy vacuum, new social movements will more than likely develop on the basis of new visions and claims to greater democratic participation. If the crisis managers crush these movements, they simply attest to their own lack of authority; if they allow these movements to thrive, they undermine their own authority.[44]

A legitimacy crisis may, however, manifest itself in more passive ways. Like people who ignore cancer warnings because they suspect that all substances are carcinogenic, citizens may feel that all political issues are crisis issues and therefore withdraw from politics altogether.[45] Massive political apathy may initially provide leaders greater maneuverability in that apathetic people do not oppose political authority. But nor do they support it. When the crisis managers call for new sacrifices, the apathetic may ignore the call, refuse to comply with it, or actively oppose it; a silent majority is not necessarily a silenced majority. At best, crisis managers can expect instrumental public compliance rather than legitimacy.

Consider now a political society in which (1) materialism and mixed belief systems displace older views on natural law, (2) government becomes centralized and distant from individual choices, and (3) leaders present themselves as little more than crisis managers. In this historical context, individuals will not necessarily withdraw their "consent" from political authority; they may continue to vote, participate in party and interest-group politics, and engage in local activism in the hope of reforming the political system and solving social problems.[46] However, individuals may invest their participation with little or no moral value, viewing "consent" as an expedient means to bring about change but not to legitimize political authority. Paradoxically, individuals may be "consenting" more, yet feeling less bound to political authority than previously.[47] In the next section, I suggest that America has evolved into such a political society.

The Evolution of Consent in America

The doctrine of consent was an extremely effective legitimation device during the early part of American history. But as the context of American politics changed during the next two hundred years, the doctrine began to lose its effectiveness. The fact that Americans continue to "consent" through their political participation is neither an indication that they feel morally obligated to obey political authority nor an example of their "false consciousness" in being accomplices in their own subordination.[48] Instead, "consent" today signifies little more than a temporary willingness not to disobey.

The early American Puritans serve as a convenient bench mark for gauging the evolution of consent in America. They anticipated consent's believing skepticism by holding that the truth of God's natural law must be voluntarily subscribed to by the individual seeking salvation. This subscription constituted a covenant that obligated the religious pilgrim to obey. The Puritans then extended the idea of covenanting to political society. Wilson Carey McWilliams writes:

> In Puritan analysis, every society or polity was based on a "Covenant." Not a utilitarian contract, the Covenant was defined by the values and goals to which members committed themselves and which gave to individuals within it a "common soul." Covenants made men brothers, in however limited a sense.[49]

Membership in the political community was based on a consensus of values and the individual's consent to abide by the religious norms of leaders in these decentralized theocracies. Consent was generally signified by acquiescence to the commands of community leaders and by continued residence.[50] One factor that makes Nathaniel Hawthorne's *The Scarlet Letter* such a compelling story is that Hester Prynne voluntarily remained in her community to suffer punishment even though she was free and able to leave it.

Religious values and consent were the basis for political authority, resulting in a hierarchical, powerful system of governance:

> Economic regulation, the control of wealth and prices, the effort to provide employment and to guarantee the individual against natural catastrophe were all part of the duty of the Puritan state. . . . Puritan analysis, in fact, is often directly opposed to the formulations of those who would see Puritanism as a precursor to capitalism.[51]

The Puritan state could exert tremendous authority over individual members, but it could not do so arbitrarily. Its control over local material life, for example, was limited to regulating wealth in ways that freed individuals from material temptations and from consuming fears of impoverishment. While Puritan leaders often disputed the best means to this end, their political legitimacy allowed them a great deal of leeway in attempting to move toward it. Ultimately, individuals would comply because they perceived obedience as the basis of their freedom and ability to seek salvation.

The Founders also began with God, natural law, and republican notions of public virtue. But between 1776 and 1787, their religious concerns increasingly gave way to utilitarian materialism.[52] God had mapped out America's destiny as a unique experiment in religious tolerance, political liberty, and especially material prosperity. He was called upon to provide a transcendental justification for the U.S. Constitution. But then he was safely eased out of everyday politics to be recalled only when rededication to national destiny was expedient. The Puritans' God demanded duties; the Founders' God justified the right to material aggrandizement. Individuals would consent to the new political authority because it would free them from traditional constraints and free them to exploit the natural wealth of the land.

The Founders' new state had extraordinarily limited political authority. Separation of powers, checks and balances, federalism with considerable local autonomy, a complex system of direct and indirect elections, staggered terms of office, and popular fears of tyranny combined to assure Americans that their government would do little more than protect national boundaries, manage internal conflicts, and protect the right of private accumulation.[53] The state was intended to be little more than a superstructure for individuals who would choose their own religious values, participate in local politics, and realize the vision of prosperity by breaking new land, starting small shops, and opening new trade routes. Ultimately, the nation's future would lie less in the hands of political leaders and more in the efforts of free individuals, Hamiltonian statism and mercantilism notwithstanding.

In the process of developing this state, the Founders profoundly altered the traditional practice of consenting to political authority. For both Locke and the Puritans, consenting was a passive, one-time affair in which individuals pledged their allegiance to political society; the leaders of society, in turn, would entrust political authority to those born and educated to rule. The Founders altered this by attaching consent directly to government and indirectly to the electoral process. The Declaration of Independence, for example, states that "governments are instituted among men, deriving their just powers from the consent of the governed."[54] This statement came to have two meanings in the constitutional period and thereafter. One meaning was that individuals must directly consent to the Constitution itself through special ratification conventions. A second meaning was that individuals must directly consent to government personnel through periodic, popular elections. While none of the Founders explicitly believed that voting was the sole or necessary basis for consent of the governed, this idea soon became a conventional norm. After all, how could individuals be represented and protected against illegitimate tyranny if not through free elections? By the 1830s, when state property restrictions on suffrage were finally eliminated, consent and voting were almost indistinguishable in the public mind.[55]

How did the Founders motivate Americans to ratify the new Constitution? *The Federalist Papers* suggest that Madison, Hamilton, and Jay went out of their way to show that the permanent crises of humankind were the major factors. The crisis of religion played a minor role, but Madison, on page after page, evoked the crisis of violent human conflict and transformed it into a vision of peaceful pluralist competition.[56] Moreover, he and especially Hamilton argued that the various economic crises of the Articles of Confederation period, with the proper political authority, could become the basis for a thriving commercial economy.[57] Here then was a government without the political authority to deny individual rights but with the power to ease the crises of everyday life. The alternative was the disorder of more Shays' rebellions and the economic insecurity of paper money schemes, land speculation, and debt suspension. In so many words, the message of the framers of the Constitution was that a new political authority based on consent would provide individuals the "freedom to" participate in a great national experiment without losing the "freedom from" unjust interference.

If the Founders succeeded in legitimizing the new political system, they also succeeded in setting the stage for a new series of legitimacy problems. First, if God and natural law were substantially replaced by a materialist consensus, then political authority increasingly rested in the realm of uncertain human choice. One could begin to ask if political authority was or was not successfully bringing Americans closer to prosperity and doing it in appropriate ways. In this context, Hamilton was a forebearer of the many Americans who would call on government to take a more positive role in the economy.[58] Second, if consent was now manifest in activities like voting or participating in the new political parties, perhaps more direct forms of consent (in a Jeffersonian ward system?) would be justified. Third, if a more active form of consent was the primary basis for political legitimacy and individual obligations, then it could be argued that governmental decisions were not binding on the minorities and women who were not allowed to vote or to participate more directly. In short, the doctrine of consent within the context of early America was useful for legitimizing the new system of political authority but also provided a justification for stronger government, new forms of public participation, and the politicization of previously excluded groups.

In the nineteenth century, the Founders' materialism became embedded in American political culture. God virtually disappeared from politics and was soon replaced by a "natural" law of material selection. For example, John C. Calhoun anticipated the growth of Social Darwinism when he wrote of "the great law of self-preservation which pervades all that feels, from man down to the lowest and most insignificant reptile or insect. In no one is it stronger than in man."[59] God and national destiny were increasingly absorbed in the notion of individual self-interest in survival. And in this struggle for survival, traditional and ascriptive forms of authority were considered barriers. What Louis Hartz calls the "Whig Dilemma" was finally solved:

> American Whiggery, when it gave up the aristocratic frustrations of Hamilton and catered openly to the acquisitive dreams of the American democrat, uncovered by a strategic accident the historical ethos of American life: its bourgeois hungers, its classlessness, the spirit of equality that pervaded it.[60]

The struggle for survival overlapped with individualistic desires for wealth. Everyone was now equal in the capitalist sense that everyone was now free to exploit nature and one another.

The consensus on materialist belief, however, was limited. God did not altogether disappear. During the Jacksonian era, he became a cosmic determinist who assured individuals that their acquisitiveness was sanctified.[61] But he also became the Transcendentalists' spiritual god who condemned materialism and sanctified nature and conscience.[62] And as abolitionism and feminism developed, he became a Jeffersonian god who made it everyone's duty to recognize the divine rights of all individuals, including blacks and women.[63] In a land that nurtured individualism, no value consensus would ever appear without significant skepticism.

The predominance of materialist values as well as the accompanying skepticism had two major implications. First, one could draw from materialism a vision of national greatness, but one could also draw from it a sorrowful image of the painful struggle for survival in which there are always winners and losers. Consequently, if national prosperity were to become a reality, the price would necessarily include widespread poverty. What could be done to control the discontent of the losers? Government coercion and Christian charity were two alternatives that continued to imply limits on political authority. But by the Progressive era, it was clear that many Americans, including captains of industry, desired that government play a more positive role in regulating economic life and in dealing with social discontent.[64] In short, many groups in society exerted pressure in the hope that political authority would take the responsibility to satisfy the multitude of interests developing in industrializing America.[65]

Second, political leaders were confronted with the difficulty of maintaining their legitimacy within a new context. On the one hand, the materialist ethic nourished radical individualism and fed the fires of class conflict. On the other hand, a variety of religious ethics and egalitarian movements challenged materialism as an appropriate basis for political and social life. Whereas the Founders had more or less succeeded to strike a balance between tyranny and anarchism, their late-nineteenth-century heirs lacked the consensus of belief that might justify a new balance. Ultimately, political leadership expanded its responsibilities to include arbitration of interests and regulation over social life. Value-based groups simply became another set of interest groups and prior areas of privacy became politicized.[66] This allowed populists, progressives, and socialists to question the fairness of arbitration as well as the relationship between political authority and individual liberty.

The meaning of consenting was revised again in the nineteenth century. Was one obligated to obey political authority if one could not vote? Abolitionists, minorities, and women sometimes answered no.[67] Is the vote an adequate manifestation of consent? Again, many began to answer negatively. Calhoun's theory of the concurrent majority, though intended otherwise, implied that voting must be accompanied by group veto power to constitute fully binding consent.[68] Many radical thinkers and activists suggested that direct forms of participation, especially workers' control over the means of production, were essential. Socialist Daniel De Leon recalled Jefferson in this context:

> Drawing a breath from an Age far in advance of his own, the breath of Socialism, holding that a free people must be an alert people, Jefferson advanced the theory that the consent of any generation to the organic laws that rule it should not be passive, but an active consent.[69]

And to radicals like De Leon, Debs, and Haywood, an active consent included the right of workers to participate in all aspects of political and social life. A system of authority that denied people that right was one that justly suffered the dissent of the governed.

In many respects, nineteenth-century America can be considered a reenactment of the basic crises of humankind: Puritan spiritualism confronted materialism; the North and South fought a violent struggle for national hegemony; and the economic monopolies faced a very radical labor movement. Sin, violence, and impoverishment, even in industrializing America, continually provided leaders a source for renewing consensus and consent. Perhaps most eloquent of all, Lincoln's Gettysburg Address played on these crises to renew the sense of union. H. Mark Roelofs states: "The Gettysburg Address . . . states the myth of American democratic egalitarianism in all its fullness. . . . The Address is a replica in exact detail of an ancient Hebraic covenant renewal ceremony."[70] By the end of the century, however, these traditional crises had lost much of their motivational value. Materialists worried little about sin; interests were ready to defend themselves with violence; and radicals willingly suffered material deprivation in the hope of a *shared* future affluence. Meanwhile, leaders searched for and readily found new crises upon which to rebuild the national consensus and to renew popular support. The "moral" crisis of the cities spawned the

Progressives' vision of rational bureaucracy and expertise. The worldwide crisis of the Great War generated Wilson's vision of America's international leadership. And the Great Depression gave birth to a New Deal. As the crises of the twentieth century multiplied, the visions of renewal grew in scope, attached greater responsibility to political authority, and yet delivered little respite until the eruption of new crises. The law of diminishing returns was beginning to manifest itself.

Consent and Apolitical Politics

Belief diminished and skepticism grew in the twentieth century. Rational administration resulted in a bureaucratization that made Americans feel increasingly dependent on government. America could not free the world for democracy or rid the world of violence. And its New Deal turned out not to be so new after all, for poverty and want managed to survive. American political leaders found it increasingly necessary to present themselves as "pragmatists": bureaucracy may be inefficient, but it is necessary in a large society; American foreign policy might not free the world for democracy, but it can at least prevent the spread of totalitarianism; national affluence may not eliminate poverty, but the welfare state can minimize poverty's impact.[71] Rather than lead Americans toward the accomplishment of national visions, modern politicians tend to suggest that they can help prevent further deterioration if only the public will cooperate.

This skepticism regarding forward progress left a vacuum of belief that was soon filled with antagonistic ethics. Conservatives called for renewed affirmations sometimes of the god of natural law and duties and other times of the god of individual rights. Radicals, too, used religious arguments to challenge leaders' pragmatism in the name of civil liberties and egalitarian revolution. This was especially the case among minority movement protests. Still other groups that transcended conventional ideological labels called forth new natural laws (for example, ecological harmony), new natural rights (for example, the right to a decent job and salary), and new material demands (for example, women deserve the full product of their labor). In short, while American leaders and much of the American public settled into a welfare state pragmatism, to accept the "end of ideology" in Daniel Bell's phrase, other groups were building a firm basis for rejecting conventional materialism in the name of other values.

Value skepticism and dissensus reproduced themselves in the political system. First, without a consensus on value priorities, the power of central government grew dramatically. It was now responsible both for preventing the deterioration of past gains and for the multitude of social problems that characterized everyday life. Federal government found itself the object of more demands than it could conceivably satisfy, but it nevertheless responded with new agencies and programs that promised to satisfy. The cost of this expansion included a loss of national faith in the ability of federal government and a resentment of the power of central government. Citizens were more isolated from the processes of decision-making than ever before. Second, sensing this isolation, many Americans demanded a greater role in political decision-making as the basis for their consent. Theories of "democratic revisionism" that relegated citizens to passive voters were replaced by theories of "pluralism" that provided citizens an active political role between elections. But as more and more Americans perceived pluralism as a political marketplace in which elite interests dominated, they replaced it with theories of "participatory democracy" and "community activism" that called for a decentralization of political power and an expansion of the public's role into all areas of social decision-making.[72] Maximum feasible participation did not allow for enough participation.

The 1960s were not simply another "surge of democracy" as Huntington argues. The decade was instead a culmination of two centuries of concern regarding what constitutes consent: acquiescence, the vote, interest-group activity, maximum feasible participation, community control, to name a few. As American federal government became more centralized and isolated from Americans' everyday life, the American public has demanded greater access to decision-making in more areas of social life. However, to the extent political power continues to be centralized, virtually no new means of participation will provide individuals effective influence in politics; to the extent Americans began to recognize this in the 1960s and 1970s—and their skepticism of political authority suggests that they have done so—they may engage in an "apolitical politics." That is, they may continue to participate in politics to prevent the worst of two evils from prevailing without feeling that these acts ultimately have much impact or that they engender obligations to comply with outcomes. Politics here is symbolic, ritualized, and therapeutic, but it lacks the element of moral commitment.[73] And without that moral commitment, no system of political authority can be considered secure.

The practice of apolitical politics tempts political leaders to invoke crisis after crisis to maintain political legitimacy. The 1970s marked the premier decade of crises: the energy crisis, the economic crisis, the tax crisis, the schooling crisis, the housing crisis, the crime crisis, and the health care crisis. These are only a few of the innumerable "crises" that American politicians evoke daily and that American media experts hurl at the public. And these crises were simply the links that connected the Vietnam crisis at the beginning of the decade to the Iranian hostage crisis and the Afghanistan crisis that ended the decade. Taken altogether, the explosion of crises in the 1970s was especially noteworthy for two reasons. First, American leaders have been unable to transform these crises into visions. Whereas Lincoln could elicit progressive visions from the ruins of the Civil War, politicians today promise little beyond preventing worse crises from emerging. "Belt tightening" in the "era of limits" means preparing for a bleaker future. Utilitarian visions of prosperity are increasingly anachronistic. The relatively wealthy college students of the 1960s had the affluence that allowed them to reject materialism; the relatively insecure work force of the 1970s sees less and less chance of attaining material fulfillment. Meanwhile, political leaders have been unable to settle on an alternative vision. This vacuum is an opportunity for people like Robert Nozick to call for a radical return to the golden age of individualism or like Barry Commoner to portray a possible future of decentralized solar socialism.[74] The specter of political polarization is real enough to alert the defenders of political authority to the fragility of their present state.

Second, today's crisis management implies a continued centralization of power and distancing of decision-making from localities and individuals. When new participatory mechanisms turn out to be deceptive and when government expertise fails to solve social problems, it becomes increasingly clear to Americans that making a moral commitment to political authority is unwarranted. In part, I would suggest, the narcissism of the 1970s was a response to common feelings of distrust and impotence. One manifestation of this narcissism was that the "consent of the governed" no longer indicated a willingness to be governed by the prevailing system of authority. Americans' lack of trust in political authority today may become the basis for them to oppose it tomorrow.

Conclusion

The American Revolution and even the Constitution were premised on the notion that legitimate political authority never automatically deserved public trust. Authority should be feared and questioned. This notion was institutionalized into American politics and inscribed into the political culture by writers like Henry Adams, Mark Twain, and Herman Melville. Nonetheless, Americans generally agreed that fear and questioning of authority need not imply anarchism. A political leadership founded on common values, instituted by processes open to popular participation, and able to ease human crises would provide individuals enough reasons to consent to a system of limited authority. Consequently, Americans have believed in the need for political authority but always with large doses of skepticism.

In the past two hundred years, skepticism of political authority has steadily increased. Consensus on authoritative values increasingly disappeared; political decision-making has increasingly been isolated from individuals' influence; and crises have become daily events that have lost most of their motivating force. While America has always had a current of anarchism flowing somewhere beneath the surface of culture, anarchism has recently reemerged as a major challenge to all forms of authority. In his recent *Against Method: Outline of an Anarchistic Theory of Knowledge,* Paul Feyerabend challenges the authority of law, reason, and method in the practice of science, expertise, and politics.[75] And he is taken seriously. Outside of the academy, fictional figures like Tom Robbins's Amanda speaks for many young Americans when she says, "The only authority I respect is the one which causes butterflies to fly south in fall and north in springtime."[76] Without the belief that consent *and* moral commitment to political authority will result in great community and individual autonomy, Americans' skepticism tends toward radical individualism and cultural anarchism.

Huntington's call for a new balance between individual and authority now appears in a new light. Unable to draw from a consensus on authoritative values or from a public willingness to back up its consent with moral commitment, Huntington is reduced to requesting that Americans uncritically trust their leaders. He is therefore negating the traditional American principle that authority ought to be feared and questioned and that it ought to be restricted within specifiable boundaries determined by the consent of the governed. His answer to modern crisis management is public acquiescence, and here the dividing line between political authority and authoritarianism disappears.

Anarchism and authoritarianism appear to be the twin specters haunting America's political future. However, such apocalyptic possibilities should *not yet* be considered imminent. As a legitimation device, the doctrine of consent has proven itself able to weather tremendous political storms. In the immediate future, I expect that political leaders will try to develop new visions, suggest new modes of participation, and be more selective about the crises that they evoke. To the degree they are able to succeed, consent will appear less expedient and more binding to Americans. However, dissidents will likely try to turn the doctrine of consent against current political leadership. They may argue for a new consensus, a decentralized political system, and a radically altered social system as the basis for moral commitment to political authority. Here is the final irony: while the doctrine of consent has been used consistently to legitimize political authority in capitalist society, it can conceivably be used to legitimize an alternative political and social system based on communal norms, radical democracy, and a need-oriented economy.

Notes

1. Robert Gilmour and Robert Lamb, *Political Alienation in Contemporary America* (New York: St. Martin's Press, 1975), p. 140.

2. Samuel P. Huntington, "The United States," in Michel J. Crozier, Samuel P. Huntington, and Joji Watanuki, *The Crisis of Democracy* (New York: New York University Press, 1975), pp. 74–75.

3. Cf. ibid., pp. 113–115, and Joseph Schumpeter, *Capitalism, Socialism and Democracy* (3rd ed.; New York: Harper and Row, 1950), chap. 22.

4. Alexis de Tocqueville, *Democracy in America,* ed. Richard D. Heffner (New York: New American Library, 1956), p. 30.

5. For an analysis of this distinction, see Gerald C. MacCallum, Jr., "Negative and Positive Freedom," in *Contemporary Political Theory,* ed. Anthony de Crespigny and Alan Wertheimer (New York: Atherton, 1970), pp. 107–127.

6. This is perhaps the major thesis in Joseph Tussman, *Obligation and the Body Politic* (London: Oxford University Press, 1960). My own revision of Tussman's argument is in Mark E. Kann, "The Dialectic of Consent Theory," *Journal of Politics* 40 (May 1978): 387–408.

7. Henry Steele Commager, "Our Leadership Crisis: America's Real Malaise," *Los Angeles Times,* pt. V, Nov. 11, 1979, p. 1.

8. Huntington, "The United States," p. 75.

9. The notion that the object of consent is specific laws rather than a system of political authority was developed into a philosophical argument by Hanna Pitkin, "Obligation and Consent—II," *The American Political Science Review* 60 (March 1966): 39–52.

10. Cf. Alan Wolfe, *The Limits of Legitimacy* (New York: Free Press, 1977), and Jurgen Habermas, *Legitimation Crisis,* trans. Thomas McCarthy (Boston: Beacon Press, 1975).

11. Tussman, *Obligation,* p. 23.

12. Cf. H. Mark Roelofs, *Ideology and Myth in American Politics* (Boston: Little, Brown, 1976), and Louis Hartz, *The Liberal Tradition in America: An Interpretation of American Political Thought since the Revolution* (New York: Harcourt Brace and World, 1955).

13. This label is drawn from Robert Booth Fowler, *Believing Skeptics: American Political Intellectuals, 1945–1964* (Westport, Conn.: Greenwood Press, 1978).

14. For example, see Alan Gewirth, "Political Justice," in *Social Justice,* ed. R. B. Brandt (Englewood Cliffs, N.J.: Prentice-Hall, 1962), esp. p. 160.

15. Consent's believing skepticism reproduces the determinism-free will dilemma of Christianity. Natural law (combined with utilitarian motivation) and voluntarism are analogous to grace and moral choice. Not coincidentally, John Locke was raised in a Puritan family.

16. Consent theory has been primarily associated with liberalism because of its individualistic basis. In my "Dialectic of Consent Theory," I suggest that this association is not a necessary one. See pp. 402–407.

17. Tussman, *Obligation,* p. 25.

18. For an extended discussion of this possibility, see David Braybrooke, "The Social Contract Returns, This Time as an Elusive Public Good," a paper delivered at the 1974 annual meeting of the American Political Science Association, Chicago, esp. pp. 1–5.

19. See John Locke, *Two Treatises of Government,* ed. Thomas Cook (New York: Hafner, 1974), chaps. 1–5. For an excellent analysis of the religious basis of Locke's thought, see John Dunn, *The Political Thought of John Locke* (London: Cambridge University Press, 1969).

20. Murray Edelman, *Political Language: Words That Succeed and Policies That Fail* (New York: Academic Press, 1977), pp. 47–48.

21. Cf. Tussman, *Obligation*, p. 23, and Antonio Gramsci, "State and Civil Society," in *Selections from the Prison Notebooks of Antonio Gramsci*, ed. and trans. Quintin Hoare and G. N. Smith (New York: International Publishers, 1971), pp. 210–276.

22. The major change that might be deemed structural is that consent theorists have radically diminished the realm of determinate belief and have expanded the realm of indeterminate choice. For example, see Michael Walzer, *Obligations* (New York: Simon and Schuster, 1970). As developed in the text of this paper, I believe it is more useful to view this change as a shift toward utilitarian belief and disputed belief as a more accurate representation of general trends among the American people.

23. Abstraction, non-falsifiability, and reassurance are some of the defining characteristics of political myths useful for mystifying knowledge and winning public acquiescence. Cf. Edelman, *Political Language*, p. 3, and Richard Sennett and Jonathan Cobb, *The Hidden Injuries of Class* (New York: Alfred A. Knopf, 1972), esp. pp. 156–159.

24. This partially explains the willingness of fairly affluent college students to challenge the Establishment in the 1960s.

25. See Michael H. Best and William E. Connolly, *The Politicized Economy* (Lexington, Mass.: Heath, 1976), pp. 83–90; also see John H. Schaar, "Equal Opportunity and Beyond," in *Up the Mainstream*, ed. Herbert Reid (New York: McKay, 1974), pp. 233–250.

26. Today, social mobility may mean the ability to provide one's children an education as an entrance to a career or a profession. Cf. Ira Shor, "The Working Class Goes to College," in *Studies in Socialist Pedagogy*, ed. T. M. Norton and B. Ollman (New York: Monthly Review Press, 1978), pp. 107–127, and Sennett and Cobb, pp. 229 ff.

27. These circumstances enhance the possibility of a dissident alliance between affluent college students and professionals, on the one hand, and insecure workers, on the other. The specter of May 1968 in France is one not readily forgotten by leadership.

28. The public relations aspect of recent American politics is nicely treated in Christopher Lasch, *The Culture of Narcissism: American Life in an Age of Diminishing Expectations* (New York: Norton, 1979), chap. 3.

29. See Hannah Arendt, "Lying in Politics," *Crises of the Republic* (New York: Harcourt Brace Jovanovich, 1972), pp. 3–47.

30. The "realism" embedded in skeptical democratic theory in the last three decades often implies that leadership, once again, must limit itself to protecting individual rights. The most eloquent recent statement is Robert Nozick, *Anarchy, State and Utopia* (New York: Basic Books, 1974). See also Lewis Coser and Irving Howe, eds., *The New Conservatives* (New York: New American Library, 1976).

31. This is essentially the argument of participatory democrats. A fine example is Carole Pateman, *Participation and Democratic Theory* (London: Cambridge University Press, 1970).

32. See C. B. Macpherson, *The Life and Times of Liberal Democracy* (Oxford: Oxford University Press, 1977), pp. 15–22.

33. This, in part, explains the growing public animosity toward the oil companies that reap superprofits while people wait in gas lines and pay inflated prices without much alternative.

34. For example, see Samuel Mermin, "Participation in Governmental Processes: A Sketch of the Expanding Law," in *Participation in Politics*, ed. J. Roland Pennock and John W. Chapman (New York: Lieber-Atherton, 1975), pp. 136–160.

35. Compare the Mermin article with Howard I. Kalodner, "Citizen Participation in Emerging Social Institutions," in *Participation in Politics*, pp. 161–185. Kalodner concludes that "to involve the poor in decision making . . . achieves little but frustration for those involved in the effort." See p. 180.

36. See Richard A. Cloward and Frances Fox Piven, *The Politics of Turmoil* (New York: Pantheon, 1974), p. 268.

37. This seems to be Huntington's recommendation, particularly in regard to the presidency, whose power, Huntington believes, has eroded dangerously. See pp. 93–98.

38. The tactic of delegating power to private interests and experts proliferated after World War II. See Wolfe, *The Limits of Legitimacy*, chaps. 4–5.

39. The "incremental" approach is presently a standard norm of public policy analysis. For example, see David Braybrooke and Charles Lindblom's by now classic book, *A Strategy of Decision* (New York: Free Press, 1970).

40. See James O'Connor, *The Fiscal Crisis of the State* (New York: St. Martin's Press, 1973).

41. For analysis of the dynamics here, see Edelman, *Political Language*, pp. 45–49.

42. Liberal pluralism does not imply a pluralism of determinate beliefs, only a pluralism of interests.

43. Liberal leaders who are crisis managers ultimately act as conservatives in politics. This conflation of ideologies tends to suggest that America's liberal and conservative political parties do not offer significant alternatives. Hence, we today experience a crisis in party politics. For example, see Everett Carll Ladd, Jr., *Where Have All the Voters Gone? The Fracturing of America's Political Parties* (New York: Norton, 1978).

44. Legitimacy is thus a nexus point where coercion and consent interrelate.

45. The voting studies of the 1950s and early 1960s treated public apathy either as an unfortunate by-product of American politics or as a positive support to American politics. That apathy could be a rational response and a potential basis for later radicalism was not clearly recognized until the civil rights and antiwar movements expanded. It is not unlikely for modern political leaders to fear that the 1970s were like the 1950s: a time of passivity that could easily erupt into dissidence.

46. Many 1960s radicals did not follow their leaders to Indian gurus; instead they engaged in quiet and sometimes effective community organizing. See Janice Perlman, "Grassrooting the System," *U.S. Capitalism in Crisis* (New York: Union for Radical Political Economics, 1978), pp. 306–322.

47. See Wolfe's chap. 9, entitled "Alienated Politics," in *The Limits of Legitimacy*, pp. 288–321. Also see Edelman's sections on "Intense Politicization" and "Antipolitics," in *Political Language*, pp. 126–133, 136–139. Both point out that participation and nonparticipation alike may entail no significant feelings of effectiveness or political attachment.

48. One of the messages of Sennett and Cobb's *The Hidden Injuries of Class* is that workers do not necessarily suffer from false consciousness. Rather, they suffer from a lack of alternatives and therefore try to find ways of maintaining self-dignity within the prevailing order. See pp. 3–50.

49. Wilson Carey McWilliams, *The Idea of Fraternity in America* (Berkeley: University of California Press, 1973), p. 123.

50. Ibid., p. 129.

51. Ibid., p. 127; also see Lasch, *The Culture of Narcissism*, pp. 107–108.

52. See Roelofs, *Ideology and Myth*, pp. 83–105.

53. Wolfe puts it this way: "One had to have the power of the state in order to make it impotent" (*The Limits of Legitimacy*, p. 22).

54. The direct connection between government and consent is more than an interesting philosophical question. It symbolizes the growing historical sense that government somehow must represent the will of constituents. Burke's trusteeship was soon to approximate popular notions of delegate representation.

55. See Douglas Rae, "The Limits of Consensual Decision," *The American Political Science Review* 69 (Dec. 1975): 1271–1273, for a brief discussion of the logic by which consent to a regime is transformed into consent to particular governments through voting.

56. See James Madison in Alexander Hamilton, Madison, and John Jay, *On the Constitution*, ed. R. H. Gabriel (Indianapolis: Bobbs-Merrill, 1954), pp. 10–19.

57. See Alexander Hamilton in *On the Constitution*, pp. 20–23.

58. Ibid., pp. 92–94.

59. John C. Calhoun, *A Disquisition on Government*, ed. C. G. Post (Indianapolis: Bobbs-Merrill, 1953), p. 5.

60. Hartz, *The Liberal Tradition*, pp. 205–206.

61. For example, see John William Ward, *Andrew Jackson: Symbol for an Age* (New York: Oxford University Press, 1962), p. 210.

62. For example, see Charles Mayo Ellis, "An Essay on Transcendentalism," in *The American Transcendentalists*, ed. Perry Miller (Garden City, N.Y.: Doubleday, 1957), pp. 21–35.

63. For example, see the "Declaration of Sentiments and Resolutions, Seneca Falls," in *Feminism: The Essential Historical Writings*, ed. Miriam Schneir (New York: Vintage, 1972), pp. 77–82.

64. See James Weinstein, "Corporate Liberalism and the Monopoly Capitalist State," in *The Capitalist System*, ed. Richard Edwards, Michael Reich, and Thomas Weiskopf (2nd ed.; Englewood Cliffs, N.J.: Prentice-Hall, 1978), p. 232.

65. See Edward S. Greenberg, *Serving the Few* (New York: Wiley, 1974), pp. 89–103.

66. The classic expression of this perspective is Arthur F. Bentley, *The Process of Government* (Granville, Ohio: Principia Press, 1908).

67. For example, see "The United States of America vs. Susan B. Anthony," in Schneir, *Feminism*, where Anthony recalls the revolutionary saying, "Resistance to tyranny is obedience to God" (p. 136).

68. Calhoun, *Disquisition on Government*, esp. p. 35, where he also suggests that the norms of a concurrent majority can "admit, with safety, a much greater extension of the right of suffrage."

69. Daniel De Leon, *A Socialist in Congress* (New York: New York Labor News, 1963), p. 8.

70. Roelofs, *Ideology and Myth*, p. 146.

71. On the whole, John Dewey's optimistic expectations for the use of the state have given way to tremendous skepticism of what government can accomplish. Cf. John Dewey, *Liberalism and Social Action* (New York: Capricorn Books, 1963), and Judith Shklar, *After Utopia: The Decline of Political Faith* (Princeton: Princeton University Press, 1957).

72. See my "A Standard for Democratic Leadership," *Polity* 12 (Winter 1979): esp. 204–211.

73. Cf. Edelman, *Political Language*, chap. 8, and Lasch, *The Culture of Narcissism*, chap. 4.

74. Cf. Nozick, *Anarchy, State and Utopia*, chap. 4, and Barry Commoner, *The Poverty of Power* (New York: Alfred A. Knopf, 1976), chap. 9.

75. See Paul Feyerabend, *Against Method: Outline of an Anarchistic Theory of Knowledge* (London: Verso, 1978), esp. chaps. 1–4.

76. Tom Robbins, *Another Roadside Attraction* (New York: Ballantine Books, 1971), p. 251.

PART TWO

Literature and Authority

"Where shall we find authority the instruction of which our natures demand?" asked John Dewey in 1891. "Shall we cease to find it in philosophy, or in science, and shall we find it in poetry?" Dewey's speculation that one might have to go beyond traditional philosophy to literature for answers to questions formerly belonging to the domain of political thought seems a little curious, especially for a philosopher who believed that all knowledge derived from experience. The experience of Western intellectual history offers no clear guidelines for such an enterprise. Plato called the poet a liar, and Emerson called the politician a cheat. Perhaps that is all that needs to be said for an "interdisciplinary" approach to the problem of authority.

Yet there are many reasons why literature can be explored to examine the various meanings of obligation and disobedience. Indeed, it might be said that in the latter half of the nineteenth century it was the literary artists—Melville and Twain in America, Dostoevski and Dickens in Europe—who wrestled with the problem of authority as the legitimate exercise of power, while political scientists were writing about property, contract, and civil service reform. Oliver Wendell Holmes, Jr., told his contemporaries that legal justice meant little more than what the courts said it was and what the police could enforce; William Butler Yeats exhorted the poet to capture "reality and justice in a single thought." The former granted authority to those thoughts that could succeed in getting themselves accepted into the "marketplace of ideas"; the latter asserted that authority could be justified only as an aesthetic phenomenon or it could not be justified at all. How, then, could the writer justify it?

If the intellectual in general provides the ideas that either legitimate or undermine authority, the literary intellectual in particular—the essayist, playwright, novelist, and poet—experiments with the very words through which such ideas are conveyed. In the beginning was "the Word," the Bible tells us. "But I say unto you, that every idle word that men shall speak, they shall give account thereof in the day of judgment. For by thy words thou shalt be justified, and by thy words shalt be condemned." The truths about authority can only be known through words, by the signs, images, and symbols invoked in linguistic construction; and insofar as literature may influence our perceptions and affect our conduct, the writer can present an imaginative discourse on authority in full conviction that his creation is intimately related to life. Whether or not the truths of literature are shaped by the forms in which they are expressed, or whether or not the poet can tell us something about the political world that we can discover nowhere else, surely he can make meaningful—indeed insightful—statements about the nature of authority:

> Thou has seen a farmer's dog bark at a beggar? And the creature run from the cur? There thou mightst behold the great image of authority: a dog's obey'd in office.
>
> *King Lear*

In the study of culture, literature is also useful as "symptomatic criticism," a body of thoughts and reflections that scholars may scour for signs of the defects of modern civilization. The three literary figures discussed in Part Two—William Faulkner, Ezra Pound, and T. S. Eliot—offer valuable perspectives on the problem of authority mainly because none could see genuine authority functioning in traditional American institutions and ideas. No doubt there are many differences that separate Faulkner, Pound, and Eliot, but they all shared a common alienation from American political thought and values, and to a large extent it was their agonizing estrangement, rooted deeply in the post-World War I malaise of the "Lost Generation," that led them to attempt what might be called the political reeducation of America through literary endeavor. Let us consider what they felt could not be salvaged in order to reconstruct the foundations of authority.

First of all, Faulkner, Pound, and Eliot all wrote against the main currents of liberal democracy, the historical and contemporary implications of which have been discussed in Part One. They also rejected many of the premises of the eighteenth-century Enlightenment in order to reaffirm either Christian values that enable man to transcend the immediacy of desire or pagan virtues that enable man to grasp the wisdom of the Orient. In this respect, Faulkner, Pound, and Eliot might be regarded as the heirs—spiritual if not political—of Henry Adams, another alienated intellectual who believed that the principle of authority could reach symmetrical perfection only as an act of the literary imagination that would take the writer outside the mainstream of American political thought. Faulkner, Pound, and Eliot also felt deeply the burdens of history, especially an American past that remained seemingly innocent of tragedy, guilt, and sin as it espoused reason, progress, and hope, and a liberal tradition too proud to acknowledge the need for authority as an answer to "the human condition." Moreover, the three writers regarded society—the very source that sociologists had looked to as the nurturing fount of authority—as the actual destroyer of such human values as love, courage, integrity, goodness, and compassion, values that might command the citizen's allegiance and thus generate an understanding of true moral authority as a commitment to principles and ideals that stand opposed to a liberal political culture based on interests and power. In the writings of all three authors American society is often depicted as having overthrown the older restraints and inhibitions only to surrender to the "spirit" of capitalism without the restraining "ethic" of genuine religion. Hence Faulkner's predatory Snopes clan, Pound's diatribes against usury, and Eliot's efforts to define "The Idea of a Christian Society" that might quiet the restless activism of modern man alienated by his own acquisitiveness. All three writers looked to some form of moral order to arrest the destructive tendencies of modern society; all deplored the absence of a common authority in America, a vacuum that Eliot depicted as a spiritual emptiness:

> Oh Father, father, gone from us, lost to us,
> How shall we find you, from what far place
> Do you look down on us? You now in Heaven,
> Who shall now guide us, protect us, direct us?
> After what journey through what further dread
> Shall we recover your presence?

As John Schaar demonstrates in his essay, Faulkner succeeded in recovering the presence of authority in the code of the hunt. In *The Bear* the meaning of human relationships can best be understood in terms that derive not from the abstract Bill of Rights but from the interactions of leaders and learners in an intimate community of shared values. A political theorist, Schaar is concerned

with two vital issues: what is the nature of genuine moral authority, and how is it transmitted? Faulkner's attitudes as explicated
by Schaar resemble Jefferson's idea of a "natural" as opposed to
an "artificial" aristocracy: any authority worth its name does not
deserve automatic respect; on the contrary, it must earn its status
based on proven talent and virtue. This form of authority, expressed in the visible deeds of human character, is transmitted from
person to person, and it enlarges and elevates behavior rather than
merely restricting and coercing it. In this respect Schaar's definition of authority is closer to the idea of "spiritual" authority discussed by Diggins than to the idea of "interdictory" authority discussed by Philip Rieff. Schaar also demonstrates how Faulkner's
belief in personal, moral authority is constantly threatened by the
human urge to possess, a tendency that had its most brutal historical manifestation in the institution of slavery that came near to
destroying the American republic. With the abolition of slavery
the urge to possess and dominate still expresses itself in the
desire for land as a means to wealth, and few of Faulkner's characters can restrain that desire. Thus Schaar's analysis of Faulkner's idea of authority goes against the mainstream of American
liberalism, where property had been regarded as the essential
institution without which man would be incapable of affirming his
moral integrity and political independence. Faulkner's *The Bear*
asks us to face squarely the traditional idea of American freedom,
based on independence, self-reliance, and the cupidity of opportunity,
so that we may better understand what is being denied and
ultimately destroyed: the mutual dependence of man upon man and
the authority of commonly shared values derived from uncommon
virtues.

If we may look to Faulkner for political instruction, for some
glimpse of human wisdom about authority that one seldom finds
in formal political philosophy, may we do the same with Ezra
Pound? Alfred Kazin's essay, "Language as History: Ezra Pound's
Search for the Authority of History," suggests why the poet is
perhaps better left where Shelley found him: the "unacknowledged"
legislator and political seer. It is not that Pound tried to establish
the authority of poetry over society, as did Whitman; or that he
became obsessed with money as a conspiratorial power, as did
Marx, with, admittedly, a little more sophistication; or even that
he became a political reactionary, as did, to only a slightly lesser
extent, Eliot, Yeats, Wallace Stevens, and other major twentieth-
century literary figures. The problem of Pound for the political

thinker is that he convinced himself that history was simply whatever happened inside his own head, a poetic conceit that made his own eccentric mind the veritable seat of authority. No doubt there is a whole tradition of poetic discourse that supports the claims of the literary imagination, and indeed the very term "authority" implies the ability to author and authorize. As translator of languages as well as creator of verse, Pound expresses ideas that are not answerable to a world outside of himself. "The sense of authority that comes from knowing that you can do just whatever you like with language will extend itself to more than literature," warns Kazin in his critical evaluation of Pound's "language intoxication." Convinced that the true is that which is made, Pound created his own version of John Adams and John Quincy Adams in the *Cantos,* and it is not the house of Adams that we entered into in Chapter 1, where authority is regarded by John and Henry Adams as something that should and must lie beyond the range of human deeds, a "natural" truth or law that may constitute a judgment on behavior by virtue of standing above it. The career of Ezra Pound presents a cautionary tale of the excesses of the poetic imagination. Comparing Alexander Hamilton and John Adams, Pound set himself up as historian, judge, and executioner:

> and as for Hamilton
> we may take it (my authority, ego scriptor cantilenae) that he
> was the Prime snot in ALL American history

Deeming authoritative anything he wanted to authorize, Pound mistook power for authority, aesthetic tyranny for ethical theory, the sheer ability of an idea to assert itself for its capacity to demonstrate its relation to a fact or truth beyond itself or to some legitimating principle that justifies the idea being asserted.

With T. S. Eliot such a legitimating principle could be found in "Tradition and the Individual Talent" (1919). Here Eliot argued that the poet can write only if he possesses "a feeling that the whole of the literature of Europe from Homer and within it the whole of the literature of his own country [is] . . . in his bones." In this early declaration, Eliot expounds a view of history in which literature is constituted as a harmonious whole, a seamless web of meaning to which all present and future works must conform. In subordinating himself to the tradition of history and culture, the poet may find an "ideal order" in the artistic feats of the past and an idea of authority based on the recurrence of symmetry. Like Faulkner, Eliot sides with Filmer over Locke (to use

Schaar's comparison): no man is born free of the past. Instead of
the past being a Sisyphean burden, however, Eliot initially called
upon man to immerse himself in a meaningful past in order that a
meaningless present might be redeemed. What Eliot's dictum required was nothing less than the renunciation of the conceit that
one possessed an absolute self, that preoccupation with the ego
that is referred to in Part Three as "the narcissistic personality."
To find true authority, Eliot seems to suggest, one must relinquish
false identity. "What happens is a continual surrender of himself
as he is at the moment to something which is more valuable. The
progress of an artist is a continual self-sacrifice, a continual extinction of personality."

William Arrowsmith's close analysis of "Sweeney Erect" reveals not only how Eliot sought to absorb himself in a text that
itself engaged eternal myths, as the poet adds his own creation to
the continuous accretions of the whole body of literature; it also
illuminates the peculiar way Eliot approached the problem of authority in the modern world. At the risk of reducing a complex
poem to a simple proposition, one could say that in "Sweeney
Erect" the problem of authority becomes the problem of man—the
ultimate nature of human nature. This subject, of course, preoccupied the philosophers of the Enlightenment, and its very existence
suggests that the self-appraisal of man implies doubt, distrust, and
misgiving about human possibility (see Arthur O. Lovejoy, *Reflections on Human Nature*). Rousseau's discourses are crucial to
this poem, as Arrowsmith demonstrates, for Rousseau forces us to
think about what has been lost and gained when man forsakes the
unreflective innocence of the state of nature to develop the artifice
of conventions as he submits himself to external authority.
Although Rousseau himself did not advocate a simple return to the
state of nature, his writings did much to advance the conviction
that nature constituted the norm for all human conduct and that
the adjective "natural" implied the highest estimate of man's
essentially rational and moral self. Opposed to natural man stood
modern civilization, which supposedly disfigured original human
nature with its restrictions and repressions imposed upon man's
pleasure-seeking impulses. In "Sweeney Erect" Eliot presents a
thesis that turns Rousseau on his head and challenges the premises
of the Enlightenment. Here modern man is depicted as the "recurrent type of carnal or natural" creature whose morning stirrings
suggest the concealed survivals of barbarism that hide beneath the
veneer of civilization. If the orang-outang is father to the man,

then clearly man's primal nature is an embarrassment to all arguments for absolute freedom that ignore the limitations of man as a
rational animal. That Sweeney is "erect" implies that he is both
man and beast, capable of freedom and perfectibility but also prone
to revert to his original animalistic nature in which no scheme
of authority exists to control the brutish instincts. What kind of
authority man needs depends upon what kind of nature man possesses, and Eliot makes it clear that even the fully erect *Homo
sapiens* is at once violent, sensual, narcissistic, and incapable of
redemption by means of intellect and reason alone. For Eliot authority must be found in an external idea or institution that represents something more than the lengthened shadow of man.

A study of the literary intellectual could well suggest that it is
the cultural rebel, and not the political revolutionary, who best
ponders the dilemmas of authority. While the revolutionary desires
to destroy in order to impose a new order ("We must organize
everything"—Lenin, 1918), the rebel desires to question and
assault without necessarily pretending to know what ideas or institutions can replace traditional authority. Between the collapse of
authority and the search for its substitute falls the shadow of modernism. Faulkner, Pound, and Eliot felt deeply that man had been
cut off from authority by the very need to rebel against it.
Pound's dispute with the forces of modern history led to the creation of a mythical past in which the spirit of John Adams could
somehow be joined with the utterances of Benito Mussolini in
order to bring economic enlightenment into the world. Faulkner
called upon the writer to unlearn what he had been taught, especially those easy scientific convictions about reason and progress,
in order that the conflicts within the human heart can be explored
and man can be seen not as a puny "sound" that will endure but
as an inexhaustible "spirit" that will prevail. Eliot similarly rebelled
against the authority of modern science that divorced thought
from feeling in order to deny the claim, so prounounced among
the naturalists and Marxists of the 1920s, that poetic endeavor
must yield to empirical analysis the task of interpreting experience. All three writers were attempting to restore through poetic
means the spiritual and moral truths that once rested on religious
thought and political theory. The old and revered idea of human
consent, the idea that man has the natural right to approve of the
power exercised over himself, stirred Pound to fulminate against
usury and espouse a popular dictator like Il Duce. Faulkner
wanted to see personal liberty and freedom rooted once again, as

it had been in Jefferson's dreams, in the openness and plenitude of the natural environment. And Eliot wanted to restore an unbroken image of authority as the continuity of literature and culture in order to heal the "broken image" of modern man.

We should not, however, press these similarities, for the differences are more telling, and this is particularly true when we compare the three writers' views of history, society, and nature. For Pound the past and present seemed to be at the mercy of his own imaginative whims, and poetry enables man to see the truth of things simply by its authority of assertion. In Faulkner and Eliot the past and present also merge, but the continuing presence of history is more threatening and seemingly cannot be extirpated by the literary imagination alone. Faulkner depicts history as the nightmare of a collective conscience, an unescapable burden of guilt and sin rooted, in his case, in the historical institution of slavery. Thus "the past is never dead; it's not even past." Eliot presents history as the consciousness that derives not so much from human deeds as from the shock of recognizing one's true ancestry: "The backward look behind the assurance / Of recorded history, the backward half-look / Over the shoulder, toward the primitive terror." For Faulkner, then, wilderness and the natural environment still hold out the promise of redemption, for slavery and oppression are manmade evils, alien to the world of the bear and deer. With Eliot, in contrast, man is continuous with nature, not separate, and nature itself is fallen and corrupted and man, the orang-outang, is the beast that needs to be controlled. Faulkner sees modern social man alienated from nature, while Eliot sees all the "hollow men" as incapable of communion with nature that represents the meaninglessness of death as well as the cycles of life. Something more than the "primitive terror" of nature must confront man before he can submit to genuine moral authority, and that requires a will to believe that Eliot's characters could never experience. Perhaps more than any other writer Eliot compels us to consider a question that every contributor to this anthology must face: can authority live without truth?

4

Community or Contract?
William Faulkner and the Dual Legacy

John H. Schaar

I want to take William Faulkner's *The Bear* as an occasion for thinking about some of the modes and meanings of authority and membership.* That will surely seem an awkward and unwelcome move to some readers of *The Bear,* and their view may be correct: perhaps it is wrong to "use" a story in any way even remotely like the way I intend to use this one. I hope not to wring from the story too many meanings that others cannot find in it, or to wrench it out of shape so it will fit my private purposes, but I know the risk is there. Others will decide whether I have avoided it.

Furthermore, I claim no authority as a reader of Faulkner. I have no academic license to hunt Old Ben, no special permission to enter the big woods, and no dog able to hold the bear even if I had the license to hunt and the permission to enter. I am aware that many critical hunters more skillful and better armed than I have gone after Old Ben and that some of them have been mauled as badly as Boon Hogganbeck. That provides a counsel of caution.

I

The final version of *The Bear* stands as Faulkner's major effort to work out in juxtaposition, showing their bearings on each other, two of his major themes and concerns: the wilderness, and what can be learned from right and wrong relationships to it, and the theme of slavery and possession, which are the founding crimes of civilization.[1] The story is woven around the ancient dualism of nature versus culture, wilderness and civilization. In the story we see Isaac McCaslin, first as a young boy growing up and then as a young man of twenty-one. Ike has two inheritances or legacies: the legacy of nature, the wilderness, and the hunt, and the legacy of civilization, the plantation that had been hacked out of the wilderness by his

---

*My understanding of *The Bear,* and of Faulkner altogether, for that matter, owes very much to conversations over the years with my friend, Randall Reid.

forefathers. The two inheritances are different in time and in kind, and Ike must learn the terms and uses of each, discover their provisions, and decide how to live with them. He must determine what his fathers, his authors both spiritual and biological, have left to him and how those legacies have shaped and will continue to shape his life. The story, then, invites us to meditate on history and paternity, on the past as both gift and burden, and on how the past congeals into the present and shapes the possibilities of the future.

So Ike must discover and decide the provisions and meanings of his dual legacy. But the question is not merely personal; the outcome matters beyond himself. Ike has also inherited an American condition. His story condenses a collective story.

From an early time, leaving the Puritans aside, the newcomers to these shores told a story about themselves that set them apart from those who lived elsewhere. The heart of the story was the idea that people in America enjoyed a special bond with and experience of nature that the residents of an old, tired, crowded Europe could never enjoy. Crèvecoeur opened the theme in 1782. "Men are like plants," he announces early in his *Letters from an American Farmer,* and when even the scraggly human weeds of Europe are transplanted in the good soil of the New World, they cannot fail to grow into strong and productive maturity. When Buffon alleged that America teemed with degenerate species (including Indians), Jefferson replied that the contrary was the case: the New World produced growths more vigorous and promising than anything the Old World could show. Tom Paine remonstrated with the French not to kill Louis XVI but to send him instead to America, where the simplicity and naturalness of life, which constituted both its health and its power to heal, could reform even a Bourbon despot. Cooper shaped the material into a national myth, and hundreds of writers, painters, and publicists since him have worked their variations on the theme. The Americans are specially blessed by a bounteous and beautiful nature. The Americans themselves are nature's favored children, and their nation is nature's own nation. Mother Nature, of course, has nurtured her children in the ways of generosity, directness, and cheerful courage and has taught them to love liberty above all. These virtues are ours by nature, and they give us a special place among the nations.

But if the source of our virtue lay in nature, our mission lay elsewhere. It lay in civilization, which meant that nature must be tamed, or even conquered, and that meant the axe, the gun and the plow, the steam engine and the dynamo, and now the nuclear reactor. Defining our virtue as coming from nature, and setting as our mission the conquest of nature, every gain on the one front meant a loss on the other. We caught ourselves in a cruel and irreconcilable opposition between destroying the source of our special virtue or failing in our appointed mission. Furthermore, this dilemma has been with us a national experience and a leitmotif of the culture, and not, as it has been among the European peoples, the anguished or sentimental lament of isolated romantics or nostalgics conjuring up visions of a lost Eden, or calling on nature in order to rebuke culture. It runs throughout our history and policy, and it has made it almost impossible for us to think and act in ways that make nature and culture complicit.[2]

II

Faulkner's *The Bear*, then, is not idiosyncratic or eccentric. It is, rather, only one of the more recent (and intelligent) explorations of the deadly paradox. I think that helps account for the story's power. Ike McCaslin's dilemma is not only his but ours too.

Ike's spiritual father and teacher in the world of the wilderness and the hunt is old Sam Fathers. Part Negro and part Indian, wifeless, childless, kinless, he is the last of his line. He lives alone in his shack in the big woods, away from the white man's eye, but still by the white man's permission. When on the hunt he is a "prince," holding by right of ability an authority that could never be his by right of lineage and law. Outside the hunt, he is just another nigger, dispossessed and dominated. The defeat of the Indians may have been unavoidable, given the whites' superiority in numbers and weapons, but the narrator insists that the vital wound to Indian authority was self-inflicted, when old Chief Ikkemotubbe was "ruthless enough" to sell land that neither he nor any other person had any right to own or to sell.

The world of the hunt has its hierarchies, and its rights and titles and privileges, just as has the world of civilization. But in the wilderness world aristocracy has a natural foundation. It rests on skill and virtue, on the proven ability to do well the things that hunters know and respect and do. Even General Compson, now old, holds his position as head of the hunt not merely because he owns the land, but because he had earlier and long proven his ability to lead men under conditions of extreme danger and hardship. Authority here cannot be faked. It lies with those who have proven themselves fit for it, and it is judged by those who know how to judge. The words of such authorities, which are "more than advice but less than command," are assessed at their true value.

The world of the hunt also has its laws and settled conventions. These laws are unwritten. They are inscribed not in statute books but in the communal memory, and they are transmitted and revised not by judges and lawyers but by storytellers. This is case law, as it were, specific as to incident and episode, but resting on a shared code of honor and a common ground of experience and needing no police for its enforcement. Furthermore, in cases of conflict, this customary law can override the formal codes and authorities of the town. A strong example of this is provided by Boon's killing of Sam Fathers, at Fatherss's request, because his time to die had come, and because he had the right to choose his own way of dying. The members of the hunt community know that Boon has killed Fathers and draw together in silent approbation of the deed, despite its illegality under the codes of civilization. The contrast between the two codes is sharpened ironically when the narrator has Boon, who ended Sam Fathers's life out of piety, end his own membership in the broken communal world of the hunt by claiming possession of all the squirrels in the Big Gum tree. Boon, the coarsest, most loutish member of the hunt community, can enforce the law of the hunt with nobility and piety. But after that community is broken, he becomes a hired guard for the lumber company that had bought the land from Major de Spain.

One's place in the wilderness world depends on ability and relationship, and the relationships are as varied as the persons involved in them. There is no equality, no abstract imperative of uniformity and homogeneity. Equals are treated equally; unequals are treated unequally. Honor and status are functions of the individual's contribution to the goals of the hunt. What one has a right to ask, claim, or expect are unique to himself and specific to the immediate setting in which the claim is made. Rights are earned, not granted by law or fixed by birth. Ike, for example, must serve his years of apprenticeship in order to earn the right to a good stand on the hunt, or to ride the best mule, or to stay in camp beyond his usual time for leaving. He makes that latter request only when he has earned the right to make it, which means he and others feel that he is not claiming a right but asserting a need and discharging an obligation. General Compson upholds the claim, even against Ike's own relatives, who are of course his rightful governors under the laws of the town. Relationship and ability are what count. Or, to say it another way, the unwritten code of the wilderness is a code for regulating conduct among familiars, while the codes of the town are for regulating conduct among strangers. We might say that the justice of the wilderness community, in contrast to that of the town, is exactly not blind and that the law there, again in contrast to the law of the town, is exactly a respecter of persons. And, of course, relationship is always troubling. Every relationship bears the double stamp of both kinship and separateness, similarity and difference.

So, there is no place anywhere in this world of the hunt for abstract and general rules of conduct. Each person is unique, so is each relationship, and so too is each situation. There is hierarchy in this world, to be sure, but the hierarchy is not fixed. Furthermore, there are many hierarchies, and the same person may occupy different ranks, according to the value or activity in question. Sam Fathers is both prince and nigger. Boon, a white man, and therefore in some settings the superior of every black man, in the setting of the hunt is a black man's kennel keeper. General Compson gives up the best mule to the youngest hunter. McCaslin and Major de Spain both command and share responsibility for Boon, but neither can command him when it comes to Lion. The poor, scurvy, marginal farmers in the Big Bottom, lowliest of all whites, have an equal right to join in the final hunt for Old Ben, for he has over the years taken many of their shoats and calves. Even the animals share in this richly textured world of relationships. Lion can be mastered, but never owned. Old Ben can be killed, but only when he has chosen the time and the terms.

The point is, there is no real ownership in this world at all, no authority or rights based merely on legal possession. Not even one's own life can be owned. Nor can freedom come to one as a legal entitlement; it too must be earned, as the account of Ike's solitary meeting with Old Ben makes clear. Authority and rights rest on knowledge and virtue, on ability and character, on promises made, actions taken, and bonds forged in the past, and no legal enactments can change that reality among familiars. There is no social or economic equality among the members of the hunt world, and no talk of justice or desert framed in such terms, but there are no exclusive claims based on legal ownership, either. Such hierarchies as there are are based on merit. Authority is visible and personal. Some voices matter more than others, but each member has a voice, and all the voices can be heard in their proper places and judged according to their quality. No member of the community is insignificant, let alone superfluous. Each member exists as a separate and unique person, yet intricately and differentially related to each and all of the others.

In this world, each is vulnerable to the others, and it takes both courage and humility to accept those mutual relationships of dependence and inter-dependence without giving in to the urge for ownership, the urge for exclu-sive mastery and control, the urge to assert the total dependence of another thing or person on the self. Within the world of the hunt, those who attempt to own, and to make claims of authority on that base, are presented as themselves slaves of that which they claim to master, and the impulse of ownership itself is said to be rooted in cowardice. This is stated sharply by General Compson in his rebuke of McCaslin for denying Ike's request to stay for a few days longer in camp in order to participate in the climactic hunt.

"All right," General Compson said. "You can stay. . . . And you shut up, Cass," he said, though McCaslin had not spoken. "You've got one foot straddled into a farm and the other foot straddled into a bank; you ain't even got a good hand-hold where this boy was already an old man long before you damned Sartorises and Edmondses invented farms and banks to keep yourselves from having to find out what this boy was born knowing and fearing too but maybe without being afraid . . . maybe by God that's the why and the wherefore of farms and banks."

Here the work of Faulkner's story joins company with a great myth— becomes itself a telling and a part of that myth—that runs through our civilization.[3] The myth runs that God, or the Creator, or Nature, had in the beginning given man a lovely and bounteous home that belonged to all in common. That home was made for all, without distinction, to be shared and enjoyed in "the communal anonymity of brotherhood," as Ike puts it in *The Bear*. This Edenic state rested on and could continue only so long as people were held together by bonds of love and trust, and only so long as they could continue to believe that there would be enough goods for all—God stood guarantor for that—and that the community would see that each member got a rightful share of those goods. But then, suspicion and fear entered: fear of shortage, suspicion that some persons got more than others or would not come to one's aid in time of need. And so some persons begin to acquire and to hoard, begin to cut off pieces of the common and call them "mine," forbidding others access and use.

The root of the weakness is fear—fear of shortage, a fear so deep that it warps perception, causing us to forget that when seen in mere or predominately physical terms, life itself is always shortage and ends in the ultimate shortage, which is death. In theological terms, this fear, and the acts flowing from it, are of course sins against God: a refusal to trust the divine promise; an effort to make oneself independent of the Creator. In political terms, the fear results in setting one's private interests above the public interest, and in failing to see how much of what one calls one's "own" is really a social and not a private achievement. Faulkner's story gains so much of its resonance from the context set by both the religious-theological and the political-secular renderings of the myth.

Now, I hope I shall not be read as saying that the hunt community, and the special relationships of right and authority characteristic of it, are flawless. They are not. For one thing, it is a world without women, and therefore unable to reproduce itself. Indeed, the only appearance of a woman in this story comes in the last part, where Ike's new wife tries to extort from him a commitment to take up his property inheritance and make her the mistress of a plantation. Ike refuses, and the price of the refusal is that he shall be forever childless.

For another, it is a world out of time, or perhaps better, a world out of history. The hunt world has its own time, which is cyclical and personal, discontinuous with the linear and objective-collective time of civilization.

Time in the hunt world is experienced partly as the rhythmic, circular turn of the seasons, and partly as the biological-moral movement of birth-development-decline-death. There are also those awesome, visionary moments when time and eternity come together, as in Ike's meeting with Old Ben. The memory of time is intensely personal: good times and bad times, happy times and sad times, times when one lived up to the demands of the moment, and times when one flagged and failed. All this is in starkest contrast to historical time—the vast, collective movements and changes of civilization—and historical time, of course, inevitably destroys the cyclical-developmental-personal time of the wilderness. Therefore, time in *The Bear* is seen mainly within the category of loss.[4]

Another and similar way in which the world of the hunt is flawed is that it is fatally vulnerable to the civilized world outside, which requires the destruction of the wilderness world as the condition of its own growth. This is what I described earlier as the Nature-Civilization dilemma, which is for us a cultural and not just a personal dilemma. Just as the artificial time of civilization destroys the natural time of the wilderness, so too does the advance civilization consume the place of the wilderness. Time and place are both located within the category of loss. Both must go, and neither can make up for the other—as a garden, for example, might make one feel the loss of springtime vigor as not just loss but also the first stage of growth and harvest, and the loss of the wilderness space as not just disaster but also the possibility of gracious habitation. But within the patterned dilemmas of *The Bear* these reconciliations are impossible.

There is still another "flaw" in the wilderness world. It is not as though life there automatically produces and sustains only noble men and good relationships. The Indians, nature's children, sold the land to others. Lion embodies a "cold and almost impersonal malignance," a "cold and grim indomitable determination"—as though in him nature had produced its own nemesis. Boon is briefly transfigured by his devotion to Lion, but he soon relapses into his constitutional coarseness and impulsive violence. There will always be Boons, and they are as necessary for some of the work that must be done in the hunt as they are useful for similar kinds of work that must be done in the towns. And as a final example, Major de Spain, captain of the hunt, sells the woods to the lumber company. So, it is not a matter of a pure Eden set against a wholly corrupt civilization. Faulkner knew better than that and said it forcefully in the interviews in Japan. That knowledge made him a deeper explorer of the Nature-Civilization dilemma than a good many other Americans who have charted the same terrain (Emerson, for example?) and constitutes part of the power of this story. For creatures such as ourselves, nature is no sufficient guide to life. In fact, our very concepts of nature are in large part functions or expressions of our social existence: a concept of nature is a masked or oblique signature of an individual and a culture.

It is a question, rather, of what, if any, virtues can be learned in the hunt—and maybe learned only there—and of how, if at all, those lessons can be brought into life in the town. What are nature's legacy and authority, and what good uses can they have in civil life?

The legacy of the hunt is spiritual. It consists of certain virtues and skills that must be learned, and learned at the right time and in the right sequence. Patience is the foundation; without it, nothing can follow. Then comes the earnest, careful development of knowledge and skills, of craft. With the skills come self-confidence and pride. But if the skills come too easily, or if men employ complicated and elaborate tools to do their work for them— putting the emphasis on elaborating the tool rather than on enhancing the skill of the tool user—then the greatest treasures of the legacy cannot develop. They are humility and courage, and they will come only to those who resolve to face the greatest tests alone, without leaning on the tools and powers of civilization—just as Ike must relinquish gun, watch, and compass before Old Ben, the living spirit of the wilderness, the embodiment of its inmost principle, will consent to meet the seeker not in fear or anger or challenge, but in pure, timeless revelation. In his Nobel Address, Faulkner said "the basest of all things is to be afraid." The seeker must give himself over to that which chooses to disclose itself, make himself fully open and vulnerable to it, even though that could mean desolation. Most of us live 90 percent by illusion and imagination—powered mainly by fear and hope— and 10 percent by fact. Only those (few) who have opened themselves to the sheer spirit of life at least once can alter those proportions and become true teachers and guides for the rest of us. To accept and pass that test of exposure, something like faith is required. And that is the final gift in the legacy of the wilderness.[5] Patience, knowledge and skill, humility and pride, courage, faith—those virtues gained, Ike is capable of living the life of a free man, which requires the acknowledgment of dependence. He has learned the right lessons from the right teachers—Sam Fathers, Walter Ewell, Old Ben, Lion, and the tightly communal but still richly personal society of the hunt. The final lesson seems to be—we have heard it before and elsewhere—that the one who would live the life of freedom must learn that there are higher things than life itself.

Now, this legacy must be learned and earned. It cannot be passed on through property deeds and testamentary dispositions. Rather, it is transmitted from person to person, through action, story, and example, and it can be given only to those capable of receiving it. From the right authorities, acting within the right natural and communal setting, one learns what to be and how to live. Without those authorities and that setting one cannot learn those things. No one in the wilderness community is or claims to be self-made, author of himself. It is worth remembering that the root of the word "authority" suggests augmentation and initiation, not just or even primarily constriction and limitation. The latter sense is the one most familiar to us, of course, just as the idiotic notion of the "self-made man" is a familiar fruit of liberal ideology and American narcissism.

Ike's legacy comes to him at the very moment when the world that nurtured it dies. First the farmers and then the loggers hacked away at the wilderness. Roads and railroads pierced into its heart. Old Ben is the last of his line. When he goes, the spirit of the place goes with him. And he is brought to bay by the strange outlaw dog, the only one of his line. The dog, in turn, had been subdued by Sam Fathers, the last of his line. It all had to happen, so it seems, for hunting means killing, and civilization means the killing even of the world where hunters do their killing.[6]

If it all had to happen, if nothing could reverse the relentless process of destruction, then the only question that matters is what attitude to take toward the process.

I do not think the author invites us to nostalgia. Nor does he hold out hope for a return to the Eden that never was Eden anyway. He does not choose for the primitive over the civilized. *The Bear* is not evidence for the view of Faulkner as a primitivist, or even a romanticist. Even if other evidence were not available—and it is, in abundance—the story itself will not sustain such a reading. I point above all to the opening and closing passages of Part 2.

Part 1 closes on the epiphany of Ike's encounter with Old Ben. Alone and unarmed, Ike has gone deeper into the woods than he had ever gone before. Then, he knows that if he is to see the bear he must give up even his watch and compass, so he hangs them on a bush and goes forward without them. He becomes lost, and in some fear but without panic, he begins to cast out in circles, as Sam Fathers had taught him, hoping to cross his back trail and follow it to the watch and compass. Then he strikes the trail of Old Ben himself, which leads him to the lost instruments. An instant after he sees them, he also sees the bear. Having relinquished all external aids, Ike has finally and suddenly come into the presence of the animate spirit of the wilderness, the object of his lifelong search.

Then, with no transition, comes the detached and, at first, objectless or referentless opening sentence of Part 2: "So he should have hated and feared Lion." *Why* he should have hated and feared Lion does not become clear until the end of Part 2, many pages later. Most of Part 2 is an account of the dog Lion, and through that account we learn that he is the dog that can hold Old Ben long enough for the hunters to come up and deal with him. *That* is why Ike should have hated and feared the dog. Part 2 closes with this paragraph, which finally provides the object or referent of the opening sentence (Part 3, remember, is the epic account of the climactic hunt, of the death of the bear, Sam Fathers, and Lion):

> So he should have hated and feared Lion. Yet he did not. It seemed to him that there was a fatality in it. It seemed to him that something, he didn't know what, was beginning; had already begun. It was like the last act on a set stage. It was the beginning of the end of something, he didn't know what except that he would not grieve. He would be humble and proud that he had been worthy to be a part of it too or even just to see it too.

"[A] fatality in it . . . the end of something . . . he would not grieve." No primitivism here. No nostalgia either. A tragedy maybe. But, most importantly, a recognition that one stage in the life of an individual, and, personified in him, of a people, had inevitably ended, to be replaced by another. We are here passing from that stage in the story of an individual, a religion, and a people where the animate forces of nature are still the gods, and thus where even the mightiest of those gods—the bear who shakes the earth—must die, as all animals must die. There is obviously no diabolism here, either, nothing even remotely like an Ahab swearing death to the god, and sealing the pledge in rum drunk from the sockets of razor-sharp harpoons. The god must die, but those who kill do not kill without reverence, do not strut and boast in victory, but are reverent and "humble and proud."

After that stage, human ritual and human community can no longer borrow nature's forms or wed nature's forces, but they can still be built in an awareness of the sanctity of the earth and in a recognition of the tragedy of all mortal life upon the earth.

Furthermore, the episode of the abandoned watch and compass suggests that the strongest human experiences and the highest human achievements are built not primarily on technique and technology, but on the right skills and virtues, above all, on courage and on a sense of the sacredness of all life and of the mysterious force at its center. The episode, I think, affirms a basic humanism, but a humanism that knows some limits—knows itself to be as much a part of as apart from the rest of being.

So the question is not one of primitivism, or of nostalgia, or of diabolism, but of what of the old ways and faith and authority can live on and sustain life in the new stage. Old Ben tests the future, just as he tested the men of the past. He might or might not teach and nurture the spirit of the future, just as the creatures nurtured not only the bodies but also the spirits of men in the past, teaching them awe and reverence and courage and pride, and the liberty that comes with those things. We might pass or fail the test. And if we fail, the failure will darken our future, and the melancholy will fall over us if not permanently, then at least in those terrible and unforgettable moments of self-recognition that can hit us even as we go about our ordinary business. I recall that shattering moment when George Catlin saw in the figure of the bunched, shaggy, stricken, archaic bull buffalo the dreadful image of blind and wrecked old Oedipus, his doom foreshadowing the doom to come.

Maybe this white race, which, even in Europe, seemed set on smashing every old way, overriding every limit, and breaking every tie with nature in its fierce will to break away and be free, could here in this new land learn reverence and limit again. Perhaps the fresh and bounteous land could teach them to trust in each other and themselves rather than in property, technology, and law. But perhaps not. Maybe this white race, in its relentless push against all limits, including the limits of nature, would not relearn the lesson. Maybe then the race itself would lose the very sense of communion and community, shaking itself out into a loose agglomerate of detached and mobile individuals, each estranged from everything that is not itself, each wanting to evade or dominate the others. If that turned out to be the path taken, then our relations with nature would not, in the end, be tragic or nourishing in any good way, but merely trivial and rapacious—nature as nothing more than a treasury to be sacked for the gratification of insatiable desires for comfort and security. Then even the mobile individual might sicken, having torn up his own roots and severed his ties with others.[7] That is the question tested in Part 4 of *The Bear*, where Ike discovers his second legacy and tries to find a way to bring his first legacy to bear upon the second, so that each might support and enlarge the other.

III

Ike learns from the old plantation commissary ledgers started by his grandfather Carothers McCaslin and continued by his father Theophilus and his uncle Amodeus that the inheritance that is his by blood and law had been founded and transmitted by violence and fraud. It was all there in those old books, "not only the general and condoned injustice and its slow amortization but the specific tragedy which had not been condoned and could never be amortized."

"The general and condoned injustice" was of course slavery. Carothers McCaslin, the founder, had inherited some slaves and bought others, including Sam Fathers and his mother, whom Ikkemotubbe had swapped to Carothers for "an underbred trotting gelding." Ike's own father and uncle had partly added to the slavery legacy (Ike's uncle, for example, had won the slave Tenni Beauchamp in a poker game), and partly tried to "amortize" it both by moving out of the unfinished big house and giving it over to the slaves and by gradually manumitting the slaves during the two decades before the Civil War.

The "specific tragedy," the one that "could never be amortized," discloses itself only gradually. Carothers McCaslin, when still young, his wife still living, had fathered a black child, Eunice. Later on, without ever acknowledging her as his daughter, he brings her from New Orleans to the plantation as a house slave. The ledgers cryptically record that she drowned herself in 1832. In 1833, Eunice's daughter Tomasina dies in childbirth, leaving behind a son. That child's father is Carothers McCaslin. To slavery have been added rape, miscegenation, and incest—marital infidelity, too, of course, though that seems hardly worth mentioning. The line thus begun continues. Sphonsiba (Fonsiba), whom Ike goes in search of in order to discharge a provision of the will, is the child of Carothers's son and a slave.[8] Hence, she is direct kin to Ike, closer to him in blood than even his cousin McCaslin.

Other laws were broken too. And not just by McCaslins, nor just by white Americans North and South, but by a line of pagans, Jews, Romans, and Christians running as far back as the record goes. Ike insists that the God who created everything

> created man to be His overseer on the earth and to hold suzerainty over the earth and the animals on it in His name, not to hold for Himself and his descendants inviolable title forever . . . to the oblongs and squares of the earth, but to hold the earth mutual and intact in the communal anonymity of brotherhood, and all the fee He asked was pity and humility and sufferance and endurance and the sweat of his face for bread.

Maybe the crime here in the New World was greater than elsewhere, for here the white race was granted a new dawn after "the old world's worthless evening," its "corrupt and worthless twilight." But maybe not. The land was already tainted by Ikkemotubbe and his ancestors, long before any white man ever set foot on it, and perhaps He had decided that another people was needed to lift the curse. That new race repeated and broadened the crime, to be sure, but it also divided and fought against itself to establish the principle that, at least, there must be no more claim by one human being to the ownership and possession of another. So,

> maybe it was more than justice that only the white man's blood was available and capable to raise the white man's curse, more than vengeance . . . when He used the blood which had brought in the evil to destroy the evil as doctors use fever to burn up fever, poison to slay poison.

The theology is a bit homeopathic, perhaps, but the conclusion is clear enough: lust for possession is the evil passion, ownership the resulting crime, and dispossession the punishment.

IV

Now it is possible to step back a little and set the material in a broader frame. Slavery is a real fact (and crime) in Southern (and human) history and in this story of the bear. At the same time, slavery and rape figure in the story as sovereign metaphors for the original and multiple and continuing violation that started with our founding and has continued to run through every aspect of our lives. That sin, of course, is domination and possession—the reduction of another person or thing to the status of an object owned or controlled by oneself. The sin is rooted in fear—fear of scarcity; fear of the vulnerabilities and vicissitudes of relationships among free and autonomous participants. At bottom, this fear is a form of cowardice and is rooted in an outlook on the world that cannot imagine security without control. This lack of imagination will usually see itself as something quite other than lack of imagination—will see itself, for example, as self-defense, or as one's duty to self and family, or as one's duty to bring order to the lives of others who are incapable of ordering their own affairs. What else than that fear and lack of imagination can produce such sentiments as President Lyndon B. Johnson expressed to American troops in Vietnam, when he told them that there were two hundred million "of us" and three billion "of them" and that "we got what they want and we can't let them have it"?

Slavery, then, is just the most intense and obvious form of the sin, the form in which human beings are reduced to property, but the cowardly lust to possess and dominate—land, goods, human beings, other peoples—runs throughout this story, just as it runs throughout much of human history. Nor does it happen only as the domination of one person over another by force and fraud. Some are willing to be possessed so that they might possess in their turn. Ike's new wife, for example, is willing to make herself Ike's whore if he will only agree to accept his McCaslin inheritance of property. Some will give up self for possession, denying and relinquishing their own integrity.

This outlook also entails a certain idea of freedom: I cannot be free unless others are under my control; freedom seen as sovereignty, or doing as one wills—even if that means reducing others to one's own possessions, or making oneself the object of another's possessive lusts for self-regarding reasons.

This conception of freedom is one of the basic strands in the whole fabric of American ideas of freedom, and Faulkner's story shows that the idea necessarily entails a denial of kinship, ultimately even a denial of one's own blood. I do not mean to say that this idea of freedom as "I own" and "I control" is exclusively American. That is obviously not the case. What I do mean to say, first, is that here we had a good chance of arriving at a better idea, having seen the disasters produced by the old idea in the old world; and, secondly, that once we failed to imagine and to implement that better idea, the familiar idea had a larger and richer field to grow in than it had anywhere else. Here, a whole, vast, sparsely peopled continent lay ready for the seed. And once planted, the idea might continue to grow until everything and everyone was either owned or owner, until everything had been so subjected to and reduced by the "I will" and "I own" that there was nothing more worth having. The hunt sections of *The Bear* end with that pitiful and bitter scene of Boon frantically claiming possession of all the squirrels in the lone Big Gum tree—all that is left of the free and bounteous legacy of Old Ben and the Big Woods, a legacy that could be preserved intact only on the condition that it be shared by all and owned by none.

The wilderness legacy is destroyed. The only legacy that remains is the legacy of the plantation. The question for Ike is what to do about that.

He repudiates it. Renounces it, rather, since, he says, it was never properly his or anyone else's to own or to repudiate. He refuses the property, leaving it with his cousin McCaslin, and chooses a fresh start. He takes up a new vocation, marries, and builds a new house for himself and his new wife. He rejects his legacy, denies the binding power of the past, and attempts a fresh start, free of all burdens save those chosen by himself.

But the path of purity and the fresh start turns out to have its own disasters. It is not so easy to repudiate or to renounce inherited burdens, even though you had nothing to do with their making. Just as Ike's first or natural birth was no fresh start, neither is his attempted moral rebirth. For one thing, while he might give up the land, the land will still be owned. Every piece of land is owned. Nothing Ike or any other individual does can change that. *You* might refuse the "sin" of possession, thereby purifying yourself, but that does not even reduce the total quantity of the sin, for someone else will eagerly and covetously take your place. Furthermore, his effort to discharge the obligation to Fonsiba laid on him by old Carothers McCaslin's will also ends in failure. Her husband spurns him. She herself turns away from his solicitude and concern with a cold "I'm free."[9] That is a particularly hard defeat for Ike, for he has learned by now that no one is ever really free, and maybe doesn't even want to be, although everyone wants the illusion of freedom, which they easily equate with being masterless, or with mastering others, or with owing nothing to any visible and personal authority. Finally, Ike's own wife refuses to become the mother of their children. The path of personal purity ends in rejection and sterility.

But Ike is not easily mocked as an innocent or purist, an "idealist" in the usual pejorative sense of that word. Nor does he judge and condemn others who fall short of his own standard. Rather, his situation itself is a nearly impossible one. Put it this way: Ike wants to do the right thing and has the will and the virtues needed to do it, even at considerable cost to himself, but he does not have the knowledge or the means.

What is the right way? How do you erase or compensate for the evils of the past when those evils constitute the present? That is the situation here: the necessary will and virtue are present, but the knowledge and resources are not. With the best will in the world, the best way is still not apparent. And neither are the means to the end.

That is not an unusual condition in human affairs, both personal and political. It is very like the situation Marx faced when he called the failed revolutions of 1848 a farce because the revolutionaries had tried to reenact 1789. Marx concluded (insisted) that the proletarians must draw their "poetry"—their vision and their methods—not from the past but from the future. But neither the proletarians nor anyone else knows how to do *that*; knows even what doing that means.

Not only is the dilemma described as Ike's in *The Bear* not an unusual one in human affairs, it may even be a peculiarly important dimension of America's self-definition. Our national birth certificate tells us that we are "born free" and endowed with "inalienable rights" to life and liberty. The author of that Declaration taught that the past had no claims on the present whatever and that every generation had the right to start anew. Similarly, we want to see ourselves as heirs of the virtues of nature. And again like Ike, we see ourselves as always intending to do the right thing. So, the right intention is there, but the requisite knowledge and means are not. That is a peculiarly bitter condition, one likely to make its victims nervous and irascible, likely also to make them seek scapegoats for failure. Ike, at least, does not do that.

The past presses on and congeals into the present. No one is born free. Filmer was of course as right about that as Locke and Jefferson were wrong. The slate is never clean, not even for the "American Adam." Is there any way to get rid of a historical burden you did not choose and do not want? There is always some amount of forgetting, of course, and if there were not, action would be virtually impossible. But forgetting is never perfect: memories can be embedded in a layer of mind below the conscious and can affect conduct in ways we cannot grasp; past actions now solidified into habit, institution, or custom can shape our present and future even though we are not aware of their doing so; and others often will not let us forget things we might very much want to forget.

Ike's way seems not to work either; and yet, it is probably the only way that could work—supposing it were possible on a societal level. Perhaps the only way to overcome the crippling burdens of the past and open new paths into the future is through asking and granting forgiveness. But that takes great courtesy and courage and humility on the part of the one who asks and an equal measure of generosity and trust on the part of the one who grants. We can hardly even imagine such a possibility on the general, societal level. Too much would have to be given up; too many risks and vulnerabilities would have to be accepted; too much knowledge would be required.

And so we continue to postpone the day of reckoning, just as old McCaslin passed on his guilty debt to his sons, charging them with making compensation for his wrongdoing. Let the future pay for the past.

We do that all the time, and in a great many ways. One of our favorite (and maddest) ways is the one offered by Jefferson—the fantasy that we can escape limits by wishing them away, by announcing and pretending that we are a new beginning. Another is the dream of unlimited production, the idea that by producing more and more of all the desired things there will some-day be enough for everybody—no losers left; no desires denied; no need for any person or group to limit consumption or to relinquish something of their own to a victimized or less-favored person or group. We are perhaps begin-ning to learn that that way might mean the destruction of nature itself, of the capacity of the earth to sustain itself and provide humanity a home.

The temptation takes still other forms, both "pragmatic" or expediential and "high-minded." This nation's leaders during the Vietnam War, for ex-ample, not only lied about the war's extent, aims, and methods, but about its monetary cost as well. The war was financed not by taxes but by govern-ment borrowing. The present inflation is partly the result of that: the future pays for the past. An example of the high-minded way: a few years ago I was a member of a college faculty that voted overwhelmingly to impose a five-year moratorium on the hiring of white males. Only women and minor-ities could be hired. That vote too followed the logic of Carothers McCaslin, for not a single person already on the faculty was affected by the morator-ium. It seemed to me at the time that the only right way to correct the injustice was for the white males already on the faculty to draw lots to determine who among us should resign, up to the requisite quota, thereby making openings for women and minority candidates. Start right *now*. It was we, after all, who were the direct, traceable beneficiaries of past prac-tices of racial and sexual exclusion and discrimination.

All such tactics of postponed and transferred rectification rest upon and express a certain conception of politics and membership. That conception was pithily stated by William Graham Sumner: A decides that B has trouble or is making trouble, and that C must be made to do something about it. You could fill in the A's and B's and C's with a hundred examples drawn from American public life. Two should make the point. Thus, lawmakers decide that a corporation must install antipollution equipment. The corporation does so and passes on the costs to consumers in the form of higher prices, thereby socializing the costs of production while continuing to keep profits and power private. Or, legislatures and courts decide that racial and ethnic imbalance in the public schools is detrimental to minority students, so busing programs are implemented. What that has meant in practice is that poor and lower-class students get moved around, while the sons and daughters of the prosperous and powerful classes go to largely white private schools or manage to stay in largely white public schools. How many members of the U.S. Congress send their children to racially integrated public schools?

These are the attitudes and these the policies of people who have never fully decided to live with each other and share a common destiny. It is exactly the ethos described in Part 4 (the plantation legacy) of *The Bear*. It is the ethos of the contractarian society built on the foundation blocks of private property, individualism, and the limited interest of each in the welfare of the whole. Against that world stands the world of the hunt, a world built on humanly meaningful authority and a community built on interdependence, loyalty, and respect for the past.

These two sets of principles still struggle for authority over the American soul, though the first, of course, is dominant. We have done no better at reconciling them in our real world than Faulkner's characters did in their fictional world. The achievement of contract is our uncertain victory; the failure of community our certain defeat.[10]

Notes

1. A shorter, simpler version of *The Bear* was published in the *Saturday Evening Post* the same year (1942) that the final version was published as a part of *Go Down, Moses*. Many characters and episodes in *The Bear* appear and reappear in works written both before and after it. The genesis, growth, mode of composition, and later uses of the story are unimportant to my purposes. The story itself suffices, and I shall not go much outside it. Nor shall I try to fix its precise location on the whole terrain of Faulkner's work.

2. Lévi-Strauss has shown convincingly that the function of much myth is exactly to mediate the nature-culture opposition, to reconcile and draw the two into complicity. Our national myth makes that reconciliation extremely difficult, nearly impossible. For an excellent brief treatment of the American theme, see Perry Miller's chapter on "The Romantic Dilemma in American Nationalism and the Concept of Nature," in his *Nature's Nation* (Cambridge: Harvard University Press, 1967), pp. 197–208.

3. "It is interesting to observe with what singular unanimity the farthest sundered nations,

and generations consent to give soundness to an ancient fable, of which they indistinctly appreciate the beauty or the truth. By a faint and dream-like effort . . . the dullest posterity slowly add some trait to the mythus. . . . The very nursery tales of this generation were the nursery tales of primeval races. They migrate from east to west, and again from west to east; now expanded into the 'tale divine' of bards, now shrunk into a popular rhyme. This is an approach to that universal language which men have sought in vain. This fond reiteration of the oldest expressions of truth by the latest posterity . . . is the most impressive proof of a common humanity. . . .

"In the mythus a superhuman intelligence uses the unconscious thoughts and dreams of men as its hieroglyphics to address men unborn." Henry David Thoreau, *A Week on the Concord and Merrimack Rivers* (1849) (New Riverside ed.; Boston: Houghton Mifflin, 1893), I, 74, 76.

4. I am not sure I have this right. I do think that time in *The Bear* is seen mainly as loss and that civilization requires that loss. But that may be among the inescapable disasters of "civilization." There are, of course, beginnings and ends. But it is an arrogance, a vanity, to think that a life has a beginning and an end—to try to isolate and characterize or define a single existence within the endless processes of nature, and to make our meager consciousness the judge of its own duration and existence, whereas it is at most a leaf floating on the surface of the river. In this sense, "beginning" and "end" are invented words for an invented concept of time, words that express the vanity of a minute consciousness that refuses to acknowledge its submergence into a larger one. That vanity may be essential to civilization, may be essential even to the concept of the human. I am not sure. But plainly, it is a vanity rooted in our unwillingness to acknowledge how much we owe the dead, how much we are the dead. Our language, our religion and customs and manners, most of our artifacts, and even our fears and joys and despairs all come to us from the dead. None of us is a new beginning though each would like to think so.

5. Not the faith that moves mountains. Rather, the faith that issues in obedience, which includes eager but patient expectation, which fills the present with the power of the future, and which binds the faithful together through shared commitment. The faith which is "the substance of things hoped for, the evidence of things not seen."

6. Hunting alone need not destroy the balance, of course. But hunting with guns usually does. And "the march of civilization" always does.

7. Alfred Kazin has called Joe Christmas the loneliest character in American fiction. And yet, he is of course free—if only to walk always within the same circle of his isolated existence, trying to fend off the demands of others that he serve their uses and confirm the perspectives of their lives. When he does finally choose a membership and a people, he seals the choice with murder and is murdered and mutilated in turn.

8. McCaslin's will had provided that $1,000 be paid to his illegitimate child—thus leaving his other (legitimate) sons the burden of paying for his violations. I will return to this theme.

9. It matters that in this episode Ike, while striving to discharge the obligations of the will, cannot take the last step and publicly acknowledge Fonsiba as his half-sister. He keeps the knowledge of kinship secret. Ike's right name, of course, is Isaac, and Isaac, of course, was the son of Abraham. But Ike's father was no Abraham—no founder and liberator. Abraham's offering of Isaac was the crowning test of his faith. And that test taught, as I understand it, both the need for a consummate sacrifice sealing the final ratification of the covenant, *and* that "J" did not, unlike many other gods, desire human sacrifices. Isaac was spared, to become a founder and leader in his turn, because his father was willing to give that which was most precious to him, his own son—even though that was not what was demanded. Ike cannot be free, and cannot become a father in his turn, because his father was unwilling to expose that which hurt him most, his secret kinship with the Negroes—even though that was what was demanded. Ike repeats the failure. It costs him nothing to give the thousand dollars, for he has

already "renounced" his own material inheritance. It would cost him much more to acknowledge kinship with Fonsiba.

10. I do not mean to say that Faulkner, were he alive today, would accept the "communitarian" argument of my final pages, especially as I apply that argument to questions of racial justice. He was opposed to the civil rights movement in its early days. He did suggest that racial harmony and justice could only come about through slow, painful, growing, mutual recognition of a common humanity. Time is the healer. For blacks, that could mean never.

5

Language as History: Ezra Pound's Search for the Authority of History

Alfred Kazin

The high pitch of interest, to his taste, was the pitch of history, the pitch of acquired and earned suggestion, the pitch of association, in a word; so that he lived by preference, incontestably, if not in a rich gloom, which would have been beyond his means and spirits, at least amid objects and images that confessed to the tone of time."

"Crapy Cornelia," by Henry James

but at least she saw damn all Europe.

The Pisan Cantos (LXXXIV)

There is no doubt—that I have been of some use—to some people.

Ezra Pound to Donald Hall, 1960

The Gods have not returned. "They have never left us."
They have not returned.

Canto 113

1908: the year (more or less), as Virginia Woolf was to remember with the authority of the modernists, when "human nature changed." Let us see. Ezra Pound from Wyncote, Pennsylvania (by way of Idaho), is in Venice, sitting on the steps of the Dogana, the custom-house. In Canto III, written sometime in the 1920s, he says that he was sitting on the steps

> For the gondolas cost too much, that year,
> And there was not "those girls," there was one face,
> And the Buccentoro twenty yards off, howling "Stretti,"
> And the lit cross-beams, that year, in the Morosini
> And peacocks in Koré's house, or there may have been.
>   Gods float in the azure air,
> Bright gods and Tuscan, back before dew was shed.
> Light: and the first light, before ever dew was fallen.
> Panisks, and from the oak, dryas,

And from the apple, maelid,
Through all the wood, and the leaves are full of voices,
A-whisper, and the clouds bowe over the lake,
And there are gods upon them,
And in the water, the almond-white swimmers,
The silvery water glazes the upturned nipple,
        As Poggio has remarked.
Green veins in the turquoise,
Or, the gray steps lead up under the cedars.

These lines are so exquisite that even if we do not get all the Venetian references, or understand why the scene suddenly shifts from Venice, where there are surely no almond-white swimmers in the Grand Canal, the water is notoriously not silvery—in fact, we have mysteriously arrived in Spain—we are aware of the young American's rapture in Mediterranean lands. There have been many golden passages in our literature on the subject of such rapture. We all remember Lambert Strether in Henry James's *The Ambassadors* telling his young friend at Gloriani's garden party that the great thing is "to live"; the opening of Hemingway's *A Farewell To Arms,* the most incongruously beautiful opening to an exposure of war's futility, is there because Hemingway said, "I'm trying to do the country like Cézanne and having a hell of a time."

Pound's velvety silky tone reminds us of them in tone. The language describes pleasures; we are at a celebration. But even when we link this very American inventory of Europe to Hemingway's passion for French-Italian-Spanish landscape (Jake Barnes in *The Sun Also Rises*: "Looking back we saw Buerguete, white houses and red roofs, and the white road with a truck going along it . . . Ahead the road came out of the forest and went along the shoulder of the ridge of the hills. The hills ahead were not wooded, and there were great fields of yellow roses. Way off we could see the steep bluffs dark with trees and jutting the gray stone that marked the course of the Irati River")—the opening of Pound's Canto III is not exclusively concerned with the pleasures of the eye alone, as when Lambert Strether registers as one the yellow in the straw-colored chablis, the *omelette aux fines herbes* and the eyes of Mme. de Vionnet when he lunches with her along the Seine.

In Pound's Canto gods float in the azure air above the Grand Canal, Bright Gods and Tuscan, back before the dew was shed. We have shifted from Venice to Tuscany, from Tuscany to Greece, where little pans and wood nymphs issue from the trees, and where the leaves are full of voices. The invocation is not of the Mediterranean but of paganism. This is serious stuff. This American poet, as his most zealous admirers will have great difficulty noticing, is for all his love of the troubadours, of Provençal, of medieval Europe, intellectually outside of Christianity, like the Fascists he will come to admire. Distinctly non-religious, unlike his great friend the Possum, as he liked in varying tones of admiration, fellowship and conde-scension to call that vulnerable and very different—because so highly per-sonal—poet T. S. Eliot, Pound will show a poetic sensibility astonishingly impersonal, slashing, hard. *His* subject is not the Romantic Ego, as you might think from his passion for word-association, but History as the pro-cession of the human mind. And what the human mind dwells on, as Pound well knew, is some desperately needed hint of immortality. If the Judaeo-Christian God no longer suffices Pound—he called the Jewish element in Christianity "the black evil"—paganism is certainly closer, he thought, to the original sources of poetry.

Paganism, polytheism, culture on culture seeking the common root: Greek, Chinese, Latin, even American! The key word in Pound's reference code will be *paideuma,* the energy-pattern of a particular culture. What we are dealing with in Pound's case is anything but the usual literary tourist's rapture of finding something older and more restful than his commercial civilization. It is the intoxication of returning to the roots of poetry and the ancient world in Asia even more than in pagan Greece and Rome. Pagan-ism: the living out of roles *in* nature, first by the gods and then by men. Paganism: an identification with the energy patterns in nature, not the mod-ern habit of seeking to study nature by dominating it. Which means: regard-ing nature as something inherently different from oneself. Which explains a certain lack of energy, a mental fatigue, ultimately due to the split between subject and object.

The twenty-three-year-old poet was to publish a first volume, A *Lume Spento,* that year in Venice. When it was reprinted in 1964, the poet recent-ly returned to Italy from almost fourteen years in a Washington madhouse called it "a collection of stale creampuffs." It is true that there is something flakey, very 1890ish—as Wallace Stevens was to complain of Pound's total output—in many of these poems. But Pound, who had announced himself as a poet at fifteen and in many respects never outgrew the role of the poet-as-adversary, began by practicing every kind of poetry he could find. When we read the early poems he kept in his collection, *Personae,* we are astonished by the absolutely faultless ear that will remain with Pound even in the most discursive sections of the *Cantos* and the somehow unaccountable intimacy with poetry in every language and of every period. The ease with which Pound assimilates other poets, other languages, every "alien" sound some-how made friendly and absorbable by Pound's ear was to give us such masterpieces from the Anglo-Saxon as "The Seafarer" and that unforgettable love poem "The River Merchant's Wife: A Letter." "*Bitter breast-cares have I abided, / Known on my keel many a care's hold, / And dire sea-surge, and*

*there I oft spent / Narrow nightwatch nigh the ship's head / While she
tossed close to cliffs. Coldly afflicted, / My feet were by frost be-
numbed. / Chill its chains are."*

This is certainly the polar world of the Anglo-Saxons in all the harsh
stormy alliterative stresses of a world with little human relief. By contrast,
the silky shy tenderness of the young Chinese wife writing to her absent
husband The River Merchant, a poem Pound tells us taken from Rihaku, 8th
century: *"While my hair was still cut straight across my forehead / I played
about the front gate, pulling flowers. / You came by on bamboo stilts, playing horse, / You walked about my seat, playing with blue plums. / And we
went on living in the village of Chokan: / Two small people, without dislike
or suspicion."*

Pound the so-called "translator" does what poets alone can do in adapting
or "imitating" the sounds of a poem that has communicated itself to the poet
without his necessarily understanding the language. The sense of authority
that comes from knowing that you can do just whatever you like with
language will extend itself to more than literature. *"Personae,"* Pound called
his collection of poems outside the *Cantos*. A poet plays roles. The most
"personal" of poets, like Whitman, writes not about his real self—whatever
that may ever be—but about an ideal visionary self who takes in all space
and time; Whitman's greatest feat was to be mistaken for America itself.
Poetry is ultimately this series of metamorphoses: language, sound, inces-
sant fantasy, real dreams, hypothetical dreams moving ungraspably in
metaphoric relation to each other.

Poetry, said Jean Cocteau, is a separate language. This must be so, since
poets often reproduce each other's subtlest art without knowing what instinct
leads them to it. Pound knew this language in all its secret strength as no
other American poet has ever known it. He had an extraordinary natural
endowment: perfect adaptability to other poets everywhere, so that he was
the early supporter of Frost and the perfect editor of *The Waste Land* and
could inform a whole generation about the art of poetry as if he were
dancing certain exquisite movements, not pontificating in a classroom—
the usual career of his followers. Pound's instinct *to* poetry was so complete that poetry possessed him, literally, to a kind of auto-intoxication.
Pound did not need drugs or alcohol in order to write. Poetry itself
drugged him, blurred the distinction between the ideal and natural worlds.
And it was just as much other people's poetry that drugged him as his
own—past the point of distinguishing between the beauty of a line from
Provençal, a Chinese ideogram, and its application to the economic problems of the 1930s. He could be almost unconscious of the slashing domi-
neering bent that the total self-confidence of his involvement with poetry
gave him. Shelly said that poets are the unacknowledged legislators of

the world. Pound would have said not *unacknowledged* but *unread:* by the multitude.

Pound was to become an amazing seismograph of the force hidden in language; he was to link this to tremors in the body politic. Since poetry is not only older than prose but stands in the same relation to it that the beginnings of life stand to the emergence of man on this planet, the greatest poets have understandably detected in themselves mystical powers, attributes of the shaman, the medium through which we touch a great mystery.

The mystery is how it is that stray filaments of emotion, which may not be known to us until we fit them into a necessary order of words and rhythm, have such a physical effect on us. The physician-poet Oliver Wendell Holmes suggested an analogue in the binary rhythm of the heart. Poetry can have such an effect as to seem *expected* by the body.

The authority of poetry over us does in fact rest on physical signs—on stresses and the sudden relief from stresses that correspond to the sensation in us of the heart and that suggest tactile knowledge. Emerson said of Dante that his verse was the nearest thing to hands and feet; Rilke said poetry was the past that breaks out in our hearts. When we look at the characteristic cross rhythms of long lines and up-springing half lines that Pound developed into such density of emotion as visual *fact* on the page—poetry as sculpture, Donald Davie called it—we recognize an energy at work in the typographical shape of the lines, an energy in human affairs that is not only the theme of the poem but is represented *by* the lines. The spacing, the sudden springing, the iconic letters in Chinese and Greek—all this is like the art of the dance to which Nietzsche, that other totally spontaneous lyric thinker, compared his own style as poet-philosopher. Thus, from *Ripostes* (1912), "The Return":

> See, they return; ah, see the tentative
> Movements, and the slow feet,
> The trouble in the pace and the uncertain
> Wavering!
>
> See, they return, one, and by one,
> With fear, as half-awakened;
> As if the snows should hesitate
> And murmur in the wind,
>   And half turn back;
> These were the "Wing'd-with-Awe,"
>   Inviolable.
>
> Gods of the wingèd shoe!
> With them the silver hounds
>   sniffing the trace of air!
> Haie! Haie!

> These were the swift to harry;
> These the keen-scented;
> These were the souls of blood.
> Slow on the leash,
>   pallid the leash-men!

Pound the restless instigator of modernism was not afraid of using obsolete words; his innate tie with the language materials of poetry in any language he encountered, even when he depended on a crib, as with Chinese, or when his own knowledge of it, as with Greek, was not so much imperfect as impatient, persuaded him that words in themselves, as Emerson put it, were fossil poetry.

The whole romantic theory of poetry as germane to the race, its unconscious resources already lying in the mind like separate pieces of type waiting to be put into rightly organized lines by the highest possible art, is one from which we have never really departed. What Pound added to this—brought out of it—was the belief that the language of poetry is not so much primitive emotion so much as it is secret knowledge. The shaman was more important to Pound than the bard. "Poem" comes from the Greek word for maker; *how* the poem is made denotes such an extraordinary amount of contraction, condensation, acceleration of human experience within a single context, that more than any other poet I can think of Pound really came to believe that the highly contracted words were occult. So the function of the poet was to teach the way back to this arcane knowledge; as poet, by displaying all the verbal shimmer he could line up in his words and the force he could reproduce in the structure of his verse.

The real Muse, we shall see, is History—but History buried in words: History as an excavation made possible only to those who know the lay of the land and where the old wisdom is hidden.

Pound's most famous single poem outside the 117 cantos is his monument, "Hugh Selwyn Mauberley," sculptured indeed in memory of the artist Gaudier-Brzeska, dead in the war. It is dear to the modernist mob created by Pound and Eliot, which learned from them to accept nothing not in their image, because it displays Pound's total disdain *For an old bitch gone in the teeth, / For a botched civilization.* Mauberley, like all of Pound's key works, is an experiment in style, detached and technical to maximum chilliness.

> Christ follows Dionysus,
> Phallic and ambrosial
> Made way for macerations;
> Calliban casts out Ariel.

All things are a flowing,
Sage Heracleitus says:
But a tawdry cheapness
Shall outlast our days.

. . .

There died a myriad,
And of the best, among them,
For an old bitch gone in the teeth,
For a botched civilization,

Charm, smiling at the good mouth,
Quick eyes gone under earth's lid,
For two gross of broken statues,
For a few thousand battered books.

The familiar post-trenches theme: contempt for Christianity, lament over departed ideals, fury at the pointless obliteration of a whole generation. Then the expatriate elite saluting itself, exasperated for having "been born in a half savage country, out of date." The most exact art alone will not suffice. "His true Penelope was Flaubert, / He fished by obstinate isles; / Observed the elegance of Circe's hair / Rather than the mottoes on sundials."

Unaffected by "the march of events, / He passed from man's memory in l'an trentiesme / De son age; the case presents / No adjunct to the Muses' diadem."

O but it does! What Pound added to the Muses' diadem was the interweaving of Greek and Latin with English, just as in his first lyric poems he "imitated" Anglo-Saxon, Provençal, Chinese, Dante and his friend Guido Cavalcanti. All this was to have an intimidating and even comic effect on an audience without those languages. This interflow of languages represented one thing in the mind of Ezra Pound, who dreamed in languages, for the languages came. It represented a totally fictitious authority in the minds of the audience.

Eliot's sense of tradition, he told us in the tumultuously experimental twenties, was Anglo-Catholic, classical, royalist. No matter that a genuine diehard, Paul Elmer More, complained of the incongruity between Eliot's stiff criticism and his poetry of fragments. More was roundly told off: criticism represents the world as it should be, poetry as it *is*. Eliot, who took his time getting to admit that *The Waste Land* was really a poem about his personal sterility, or that he might have turned Buddhist as easily as Christian, nevertheless acquired a greater authority over literature in English than anyone since Dr. Johnson. Pound, who did far more for other poets than anyone else, and was forever pushing poets, prodding poets, instructing everyone at large in books typically entitled *Instigations, Make It New, How To Read, ABC of Reading, Guide To Kulchur,* scattered his forces in London, Paris, Rapallo, was soon too heated an agitator for Social Credit and other favorite nostrums, to achieve the same lofty dignity as the Possum. The great work of his life, the *Cantos,* turned out for many of us to be the great failure as the epic it proclaimed itself to be—and finally a work of such obscene hatred as to make one weep over the manic flaw in Pound, his overbearing illusion that through his innate tie to poetry he could instruct a disordered world.

Edgar Allan Poe said that a long poem could not sustain itself; especially, he might have added, by lyricists like himself and Ezra Pound with an ideal vision not only of the classical world but of their own intellectual powers. The *Cantos* are full of miraculously beautiful lyrics; the poem as a whole, if you can call it a whole, proceeds from Pound's inner ecstasy at poetry in all languages rushing out of each other into a mind driven to frenzy by the speed-up of words and images within it. What you get in the *Cantos,* above everything else, is this inner vortex of sounds and associations, all these buried quotations and anecdotes, these pages and pages lifted without discernible order from Renaissance history, American political documents, the conversation of Benito Mussolini, newspaper articles, economic lore, etc., etc.

An epic, he told us in *Make It New,* "is a poem including history." We had better remember that as we drift through the *Cantos.* History turns out to be anything that interests Ezra Pound, that he suddenly thinks of in connection with something else, that he has read, that he can quote, that he can in fact *repeat.* But this total recall and assemblage is the reverse of arbitrary; it is as natural to Pound as eating drinking copulating defecating, and slides onto a page as if he were doing just that on the page.

The great epic—the *Odyssey,* the *Aeneid,* the *Divine Comedy, Paradise Lost*—is the poem of a whole civilization. Pound assumes the authority behind such an epic, and though the cantos are at times not so much written as accumulated, Pound does take on more than one civilization. Which is not why he fails as an epic poet: there he fails, as all long poems in America mostly fail, because they are not content with great narratives of the existing world; they want to leave it. Pound wants to take us out of the wasteland, the charnel house, the Heartbreak House of finance capitalism.

His way of doing this is to stun us: the language museum without walls: the past of China, Greece, Latin Europe in all the culture-splendor of their original words. The infliction of obscurity is so unyielding that sometime, if he is honest, the reader of the *Cantos* must ask a) how far all these quotations and references are just disdain for the ordinary world in which we live b) how much it therefore corresponds to the gap between the shaman and the tribe c) how much, in fact, none of this is consciously demonstrative but just Pound's language intoxication. In the *Cantos* this rises to a delirium of cross references just as in *Finnegans Wake*. Joyce is so absorbed in a language entirely his own that it becomes self-reproducing.

This last is the truth, which does not relieve us from the contempt that shines proudly through the brilliancies of Mauberley. There is a frivolity in any great artist—Joyce and Picasso come to mind—who take their endlessly inventive hand as the measure of reality. Yeats sadly reported his impression of the *Cantos*: "nervous obsession, nightmare, stammering confusion." Jung said of *Ulysses* that Joyce would have gone mad if he hadn't written it. It is true that Pound was an only child, famously spoiled, who kept his parents with him in Europe. But his belief in his own rightness was not just psychological, for like Beethoven he finally heard nothing but what he remembered. To this extent, not being deaf, he was "mad." We can see the extent and limits of this "madness" in the *Cantos* as well as in his Fascist pamphlets and frightful radio broadcasts from Italy during the war.

Pound's problem was never conflict with himself but an excessiveness, an incessancy of verbal self-stimulation; actually isolated in Rapallo from much of what was actually happening in the great cities of Europe, and as always living on reading, he could be more excited by anything in print than by strong drink. There has simply been no other mind like Pound's for the energy with which he assimilates, the sputtering impatience with which he turns from episode to quotation to anecdote. The shiftings of his mind are such that one feels changed by the extraordinary lyric bursts, usually in a water context which provide an extension of ordinary human sight—

> Black azure and hyaline
>   glass wave over Tyro,
> Close cover, unstillness,
>   bright welter of wave-cords,
>   . . . Glass-glint of wave in the tide—rips against sunlight,
>   pallor of Hesperus

Then one feels positively jostled by the inevitable shift.

The difficulty lies not in the huge blocks of Greek, Latin, Provençal, Chinese flung at us—or in the elusive garbled quotations relating to the plunderings and escapades of the Renaissance swashbuckler Sigismundo da Malatesta, obviously admired for his cruel Renaissance "energy." Even if we knew everything that Pound knows, we still would not know *why* in Canto VII we go from Eleanor (presumably of Aquitaine) to "poor old Homer blind, / blind as a bat, / Ear, ear for the sea-surge; / rattle of old men's voices" to Pound quoting himself on Henry James—"And the great domed head, *con gli occhi onesti e tardi.*"

All we know is that this is the order in which the voices of Pound's cherished inscriptions, memories, etc. are heard by him. They occur on the page as they occur to Ezra Pound. If the reader, informed with all of Pound's references, nevertheless asks of this automatic writing—where am *I* going with all this?—the answer is something that has to be given him by a critic; he will not decipher it himself from the dizzily shifting references.

O.K., nothing wrong in being instructed. How many of us now look at Picasso's *Les Demoiselles d'Avignon,* hear Stravinsky's *Le Sacre du Printemps,* knows that $E = mc^2$, even follow the historians' arguments about the origins of the Cold War, without having been instructed by authority? Are we against interpretation, do we want to take the bread out of Hugh Kenner's mouth if we wonder just what his instruction does for us when he writes in *The Pound Era*: "Later 1–16 and 17–27 were joined without division, and three more cantos added to make a first block of 30. The span of this no longer reaches from the Renaissance to modern times but makes a closed loop within the Renaissance, with modern extrapolations. We commence with Divus, 1538, and close with the death of Pope Alexander Borgia, 1503; close, moreover, despite this death, on a note of hope, for Hieronymous Soncinus is initiating the kind of printing activity that will bring Divus' Homer into the public domain. Even the wreck of the Malatesta is subsumed; the quotation from Soncinus concludes . . ."

But this is supposed to be an epic, and an epic is a poem that includes history! In fact the cantos are really Pound's intellectual diary, the record of his amazing reading, disgorged just when and how he feels like it. So the final authority of this epic belongs not to Ezra Pound but to his commentators. Whom we cannot choose but hear. The *Cantos* is not to be dismissed, bewildering as its many turns can be. To anyone sensitive to poetry and at the same time aware that "modern times" are equivalent to the sense of History as a problem inviting a solution—the Enlightenment legacy which only in our day has begun to discourage intellectuals—the *Cantos* is shattering in the *insistency* of Pound's mind and finally tragic. Tragic because like all ambitious efforts to present History within a single book, they yield us just another image of ourselves.

Eliot said in his most influential essay, "Tradition and The Individual Talent," that the order of the past is transformed by every new work. Everything past becomes an aspect of present taste. The greatest effect of Eliot-Pound was to abolish among the literary all sense of historicism and to coerce the whole past into the fashions of the present. African masks are viewed by the museum crowd as a stimulant to Picasso's roving imagination; Confucius the perfect teacher becomes a metaphor of the "wise ruler" in Pound's myth of the perfect society; Jefferson is a counterpart to Mussolini; and his great hero John Adams becomes absolutely meaningless in the so-called Adams Cantos, LXII–LXXI. As Professor Peter Shaw has shown in a devastating examination of what Pound did to *The Works of John Adams* (Partisan Review, # 1, 1977), Pound transcribed so mechanically that he reproduced even the misprints.* But one of the marks of what Harold Rosenberg called the herd of independent minds, the culture-vultures who nervously pace the modern museum gathering impressions, who expertly compare one recording with another without knowing how to read music, is the lack of attentiveness that Pound's ransacking method invites.

The difference between us, who nowadays accumulate all too many impressions, and Pound is that although he shares many of our touristy traits, he collects them at the pitch of genius, as Henry Adams did in the historical scene shifts of the *Education* and *Mont St-Michel*. Perhaps more than Adams, who cultivated a weary detachment, Pound is visibly tormented. History has become his agony. Joyce said: History is the nightmare from which I am trying to awaken. Joyce did flee History into the interstices of language. Pound did just the opposite: he moved from the withinness of the poem out into the terror of 20th-century history. Yet the terror is not the authoritarian state—Pound is noticeably indulgent to Lenin, as an admirer of Mussolini should be—ignores the slaughter of so many innocents by Hitler-Stalin-Mussolini-Franco—is obsessed by finance capitalism, the admitted lunacy and unfairness of the credit system. *Usura* (as he calls it) is his Inferno, not imperialism, racism, the ever-accelerating avalanche of war. The classical past, embodied in perfect language, has become the sacred icon. The present is by definition without value.

Pound the would-be epic writer has a driving sense of history but is really without history. Over and again he refers in the *Cantos* to Mussolini draining the marshes and establishing corporate guilds for labor and capital; in the *Pisan Cantos,* written with great gallantry in the appalling cage of an American Army disciplinary unit, he actually refers to Mussolini as the twice-crucified and describes Italians as maggots eating off a dead bullock. Did he not know how little the draining of the Pontine marshes represent in the history of Fascism, that the so-called Fascist corporations never really existed? When Hitler made his state visit to Mussolini, Italian submarines were ordered to make instant maneuvers that put whole crews in jeopardy; Pound quotes an informed source on the danger without recognizing what this implies.

---

*Just how dotty Pound could get when the word "Adams" swam into view is suggested by the following: "[Eliot] has renounced America ever since the time of his first departure, but if he would consider the dynasty of the Adamses he would see that it was precisely because it lacked the Confucian law that this family lost the Celestial Decree."

"A Visiting Card." (#4 of the "Money Pamphlets," published by Peter Russell, London, 1952.)

The history of the Second World War as some of us lived it and the war that Pound in Rapallo read about in Fascist newspapers bear no connection to each other. Pound was capable of saying in St. Elizabeth's that no man named Ezra could be an anti-Semite. But in the great work of his life, the *Cantos*, the successor to the great epic poems of Western man, we read of "fresh meat on the Russian steppes" and that the slaughter of the Jews was unfair only because so many poor Jews had to pay for the guilt, *schuld*, of the Rothschilds, whose name means Red Shield. Schuld, Schild, what's the difference so that you get a pun in? *"poor yitts paying for / paying for a few big jews' vendetta on goyim."* This apparently is how the Second World War started, and Hugh Kenner confirms and expands on this in *The Pound Era*.

Pound's hideous broadcasts on the Fascist radio are all available through the Library of Congress, and though the lawyers of the Pound estate tried to keep me from quoting them, the broadcasts were published by our government and so are out of copyright. Hemingway said that Pound was crazy, "all poets are," and it is a fact that Pound's broadcasts were so disordered that one Italian official suspected that he was really an American agent broadcasting to the U.S. in code.

Pound's Fascist writings and broadcasts, Pound's thirteen years in St. Elizabeth's in Washington—all this belongs to the past; no need to go over it all again, is there? Besides, everything passes so quickly nowadays, the war has been over for so long, that a student of Pound's genius may properly affirm that the Pound case, taken entire, with the flood of commentary dripping over it, represents the last act in that nineteenth-century drama: the poet as the unacknowledged legislator, the poet who presumed, once, to lead us once from history as blood and tears, *mere* history, to the Delectable Mountains.

Eliot, saluting James Joyce's *Ulysses* in the 1920s, said of the new interest in myth that it was liberation from the anarchy and futility of history. Eliot was on his way to a religious solution of his personal problem: secularism was abhorrent to him. None of this was useful to Joyce, who had no interest in returning to the Church, or to Pound, who was bored by Christianity. For a while, for quite a long while, Modernism became a kind of church, and students who knew nothing of poetry but what their teachers told them recited in unison the wonders of myth, tension, paradox and ambiguity, to say nothing of the horrors of "heresy." All that is over now, in a culture so speeded up in disposing of last year's cultural models that freshmen have never heard of Norman Mailer. Poor Ezra Pound, who believed in the authority of history, as transmitted to us through the unique authority of literature.

Pound failed himself, not the masses who never really knew or cared about History as an enchantment, idol, sorrow, trap—History that only intellectuals can afford to worry about. In the end, in Italy, this formerly quenchless mouth snapped itself shut. *Tempus loquendi, tempus taciendi* was one of his favorite sayings. There is a time to speak and a time to shut up. And indeed, indeed, he had much to be silent about. But that is not the way this extraordinarily gifted man started. Nor should the anti-climax of his old age blind us to the *radiance* with which he started. Pound was the last to believe that the poet does have authority. His manic power reminds us why Plato feared the poets and wanted them out of The Perfect Republic. They spoil their own dreams.

6

Poetic Tradition and Authority:
A Dialogue on Eliot's "Sweeney Erect"

William Arrowsmith

> Tom said . . . that he would never dream of shaving even in the presence of his wife . . . Virginia one evening tackled him . . . and told him that "he wilfully concealed his transitions." He admitted this, but said that it was unnecessary to explain; explanation diluted fact . . . What he wanted to do was to disturb externals.
>
> Leonard Woolf, *Downhill All the Way*, p. 109

FLETCHER: Good evening. Several weeks ago a group of us met to discuss T. S. Eliot's French poem, "Dans le restaurant."[1] We were interested in validating—or invalidating—Eliot's account of the traditional poet as applied to his own poetry in the period 1915–1922. *If,* we supposed, Eliot seriously practised what he declared in "Tradition and the Individual Talent"; *if* it is true that the poet gifted with "the historical sense . . . nearly indispensable to anyone who would continue to be a poet beyond his twenty-fifth year," writes "with a feeling that the whole of the literature of Europe from Homer . . . has a simultaneous existence and composes a simultaneous order"; *if* the mind of Europe is truly "a mind which changes . . . which abandons nothing *en route*, which does not superannuate either Shakespeare, or Homer, or the rock-drawing of the Magdalenian draughtsmen"; *if* this traditional poet actually writes with the whole Western tradition flowing into his fingertips; *then* everything he writes ought to provide evidence of the galvanizing presence of that tradition. The poet's *authority,* we may reasonably assume, is a function of that tradition as it enters into combination somehow with the experience and voice of the "individual talent." The original poet is original, at least partly, not only because he goes back to his sources and origins, but because these origins are revived and renewed in his work.

We concluded that, in the case of "Dans le restaurant," Eliot's poetic practice marched *pari passu* with his critical theory. The theory was, as Eliot himself observed, plainly programmatic, the critical by-product of the poetry.

Not everybody was convinced. We had, it was said, simplified our task by choosing a poem which, because of its link with *The Waste Land,* had a thematic density lacking in earlier poems, especially the quatrain poems of *Ara Vos Prec.* Could we repeat our performance with a slighter poem such as "Le directeur" or "Lune de miel" or one of the English quatrain poems? Professor Boyd rebuked us for suggesting that the complexity we saw in the poem—its *ordered* intrication of learned allusion and echo—justified it *qua* poem. Our criticism, he said, was self-serving; an effort to vindicate, not the poem, but the critical skills brought to its exegesis.

In any case, Professor Saettaro has accepted the *défi* on behalf of "Le directeur," which he proposes to defend two weeks from tonight at the next meeting of the College Moot. Our choice for this evening's discussion was Eliot's "Sweeney Erect" (1919). It was, we thought, fairly well-known; it had not, like "Cooking Egg" been overwhelmed by controversy; and, at first sight anyway, it seemed considerably less elusive than "Sweeney Among the Nightingales," even though nobody seems to know exactly what it's about. Not least, it's one of the last of the quatrain poems, contemporary with "Burbank with a Baedeker, Bleistein with a Cigar," whose allusive richness it may be presumed to share. Because the poem is based on classical accounts of Theseus' abandonment of Ariadne on the island of Naxos, I was asked to lead the discussion.

So let me lead off with a few immoderate remarks. First, I accepted my moderator's post tonight on condition that we avoid talking like a caucus of specialists. That sort of talk might not divide *us,* but it would shed precious little light on our poem. On this point I share Boyd's suspicions. Our purpose here, as I see it, is not to represent our disciplines but to pool what we know—and what we don't know. This means recognizing the inadequacy of specialist skills for reading a poem whose poet insists that a knowledge of "the *changing* mind of Europe" is indispensable to the poet. Somebody has remarked that it takes a university to read Eliot, which may explain why Eliot has been so persistently misread, under- and over-. True, Eliot is an erudite poet; but not, I think, an academic one. What matters is not the learned *impasto* but the way in which the poetry actively, poetically, *engages* the learning. To what perennial and present purpose; with what moral and intellectual power; with what technical skill adapted to what vision or idea?

Engagement is what counts. "Sweeney Erect" engages a set of texts which in turn engage a myth; myth and texts engage different cultural and

temporal situations. In their *re*combination—in the way in which the past
issues into the present, and the present resumes, without repeating, the
past—there is the irony of incongruous juxtaposition, but also a recurrent
pattern, a rhythm: now *buffo*, now serious; now aulic, now colloquial.
Formally, it's the same thing. Under the smooth controlled surface of what
looks like clever *vers de société*, something quite different signals its presence between the lines or on the fringes of vision. This emerging meaning
depends for its cumulative effect upon the texts which the poem engages.
Unless we can cope with these texts, in their active encounter with each
other, we are likely to "have had the experience but missed the meaning."

But turn to the poem itself. You have all received a line- and stanza-
numbered text of the poem. It seems to me essential that we hear the poem
as well as see it, so I'll begin by asking Professor Boyd, our official stentor,
to get the poem off the page for us. Professor Boyd.

BOYD: (reading aloud)

SWEENEY ERECT

And the trees about me,
Let them be dry and leafless; let the rocks
Groan with continual surges; and behind me
Make all a desolation. Look, look, wenches!

1	Paint me a cavernous waste shore	
2	Cast in the unstilled Cyclades,	I
3	Paint me the bold anfractuous rocks	
4	Faced by the snarled and yelping seas.	
5	Display me Aeolus above	
6	Reviewing the insurgent gales	II
7	Which tangle Ariadne's hair	
8	And swell with haste the perjured sails.	
9	Morning stirs the feet and hands	
10	(Nausicaa and Polypheme).	III
11	Gesture of orang-outang	
12	Rises from the sheets in steam.	
13	This withered root of knots of hair	
14	Slitted below and gashed with eyes,	IV
15	This oval O cropped out with teeth:	
16	The sickle motion from the thighs	
17	Jackknifes upward at the knees	
18	Then straightens out from heel to hip	V
19	Pushing the framework of the bed	
20	And clawing at the pillow slip.	

21	Sweeney addressed full length to shave	
22	Broadbottomed, pink from nape to base,	VI
23	Knows the female temperament	
24	And wipes the suds around his face.	

25	(The lengthened shadow of a man	
26	Is history, said Emerson	VII
27	Who had not seen the silhouette	
28	Of Sweeney straddled in the sun.)	

29	Tests the razor on his leg	
30	Waiting until the shriek subsides.	VIII
31	The epileptic on the bed	
32	Curves backward, clutching at her sides.	

33	The ladies of the corridor	
34	Find themselves involved, disgraced,	IX
35	Call witness to their principles	
36	And deprecate the lack of taste	

37	Observing that hysteria	
38	Might easily be misunderstood;	X
39	Mrs. Turner intimates	
40	It does the house no sort of good.	

41	But Doris, towelled from the bath,	
42	Enters padding on broad feet,	XI
43	Bringing sal volatile	
44	And a glass of brandy neat.	

FLETCHER: Let me dispose as swiftly as possible of the classical materials on which the poem is based. Not that they aren't of considerable interest; and not that Eliot's handling of them isn't worth scrutiny. But the two Latin poems involved are accessible to any reader with modest Latin or a good trot. The first—to my mind, the more important—source is Catullus 64, the lovely epyllion devoted ostensibly to the wedding of Peleus and Thetis. Even for the technically adventurous Catullus, it's an unconventional poem, above all in its brusquely effective enjambment of festive and funereal, joy and sorrow. Against the happy backdrop of Thetis' nuptials, Catullus sets the tragic tale of Theseus' desertion of Ariadne on Naxos—a tapestry narrative woven into the counterpane of Thetis' wedding-couch. Linked to this tale is its equally tragic sequel—the death by suicide by Theseus' father Aegeus when Theseus fails to hoist a white sail on his return as promised (at which Eliot glances, I suspect, in his "perjured sails")—and of course the coda in which the god Dionysus makes his epiphany and rescues the abandoned Ariadne. The poem is rounded off, movingly but strangely, with a sinister wedding-song in which the Fates foretell the death of Achilles, the son who will be born to Peleus and Thetis on this same marriage-bed. Musically and tonally, the poem as a whole displays the counterpoint of enfolded opposites which suggest the crisscrossed pattern of human existence. In short, just that combination of levity and seriousness which the ancients called *spoudogeloion* and which Eliot admired in the poetry of Marvell.

That it's primarily this Catullan version of the myth which figures in Eliot's strategy is apparent in Eliot's own mixture of modes but also in his choice of the epigraph. This passage (taken from Act II of Beaumont and Fletcher's *The Maid's Tragedy*) is itself part of a needlework narrative of Ariadne's desertion by Theseus, used by the dramatist as a mythical backdrop to the plight of Aspatia, the play's jilted heroine. But into the Catullan account Beaumont and Fletcher have woven strands from Ovid's telling of Ariadne's tale in *Heroides* 10. Far more than Catullus, Ovid stresses the loneliness of Naxos, the vast expanse of water, the lunar landscape seen by the abandoned girl when she wakes:

> *Luna fuit; specto si quid nisi litora cernam:*
> *quod videant oculi, nil nisi litus habent . . .*
>
> *. . . vacat insula cultu*
> *non hominum video, non ego facta boum.*
> *omne latus terrae cingit mare: navita nusquam,*
> *nulla per ambiguas puppis itura vias.*

[The moon was shining: I look to see if there is anything except shore. / So far as my eyes can see, nothing but the shore . . . / . . . The island is empty, uncultivated. / I see no trace of man, no trace of cattle. / The sea girds the land on every side; no sailor anywhere, no ship to make its way over the uncertain ways.]

The negatives pile up as Ariadne becomes aware of the emptiness and stony silence around her, and their reverberation in herself—the stony nothingness she now discovers is her life. Utter solitude; the hostility of nature not inanimate but dead—the coldness, the sea, wind, and sand; the effect is to evoke the sense of the desert world in the epigraph and so vivid in Catullus too:

> *nulla fugae ratio, nulla spes; omnia muta:*
> *omnia sunt deserta, ostentat omnia letum.*

[No counsel of escape, no hope: everything silent, / everything a desert waste, everything reveals death.]

In short, the world of the Wasteland; the experience of desolation and desperation which, in Eliot, is always the condition of spiritual rebirth. In the myth of Ariadne—her desertion by Theseus, her deliverance by the god Dionysus—Eliot found a legendary subject capable of being renewed in present experience. Renewed experience, renewed meaning.

Glance briefly now at the poem's overall form. The Jacobean epigraph folds easily into the first two stanzas, with their echo of Aspatia's imperatives to her weaving handmaid Antiphila (*"Do* it," *"Do* my face," ". . . *strive* to make me look / Like Sorrow's monument"). Formally, in style and diction, these two stanzas are audibly stiff and "elevated." We should note, for instance, the strongly Latinate turns, those "perjured sails," stressed not only by the pat masculine rhymes but by the rhythmical repetition; and the classicizing inflation of "anfractuous." The effect is deliberate archaism— roughly late 17th century, I would guess. And the archaizing effect is sensibly heightened through contrast with the succeeding stanzas. The break comes at the third stanza, with its roughly contemporary manner, its seamy details, its brusque no-nonsense tone. With stanzas four and five, the pretense of ordered syntax dissolves; the punctuation mostly disappears in a crescendo of sexual violence, the verses gasping and panting until collapsing convulsively into the *détente* of lines 19 and 20. The next two stanzas are clearly cool comic verse—"business" quatrains, neat and witty, with an ironic and narrative function to perform. In the ninth stanza, with Ariadne's epileptic seizure, there's a reversion to the rasping harshness of stanzas three and four; then two more stanzas, nicely mortised into each other, of clever *vers de société.* The final stanza "resolves" the poem; yet the initial adversative "But" along with Doris' action sets the stanza apart from its predecessors. The poem closes with a strong but discreet caesura in the last line. I mean: you don't order "brandy-neat" from an English bartender. You order "brandy: neat." Eliot, I feel quite sure, wants us to *hear* and ponder this caesura.

My purpose in this overview is to suggest the conditions to which our discussion of the poem's meaning should conform if we suppose that the poet knew what he was doing. Throughout his life Eliot took intense pride in his adaptation of meaning to music; a poem's music, he insisted, was an integral part of its meaning, and the reader who didn't recognize the allusions might perhaps be led by deepening musical awareness into the experience and even the meaning of the poem. For the moment, I note a few general impressions. First, past and present, archaic and contemporary, are presented not as sharply opposed but as discretely continuous. Past and present are enjambed as they are, not I believe in order to discredit the present by contrast with the past, but rather to relate them by bringing them into meaningful encounter. If they differ in style and meaning, there is nonetheless, beneath the differing styles, a persisting pattern, musically audible as the poem's continuing form, its quatrains. Second, the poem's rhythm—now relaxed, now tense; now colloquially coarse, now elevated—corresponds to the carefully structured alternation of dimension or realm: comic and tragic, profane and sacred, body and spirit.

Turn now to content. It seems reasonable to begin with the questions the poem obviously puts to us. Who, for instance, is Sweeney? What links him to Theseus but also Polyphemus? Why is Polyphemus paired so incongruously with Nausicaa/Ariadne? The problem with these questions is that the reader assumes he already has the answers, or that this poem, like other quatrain poems, is too obscure or trivial to be worth the trouble of decoding. Every reader knows, for instance, that Sweeney is Eliot's recurrent type of carnal or natural man, *l'homme moyen sensuel.* In "Whispers of Immortality" we find him shifting from ham to ham, like a baby in the bath, while the sterile theologians, "masters of the subtle schools," conjugate the abstract Word; or, in *The Waste Land,* announced by the sound of horns and motors which bring him to Mrs. Porter in the spring. The reader will also know that Sweeney is an evolving *persona.* Even in the early poems, whether we meet him as orang-outang or the apeneck among the nightingales, he already possesses an implicit tragic nature linking him to Theseus, Agamemnon, Dionysus, Christ and, later, to the Fury-hounded Orestes of "Sweeney Agonistes" and *The Family Reunion,* or the comically tipsy Heraclean shrink of *The Cocktail Party.* From the very outset he is a type of *homo duplex*—carnal and *buffo,* violent and fatuous, but with an emerging capacity for spiritual life. His bottom may be broad, but, like Shakespeare's Bottom, he has antennae which link him to another world and to what Eliot elsewhere called "the higher dream."

Finally, the reader will be familiar with Eliot's habit of making the various *personae* of his poem melt into one another, as in *The Waste Land,* "the one-eyed merchant, seller of currants, melts into the Phoenician sailor, and the latter is not wholly distinct from Ferdinand Prince of Naples," and "all women are one woman." The familiar logic of identity dissolves in order to let us see what that logic normally occludes—the higher or spiritual identity to which it points (as in "But who is that on the other side of you?"). The same dissolution occurs with time and place. Just as the past relentlessly pushes into the present, so the present assumes the past; and the resulting (Bergsonian) *durée* in turn annihilates history and locality in the nightmare perspective of a stereoscopic present:

> Falling towers
> Jerusalem Athens Alexandria
> Vienna London
> Unreal

Just *who* then is Sweeney, in this complex sense of multiple dissolving identities, and how and why does he fuse with his *semblables*? What are the *larvae,* to use a properly biological metaphor, that compose or define him? Who, in short, are Sweeney's ghosts, his shades or avatars?

The first ghost is also the nearest—the famous orang-outang of Poe's "Murders in the Rue Morgue."[2] The Maltese sailor, you'll recall, tells how he returned to his room to find that his orang-outang had escaped from the wardrobe and was standing full-length before the mirror attempting to shave himself with his master's straight-edged razor. An arresting image, but so far as I can tell, nobody has explained just what this allusion is actually *doing* in the poem. We can, of course, take Professor Bateson's line and write off these echoes as genial plagiarism by a poet who simply couldn't resist the *frisson* of learned allusiveness.[3] But if we think of Eliot as a serious poet, then we have to show just how these allusions function in the service of the poem rather than the poet.

—But I see you nodding vigorously, Ayres. You're the American Lit. expert in the room. Perhaps you'd care to comment on the Poe allusion here?

AYRES: As a matter of fact, I would. First, it's my conviction that Eliot saw in Poe a writer who, despite faults of style and sensibility, was uncannily good at evoking the nightmare world of desires, terror, and anxieties buried beneath the conscious "civilized" mind. The barbarous or primitive X beneath the superficial order of Victorian urbanity. At his worst, Poe is straight Grand Guignol, all melodramatic props and penny-dreadful sentiment. But at his best—"The Murders in the Rue Morgue," "The Maelstrom," "The Narrative of Arthur Gordon Pym"—he's unsurpassed in expressing the nameless savage memories, the animal lurking in all of us, buried at the base of the vertebrate spine. When he evokes these things and engages them seriously, *morally,* Poe is a writer of real greatness. And it was primarily this power that Eliot admired in Poe, just as he admired it in writers like Donne, Webster, and Marvell. The poet, Eliot once observed, "should be aware of all the metamorphoses of poetry that illustrate the stratifications of history that cover savagery."[4] He wrote admiringly of Frazer that he had "extended the consciousness of the human mind into as dark and backward an abysm of time as has yet been explored."[5] The words of Donne and Webster, he said, "have often a network of tentacular roots, reaching down to the deepest terrors and desires."[6] And Marvell's poetry has "a connexion with that inexhaustible and terrible nebula of emotion which surrounds all our exact and practical passions."[7]

SAETTARO: Eliot's critical eye is really astonishingly programmatic, isn't it? He seizes on just those qualities in other poets that his own poetry emulates. I think, for instance, of those splendid words on what he called

"the auditory imagination." How does it go? "The feeling for syllable
and rhythm, penetrating far below the conscious levels of thought and feeling . . ."

FLETCHER: ". . . far below the conscious levels of thought and feeling,
invigorating every word; sinking to the origin and bringing something back,
seeking the beginning and the end."[8]

SAETTARO: And then the poetry spells out the theory which, as music or
idea, animates it:

<blockquote>

I have said before

That the past experience revived in the meaning

Is not the experience of one life only

But of many generations—not forgetting

Something that is probably quite ineffable:

The backward look behind the assurance

Of recorded history, the backward half-look

Over the shoulder, towards the primitive terror.[9]

</blockquote>

AYRES: Precisely. It was just this "primitive terror" stalking the mind of
individuals and cities alike which appealed to Eliot in Poe. Sweeney, I mean,
really is "larval," as Fletcher suggests. Shade on shade, each one slightly
different, extending back and back as far as the mind can reach. His (Emersonian) shadow falls ironically across present and future, but Sweeney
himself is a shadow cast by the whole human past. Poe's orang-outang is
one of these shadows or avatars. Just as Phlebas the Phoenician drowns,
sinking down into his past, his origins, *aux étapes de sa vie antérieure,* so
Sweeney sinks into the larval forms that precede him; so Poe's orang-outang
presses into the present, giving Sweeney the stereoscopic depth of the past.
Finally, the poet who records these throwbacks is, in his own theory, a kind
of sensorium, the "vessel" of that continuing tradition by which the whole
Western past, "back to the Magdalenian draughtsmen" of human prehistory,
rises into the present memory of the mind of Europe. The poet's active,
engaged memory of the tradition is the source of his authority.

FLETCHER: The poem, then, is a constructed palimpsest. Each cultural
layer or lamina reveals a new, but analogous, organization of "the changing
mind of Europe."

SAETTARO: "The stratifications of history that cover savagery . . ." Each
stratum or layer is represented by a revealing metaphorical action or image—in the case of this poem, the action of shaving. Sweeney shaving is
superimposed on Poe's orang-outang, and—

AYRES: Hold on, Saettaro. We haven't finished with Poe yet. If I'm right,
Eliot's allusion to Poe here isn't casual. I mean, it's not literary "name-
dropping." It cuts deep, engaging not merely the echoed incident—the shav-

ing—but the whole tale. The point isn't to recognize the allusion, but the *meaning* of the allusion, the meaning which makes the allusion necesssary in the first place. The reader has to consider the connection of the two texts—their stratification, if you like. The texts are juxtaposed in order to make him *see,* to see with fresh eyes. The connection is startling only because it's instructive. The *thinking* poet asks us to *think.* In this way the erudition governing the allusion becomes a crucial element in the meaning of the poem. The poem depends upon what we understand of what we know, not what we happen to know or recognize. In his 1916 essay on Leibniz and Bradley, Eliot remarked of Leibniz (and later of Bishop Andrewes) that their erudition was an essential ingredient in their originality.[10] The same is true of Eliot, and for the same reason. The erudition is *engaged,* it's not merely ornamental.

FLETCHER: How, exactly how, do you see Eliot engaging Poe's tale?

AYRES: Here and elsewhere Poe is preoccupied with suppressed violence. The orang-outang is hidden, like a dark secret, in a wardrobe in the city of light. The ape is, I think, a symbol of the *pudendum* concealed by the rational daylight city. Suppressed and coerced, it becomes explosive, murderous. After escaping, the shaving orang-outang is surprised by his master, who fetches his whip. Terrified, the ape leaps out into the night to commit his atrocities: a mother decapitated by a single stroke of the razor, the daughter shoved up the chimney with such force that the combined strength of four men is needed to pull the body back down. Poe gives us the shock effect of random brutality, enhanced by the victims' helplessness and the terror of the primitive. But what gives the effect of *moral* shock—the episode, I think, is *seriously* shocking—is the fact that the orang-outang is shaving when surprised. The grotesquerie is crucial. Remove the shaving sequence, and Poe's tale is merely a well-plotted horror story. The moral element lies in that ambivalent razor, at once an implement of civilizing adornment and of murder, and the corresponding ambivalence of the orang-outang. Poe, I mean, is talking about *us*; and so, I take it, is Eliot when he annexes just this incident. *We* are this orang-outang Sweeney. His ghosts and avatars, his brutality is ours. But he's more than merely violent. Along with his capacity for violence, there is a corresponding instinct to evolve and shed the animal, to stand *erect.* For it's obvious, I think, that "erect" here means not only sexually, but anthropologically "erect." Poe's orang-outang, like Sweeney, has a dual nature. This dual nature, moreover, is always in active transition—in metamorphosis, from monster to man and vice versa—rising or falling, ascending or descending. And in the idea or image of *the shaving animal* we have the revealing effort to beautify by shearing away the animal, the brute, the lout, to redeem the "Old Harry." In this image Eliot galvanizes the idea of *decision*—for standing erect or falling, for civilized life or barbarism and savagery, for becoming man or reverting to animal—implied in Sweeney's ambivalent nature. There, in front of the mirror, standing Sweeney will come to first consciousness of himself as man, will see himself in the act which reveals his human face, the image in which he was made. Whether he knows it or not, Sweeney is deciding his fate. The fatefulness of the moment is increased if we remember Poe's orang-outang and what happened to him in the same situation and position. It's tense, *dramatic,* this moment of decision. Sweeney, we're told, is "addressed full length to shave." "Addressed" means "concentrated"; "full length" suggests the object of concentration: the effort to stretch oneself, to stand erect. The sudsing in line 24 to me suggests ritual cleaning, itself a dramatic act. And the suspense is increased through the parenthesis of the eighth stanza, with its suggestion of historical shadow looming ironically in Sweeney's decisive position, but above all in the melodramatic expectancy—the *metaphysical* suspense—suggested by lines 29 and 30:

> Tests the razor on his leg
> Waiting until the shriek subsides.

FLETCHER: Metaphysical suspense? I rather agree. Eliot's echo of the Poe story is surely a great deal more than a literary way of suggesting Sweeney's apelike qualities. Why, after all, I found myself thinking, an *orang-outang?* Because, physically speaking, in bone-structure especially, the orang-outang is the most nearly human, his posture the most erect, of the large primates.[11] If Eliot's point were simply to suggest the apeman, Sweeney should logically have been a gorilla. But perhaps I'm pressing Eliot's simian precision a little too hard.

BOYD: No, Fletcher, I'm afraid you're squarely on target. That curious magpie eye of Eliot's was constantly on the *qui vive* for oddities like one-eyed men, theater cats, oysters, crocodiles, etc. But also on orang-outangs, and probably for the reasons you suggest. Here, anyway, is a passage I noted in *The Use of Poetry and the Use of Criticism:*[12]

> With Shelley we are struck from the beginning by the number of things poetry is expected to do; from a poet who tells us, in a note on vegetarianism, that 'the orang-outang perfectly resembles man both in order and number of his teeth,' we shall not know what to expect.

Coincidence? I doubt it.

FLETCHER: Thanks, Boyd. But there's a further point here. And that's my feeling that the poem suggests a real link between the grisly murders of Poe's orang-outang and the savagely murderous sexual intercourse described in the fourth and fifth stanzas. The sexual act begins with that undefined "gesture of orang-outang" which "rises from the sheets in steam." Then, we get an account of sex which reads more like a mugging or execution than love-making. *Slitted*; *gashed*; that *dentate* O; the *sickle* motion from the thighs which *jackknifes upward*; and finally an orgasm as spastic as any death-agony.

AYRES: Rough stuff, I agree. Rougher in its own way, I think, than Poe's account of the orang-outang's murders. Eliot's sexual act here is, in fact, accomplished murder. The question is why.

SAETTARO: Before we proceed to that question, Ayres, I want to corroborate your analysis of the Poe allusion by providing Sweeney with still another avatar. A rather curious one, I think you'll agree. Where, I started wondering, did Poe get that orang-outang of his, if he didn't simply invent it? In his annotated edition,[13] Mabbot suggests numerous possible sources, none of them particularly persuasive. What is clear, however, is that 18th- and 19th-century Europe was haunted by tales of killer apes, wild men, civilized cannibals, etc.—a taste obviously deriving from the great explorations of the world's more primitive regions. But the *literary* sources were above all Buffon's *Histoire naturelle* and various writings of Rousseau, especially the *Discours sur l'origine de l'inégalité* (1755), the appendix to which contains Rousseau's influential remarks on the orang-outang as the earliest form of man.[14] There, you may remember, Rousseau speculates that the orang-outang might not be animal at all but man—the first man or primal savage who, simply because he lived in a state of nature, far removed from civil society, had not acquired the ability to speak. (Rousseau believed that *perfectibility,* not speech, was the distinctively human trait.) If, Rousseau concludes, it could be demonstrated that this primal savage or transitional man possessed the trait of perfectibility, he would prove to be human, not bestial. Finally Rousseau observes that these same orang-outangs whom travelers mistake for beasts must be identical with those creatures whom the ancients called fauns, sylvans, and satyrs, and to whom they attributed divinity.

FLETCHER: And Cyclopes, like Polyphemus?

SAETTARO: Hold on, Fletcher. As I was about to say, Rousseau's speculations provoked intense debate. Voltaire, writing to Rousseau (Aug. 30, 1784) called the *Discours* "votre livre contre le genre humain"; in the *Dictionnaire philosophique,* under the entry "Luxe," he scoffed at Rousseau's ideas again; and he did so once more, humorously, in *Candide*. As Candide and their party make their way upstream towards El Dorado, they see a strange sight: a couple of naked girls followed by monkeys busily nibbling the girls' buttocks. It is explained to Candide that these apes are the girls' lovers: "Why should you find it strange that in some parts of the world monkeys obtain ladies' favors? They are partly human." To which Candide replies: "I am afraid you must be right, for I remember Professor Pangloss saying that similar accidents used to happen in the old days, and that such unions produced centaurs, fauns, and satyrs . . ."

BOYD: Excuse me, Saettaro. But you're losing me. Are you seriously suggesting that Eliot was consciously using all this stuff? I'm impressed, I admit, by your orang-outang lore. But while I can see that Poe may have borrowed from Rousseau for his tale, is there really the slightest evidence that Eliot, always vehemently anti-Romantic, might have had Rousseau in mind here? If not, all this sounds quite academic.

FLETCHER: I can understand your suspicion, Boyd. But Saettaro's right. In 1916 Eliot gave two courses of extension lectures for Oxford University at Ilkley in Yorkshire.[15] One was entitled "A Course of Six Lectures on Modern French Literature." The topic of the first lecture was Rousseau; the required readings were: *Les confessions*; *Sur l'origine de l'inegalité*; and *Le contrat social*. The fact that Eliot disliked Rousseau has nothing to do with Eliot's *use* for Rousseau as an essential stage in that evolving mind which is "the changing mind of Europe." Eliot had, after all, "the historical sense." And Rousseau, like Voltaire, is in fact one of the more prominent "voices" in Eliot's work.

Let me offer you what strikes me as a very revealing example. I have in mind the famous line from the third section of *The Waste Land*:

By the waters of Leman I sat down and wept

Commentators point out the obvious echo here of the lament of the Israelite exiles in Babylon from the *Psalms,* and the fact that Eliot wrote much of *The Waste Land* while undergoing psychiatric treatment near Lausanne on Lake Leman. But so far as I know, nobody has noticed the allusion here to Rousseau—an allusion that seems to me beyond dispute and also of great thematic importance for the poem as a whole. In the fourth book of the *Confessions,* Rousseau tells of his passionate yearning for the countryside near Lausanne along Lake Leman:

The view of the Lake of Geneva and its lovely shores had always a particular attraction in my eyes, which I cannot explain and which does not depend only on the beauty of the sight, but on something more compelling. Every time I approach the country of Vaud, I feel an impression composed of the memory of Mme de Warens, who was born there, of my father who lived there, of Mlle de Vulson who reaped there the first fruits of my love . . . and some other source still more secret and powerful than these. When that burning desire for the mild and happy life which eludes me and for which I was born, returns to fire my imagination, it is always there in the country of Vaud, near the lake . . . that it fixes. On this trip to Vevey, in strolling along these beautiful banks, I abandoned myself to the gentlest melancholy . . . I was moved, I sighed and cried like a child. How many times, stopping to cry with more ease, have I not been beguiled to watch my own tears falling into the water . . .[16]

Between the Israelites in Babylon and Eliot in Lausanne, each mourning his exile, stands Rousseau. Typically, Eliot gives us three linked "nodal" allusions, in each of which an exiled nomad mourns for the Earthly Paradise (or true Paradise *al di là*) from which he has been expelled. But combined with this, especially in the Rousseau allusion, is the image/theme of Narcissus looking at his own reflection in the water. As we know from *The Facsimile Transcript of The Waste Land*, Eliot originally intended to include the poem now titled "The Death of St. Narcissus"; whence, in part, the persistent mirror-imagery of the larger poem. The point isn't of course Rousseau's intense narcissism, but his power of self-dramatization. Above all else, Rousseau aspired to be a composer; his first opera was entitled *Narcissus*. And Rousseau was obviously its real protagonist. Eliot's astonishingly acute eye for this sort of detail, as well as the larger parallel, has caught Rousseau literally *enacting* his own first musical work. Here is Rousseau, like our Sweeney, suddenly confronting himself in the mirror, face to face, *seeing* himself, dramatically, in the instant just preceding actual self-consciousness.

SAETTARO: Excellent, Fletcher. I refuse to plead guilty to Boyd's charge of pedantry. Anyway, if I read Eliot rightly, Rousseau's orang-outang is an essential part of "the backward look . . . towards the primitive terror." The issue between Rousseau and Voltaire is, after all, the nature of man, nothing less. Here in essence, is the debate which divided Europe for the next two centuries: feeling vs. reason; individual vs. society; nature vs. law; the natural vs. the social. Orang-outang lore it may be, but the definition of the orang-outang involves the definition of Man. Rousseau's orang-outang, like our Sweeney, is also man-in-transition. Upwards or downwards, as the case may be. Upwards in Rousseau's case. He looks at himself (or Man) in the mirror and, like Narcissus, admires what he sees. Not the monstrous predator or primitive, but the Noble Savage.[17] Poe's orang-outang derives perhaps from Rousseau, but the Romantic's *beau idéal* has become the Victorian's nightmare. Similarly, Sweeney and Rousseau's orang-outang are not the same, but they're linked. The *image*—the ape with a razor—persists, overlapping; but each image expresses a different stage in the evolving "mind of Europe." The Noble Savage isn't Mass Man. But *if* the ape is Rousseau's ideal of "original, uncorrupted Man"; *if* Rousseau believed what he wrote when he said that "a state of reflection is a state contrary to Nature," and that "a thinking man is a depraved animal," then Rousseau's orang-outang is a direct *step* in the process that leads historically to Sweeney.

AYRES: Things are converging. Here too, at least in germ, is Eliot's doctrine of "dissociation of sensibility"—feeling cut off from intellect, at war with it even. Look *forward* from Rousseau's orang-outang, to Poe's, to Sweeney—

BOYD: And Sweeney Todd perhaps, the demon barber of Fleet Street? And to that "Sweeney" or M'Sweeney" from whom Henry Crippen procured the poison with which he killed his wife?

AYRES: Why not? Anyway, look forward from Rousseau's orang-outang to Poe's, to all the modern Sweeneys, and we literally come to consciousness of ourselves. Meeting our avatars, we meet that part of our past which inhabits us as it also inhabits the present. We know more than the dead, Eliot remarked, "and they are that which we know."[18] Thanks to this historical perspective, we inhabit a conscious present; we have, in Eliot's words, "an awareness of the past in a way and to an extent which the past's awareness of itself cannot show." Look *backward* now from this conscious present, from the complacent cocksman Sweeney in Mrs. Turner's "house" to Poe's ambivalent primate and Rousseau's natural man, and we see ourselves becoming conscious of ourselves. Behind Rousseau's orangoutang—the word means "wild man of the woods"—stands Swift's Yahoo, and the Wild Boy of Hanover, and Caliban, that "thing of darkness":

> Rings of light coiling downwards, leading
> To the horror of the ape.[19]

Further backward still, Rousseau suggests, lie more primitive avatars, none of them wholly superseded—all those satyrs, fauns, centaurs, and other human hybrids—

BOYD: And "the old Adam," and *l'homme primitif* of Scripture. And Plato's apeman, Thersites.[20] And—

AYRES: And Polyphemus, I suppose?

FLETCHER: You're stealing my thunder, Ayres. But you're quite right. The Cyclops *is* the ancient avatar of the simian or savage Sweeney. But Eliot's Polyphemus is *not* Homer's monster nor Euripides' cannibal sophist nor Theocritus' lovesick shepherd. Rather, he's the complex shadow of all of these which, merging with other versions, appears in Ovid's lovelorn pastoral-comic Polyphemus in the tale of Acis and Galatea at *Metamorphoses* 13, 738–897. Just why this certain source of Eliot's poem hasn't been recognized, I can't say.[21] The passage is mainstream Ovid at his wittiest and most graceful; its poetry has been admired and imitated by English poets from Chaucer on; it almost certainly inspired Marlowe's "Come live with me and be my love." There can't be the slightest doubt of the echo; the whole Ovidian episode constantly informs the Eliot poem. And the echo was *meant* to be recognized.

Ovid begins with Galatea confiding her amorous troubles to the sea-witch Scylla. Passionately in love with the shepherd Acis, it is her misfortune to be loved by the monstrous Polyphemus:

> *nec, si quaesieris, odium cyclopis amorne*
> *acidis in nobis fuerit praesentior, edam:*
> *par utrumque fuit. pro! quanta potentia regni*
> *est, Venus, alma, tui! nempe ille inmitis et ipsis*
> *horrendus silvis et visus ab hospite nullo*
> *impune et magni cum dis contemptor Olympi,*
> *quid sit amor, sensit validaque cupidine captus*
> *uritur oblitus pecorum antrorumque suorum*
> *iamque tibi formae, iamque est tibi cura placendi,*
> *iam rigidos pectis rastris, Polypheme, capillos,*
> *iam libet hirsutam tibi falce recidere barbam*
> *et spectare feros in aqua et componere vultus.*
> *caedis amor feritasque sitisque immensa cruoris*
> *cessant, et tutae veniuntque abeuntque carinae.*

[I cannot tell, if you ask me, whether my love for Acis or my hatred of the Cyclops was stronger: both passions were equally violent. O gentle Venus, how powerful is your dominion! For that savage monster Polyphemus, an object of terror even to the wild woods, a danger to any stranger who met him, a creature who despised great Olympus and the gods too—even he understood what Love means. Seized by violent passion, his heart on fire, he forgot his flocks and caves. O Polyphemus, it was at that moment that you begin to take care of your appearance, to be anxious to please; you combed your bristling hair with a rake, and joyfully cut your shaggy beard with a sickle, examining your bestial features as they were reflected in the water, and composing their expression. Your lust for killing, your savagery and insatiable thirst for blood, were all forgotten, ships went and came, unmolested.]

There it all is, trait for trait, theme for theme, repeated or reversed: the evolving present implicit in the past, the past edging into the new consciousness of the present. The orang-outang looms in the ancient monster, whose cosmetic sickle corresponds to the ape's razor; the civil passion of Ovid's one-eyed wild man looks forward to Rousseau/Voltaire's amorous monkeys, the murderous lust of Sweeney Todd, and Eliot's Theseus/Sweeney. Even the Narcissus mirror is there—the water in which the Cyclops gazes admiringly; the mirror in which Poe's orang-outang shaves; Lake Leman watered by Rousseau's tears. Here, in brief compass, is the characteristic texture of

Eliot's poetry after *Prufrock* and through *The Waste Land*. Not random echoes of fragmentary texts, but an intricately structured arrangement of texts and *topoi* designed to reveal, stratum by stratum, the complex archaeology of "the changing mind of Europe." The poem as palimpsest.

BOYD: I have to agree, Fletcher, that the Ovidian passage fits. It can't be just coincidence. But there's a problem surely. Your Ovid passage deals with Galatea and Polyphemus, whereas Eliot's explicitly concerned with "Nausicaa and Polypheme." So it's not surprising that your allusion hasn't been recognized. Admittedly, nothing in Homer or any ancient author links Nausicaa with Polyphemus. It's odd, but she seems to have no existence outside the *Odyssey,* no later literary "shadow."[22] So what's Eliot's point? Why didn't he simply say "Galatea and Polypheme" at line 10? Why Nausicaa?

FLETCHER: Good question. But I don't have the answer.

AYRES: Surely the connection has to be Odysseus. It's his travels after all which link the Nausicaa and Polyphemus episodes in Homer. And there's a similarity between Odysseus and Theseus; they're both heroic sensual adventurers—

SAETTARO: Maybe. But I think you're barking up the wrong tree. In fact, it looks to me as though Boyd may have answered his own question. The point, as I see it, is that Nausicaa's unique. I mean, she can't be confused with anyone else. Narratively and thematically, that's important to Eliot's situation here. What his tale requires is a fresh and innocent girl—a virgin, in fact. But above all a *human* virgin, a real virgin. Not one of Ovid's promiscuously interchangeable sea-nymphs, like Galatea, or Doris, or one of Prufrock's mermaids, or Cleopatra's Nereids, or some flirtatious Rhinemaiden. Eliot's story, as I see it, is a tale of seduction and desertion. The sex here is *serious*; it has consequences, at least for the girl. There's no consequence whatever to a tumble in the waves with a Nereid. And it's just this girlish innocence and nubile virginity that Nausicaa provides. She's the quintessential human virgin, no Amazon, trembling on the edge of woman-hood. Virginity's the point. Eliot's tale, like Beaumont and Fletcher's play, is a *maid's* tragedy. Eliot's not simply retelling the story of Theseus and Ariadne; he's recasting it, making a parallel contemporary tale of his own, both like and unlike the old story. Wasteland Naxos is transformed into its modern equivalent—a shabby-genteel boarding house or house of assigna-tion run by a bawd called Mrs. Turner.

AYRES: Her name *declares* her a bawd, doesn't it? At least that's the Elizabethan/Jacobean sense. When the Messenger in *Antony and Cleopatra* reports Antony's marriage to Octavia, he puns on Cleopatra's "For what good turn?" by answering, "For the best turn 'i the bed." There must be dozens of examples.[23]

SAETTARO: Thanks, Ayres. Anyway, to this urban Naxos our Sweeney brings his Nausicaa/Ariadne. The poem, as line 9 informs us, begins with morning; we're meant perhaps to imagine the preceding night. What's actually being described in stanzas four and five is, I believe, the deflowering of a virgin. Hence the violent, even murderous language, deriving at least as much from the situation as from Eliot's supposed squeamishness about sex. There's a remarkably similar passage describing just this situation in Eliot's "Ode" (a poem published in the first edition of *Ara Vos Prec* but subsequently omitted):

> When the bridegroom smoothed his hair
> There was blood upon the bed.
> Morning was already late
> Children singing in the orchard
> (Io Hymen, Hymenae)
> Succuba eviscerate.

The details, but above all that *succuba eviscerate* with its suggestion of accomplished murder, follow the violent thrusting of "jackknifes upward" and the sexual crescendo of our poem.

FLETCHER: There's another remarkably parallel passage, Saettaro, from a fragment in *The Facsimile Transcript of The Waste Land* (p. 111), which actually equates husband and wife with knife and victim:

> I am the Resurrection and the Life
> I am the things that stay, and those that flow
> I am the husband and the wife
> And the victim and the sacrificial knife . . .

BOYD: And of course Sweeney's famous lines in *Sweeney Agonistes*:

> I knew a man once did a girl in
> Any man might do a girl in
> Any man has to, needs to, wants to
> Once in a lifetime do a girl in.

And there's also Harry (Hairy?) Monchesney in *The Family Reunion*, the English Sweeney/Orestes who's hounded by Furies because he murdered (or thinks he's murdered) his wife.

AYRES: I noted still another parallel, which I think has obvious bearing on our poem. It comes from the published but uncollected (why doesn't someone collect these things and publish them?) piece called "Eeldrop and Appleplex" (1916).[24] Eeldrop is speculating on the effect of a fatal, irreversible act, like murder or sex, and the agent's new consciousness of sin and damnation:

> In Gopsum Street a man murders his mistress. The important fact is that
> for the man the act is eternal, and that for the brief space he has to live,

he is already dead. He is already in a different world from ours. He has crossed the frontier. The important fact is that something is done which cannot be undone—a possibility which none of us realize until we face it ourselves.

The ideas expressed in this passage—the irreversible fall from innocence, the fatal act by which the human soul is born and by which it enters time and history, the sense of having "crossed the frontier"—reverberate throughout Eliot's work. I think particularly of the Sweeney of *Sweeney Agonistes,* who's crossed the frontier of experience separating him from those who have not acted ("I gotta use words when I talk to you"), and who waits for the fatal knock on the door, that "KNOCK KNOCK KNOCK" announcing the appearance of another world ("Behold, I stand at the door and knock"). And I think of course of *The Waste Land*:

> *Datta*: what have we given?
> My friend, blood shaking my heart
> The awful daring of a moment's surrender
> Which an age of prudence can never retract
> By this, and this only, we have existed

The concentration is impressive. Almost obsessive.

SAETTARO: I agree. Curious, isn't it, that Eliot's sense of the Fall should be so overwhelmingly sexual? Again and again the poet's appletree Eden of "Children singing in the orchard" is juxtaposed, with obviously purposive violence, against the "succuba eviscerate" of adult sexuality. The sexual act, especially the first, *is* murder. In *The Mystic Rose*[25] Ernest Crowley remarks that "in Jersey I used to hear of a bride who ran to the window and screamed 'Murder!' on the wedding-night." But in Eliot man and woman, murderer and victim, seem to fuse into a single sexual "death," by mutual decision or surrender, by nature irrevocable. Surely because sex is viewed as a fundamentally religious event. Eliot's critics often seem to suggest that his religious perspective is, in this respect, the product of his sexual anxiety; but I wonder if it isn't the other way around. I mean, I rather doubt that the general unpleasantness of sex in Eliot is wholly due to the poet's supposed squeamishness. Nobody objects, after all, when Dostoevsky detects in sexuality "the impulse of that cruel sensuality which overcomes almost every man on this earth, all and each, and is the source of almost every sin of mankind on this earth," as he does in *Dream of a Ridiculous Man*. Baudelaire's views are similar, born also of a fundamentally religious outlook:

Love is very like torture or a surgical operation . . . Do you hear those sighs . . . those cries, those throat-rattlings? Who hasn't breathed them forth, who hasn't irresistibly evoked them? And what worse do you find in the torments applied by painstaking torturers? Those faraway sleepwalker's eyes, those limbs whose muscles twitch and tauten as under the action of a galvanic battery . . . And the human countenance, which Ovid thought created to reflect the stars, look! it speaks only of insane ferocity or is spread in a species of death . . . The one and the supreme bliss of love rests in the certainty of doing evil. Both man and woman know, from birth on, that in evil lies all bliss.[26]

I noted this passage because it struck me as powerfully bearing on, or at least illuminating, our poem. As for its impact on Eliot himself, we have his own word for it in the later (1930) essay on Baudelaire. Especially important, I think, is Eliot's insistence upon *action,* on the ultimately positive quality implicit in all action, even evil:

Baudelaire has a great deal to say of the love of man and woman. One aphorism which has been especially noted is the following: *la volupté unique et suprême de l'amour gît dans la certitude de faire le mal.* This means that Baudelaire . . . has perceived that what distinguishes the relations of man and woman from the copulation of beasts is the knowledge of Good and Evil (of *moral* Good and Evil which are not the natural Good and Bad or puritan Right and Wrong). Having an imperfect, vague Romantic conception of God, he was at least able to understand that the sexual life as evil is more dignified, less boring, than is the natural 'life-giving' cheery automatism of the modern world . . . So far as we are human, what we do must be either evil or good; so far as we do evil or good, we are human; and it is better, in a paradoxical way, to do evil than to do nothing: at least we exist. It is true to say that the glory of man is his capacity for salvation; it is also true to say that his glory is his capacity for damnation.[27]

Like Baudelaire, Eliot's Sweeney brings to sex not only the animal brutality apparent in his history and forebears, but the murderous violence bound up with sexual pleasure, which is itself the most apparent "mark of the beast." Original sin *in action,* risking damnation and, therefore, the first step on the path to salvation. Redemption here, as I see it—

FLETCHER: Forgive me, Saetarro, for interrupting your reflections on redemption. But time's running short, and we're in danger of letting the poem get away while we pursue Eliot's allusions and our reactions to them, always a danger with these labyrinthine poems.

Ayres has introduced the idea of the Fall as central here, and I think she's absolutely right. If Saettaro's correct in his explanation of Nausicaa, then "Sweeney Erect" is at least partly the tale of a "fallen woman." She "falls" physically, but also spiritually; and her fallen state is throughout presumably in contrast to Sweeney's upright posture. At first, in bed, he's sexually erect: Sweeney as the one-eyed cocksman, even the Cock incarnate— Sweeney/Phales. But in the second half of the poem he's anthropologically, not sexually, erect. He *stands* upright—the ape evolved into man. But there's more. For Nausicaa/Ariadne is epileptic, we discover. And epilepsy is traditionally known as "the falling sickness" because the effect of the attack was to fell the sufferer. There's a fine example in Shakespeare's *Julius Caesar.*—Boyd, do you recall the passage?

BOYD: You mean the conversation between Brutus and Casca in Act I, about Caesar? Of course I remember it:

> *Casca*: He fell down in the market-place, and foam'd at mouth, and was speechless.
> *Brutus*: 'Tis very like; he hath the falling sickness.
> *Casca*: No, Caesar hath it not; but you, and I, And honest Casca, we have the falling sickness.

The effect of this exchange is to prepare for Cassius' account of Caesar's death, where the two senses of "falling" converge in a third:

> Even at the base of Pompey's statue
> (Which all the while ran blood) great Caesar fell.
> O, what a fall was there, my countrymen!

FLETCHER: Thanks, Boyd. But I'd like to defer for a moment the meaning of epilepsy in Eliot's poem. I'm content if you accept my notion that the contrast between the standing Sweeney and the fallen woman is schematic, even studied, since this tells us a good deal about the poem's structure and meaning.

Return now to the violence of the sexual act. Saettaro suspects the influence of Baudelaire here, and he may be right. Certainly it *looks* as though Eliot were echoing Baudelaire's description of intercourse as a surgical operation or an execution. It has the violence, I suggested earlier, of a mugging. But I want to urge you to look behind these metaphors of surgery and execution to another kind of action—an action which resembles them in its violence but which is done for a very different end, much more in keeping with Eliot's thought here and elsewhere. I mean: *sacrifice*. Defloration as sacrifice will in fact be a kind of sacred violence practiced by a murderous priest (who does not regard himself as a murderer), in search of salvation of some kind, on a willing victim.[28] The ritual of sacrifice involves the effort to secure life, even everlasting life, by means of death. But it's also an attempt to create, through the agency of the dying victim, a link between this world and another, between the profane and the sacred. Here, for instance, is the classic account of sacrifice by Henri Hubert and Marcel Mauss:[29]

> Sacrifice consists in . . . *establishing a means of communication between the sacred and profane worlds through the mediation of a victim, that is, of a thing that in the course of a ceremony is destroyed* . . .

Sacrifice can therefore impart to the victim most varied powers. . . . The victim can also pass on a sacred character of the religious world to the profane world, or vice versa . . .

There is no need to explain at length why the profane thus enters into a relationship with the divine: *it is because it sees in it the very source of life* . . . How does it come about that the profane only communicates with the sacred through an intermediary? The destructive consequences of the rite partly explain. . . . If the religious forces are the very forces of life, they are themselves of such a nature that contact with them is a fearful thing for the ordinary man. . . . That is why between these powers and himself he interposes intermediaries . . . If he involved himself in the rite to the very end, he would find death, not life. The victim takes his place. It alone penetrates into the perilous domain . . . it dies there, and indeed it is there to die. The sacrificer remains protected: the gods take the victim instead of him. *The victim redeems him.* . . . There is no sacrifice into which some idea of redemption does not enter.

This account, I insist, is not *an* account, designed to fit my interpretation, but the classic account which informs dictionaries and encyclopedias still. Sacrifice, then, modifies the life of the sacrificer to the degree to which it confers sanctity or purity, its analogue, on the victim. Its sacred effect derives from the contact it establishes between two worlds otherwise discrete and sundered. For instance, in Eliot's *Cocktail Party*, Celia dies by being sacrificed alive on an anthill; this death confers sacramental meaning on the secular communion called a "cocktail party," just as it gives life to, and purifies, the communicants. So here the blood of the virgin "sacrificed" by Sweeney sets in motion forces beyond his or his victim's control, giving him the life he unconsciously sought and releasing her, by the "death of the body," into a new life. They're renewed, purified.

SAETTARO: Of course! And that's why the sexual act is immediately followed by the purifying action of lathering and shaving. The same cleansing ritual occurs, you recall, in "Dans le restaurant," with the injunction to the slobbering, broad-bottomed waiter—clearly a middle-aged French Sweeney, *à la croupe arrondie*—to go take a bath and dredge the filth from his skull: "Tiens, voilà dix sous, pour la salle-de-bains." Even the Hippopotamus, we're told, will be cleansed of his mud—"washed as white as snow,/By all the martyr'd virgins kist."

AYRES: And there's Phlebas' death-by-water, purified by drowning. Or Sweeney in "Mr. Eliot's Sunday Morning Service," paddling in the baptismal font while the theologians chop logic with the Word.

SAETTARO: Purification . . . The point's regeneration. In "Sweeney Erect" it's admittedly glancing and ironic, but the entire ritual is still subtly controlled by the image of Sweeney's sudsing and shaving avatars. Unknowingly, incipiently purgatorial man: his shaving is his effort to efface "the mark of the beast," to cleanse the stain of original sin.[30] True, Sweeney remains essentially what he was: gross, fatuously and coarsely confident of his sexual prowess. But *something* has changed; *something* is stirring, as we say. A soul perhaps; that *Geist* which, for Hegelians and Bradleyans, is synonymous with self-consciousness; or a shadow, the same shadow that later falls across the bed (I'm filling in Eliot's narrative ellipsis) and triggers the epileptic seizure of his "victim." Tenuous or not, I can't help but see in Sweeney's nakedness—"pink from nape to base"—a suggestion of babylike skin.

BOYD: Good. But the essential point, I take it, is that this regeneration, or tenuous hint of it, is the result of Sweeney's having *acted*. Whether for good or evil, he's acted; and in turn something else is acting upon him, even though he doesn't know it. He *hesitates,* the razor poised to begin, waiting until the epileptic's shriek is over. If he hasn't quite crossed the frontier, he's preparing to cross it, his whole carnal self concentrated on the act of shaving. Which means, I agree, shearing away the animal.

AYRES: But what about Sweeney's victim? Or don't you men *care*? The poem presents us with paired tales and tangled lives. So what about Ariadne/Nausicaa? What's it like to be the victim of a sacrifice? To be done to death sexually, to bleed from the sickle cut, and the upward-stabbing knife? She crosses the frontier too, doesn't she?

SAETTARO: That's my sense of it. The sacrificial victim experiences death, and the *pain* of death. But that pain is mingled with pleasure. The victim is, as we say, *mortified*; she too, I agree, crosses the frontier. In the case of the willing sacrifice, death is desired; the spirit desires the death, by mortification, of the flesh that desires. Without the "death of the body"—the desiring self—there can be no union with the world of the sacred, with God; no transcendence. So we have a physical death *and* a spiritual birth, and these produce an intense mingling of pain and pleasure, as in the mystic's erotic ecstasy. We're lucky to have numerous accounts of this ecstasy of passage from this world to the world beyond. But two of them are especially pertinent to this poem. The first is the celebrated account by St. Teresa of Avila:

> Our Lord was pleased that I should at times have a vision . . . I saw an angel close by me . . . I saw in his hand a long spear of gold, and at the iron's point there seemed to be a little fire. He appeared to me to be thrusting it into my heart, and to pierce my very entrails; when he drew it out, he seemed to draw them out also, and to leave me all on fire with a great love of God. The pain was so great that it made me moan; and yet so surpassing was the sweetness of this excessive pain that I could not wish to be rid of it. The soul is satisfied now with nothing but God. The pain is not bodily, but spiritual, though the body has its share in it, even

a large one. It is a caressing of love so sweet which now takes place between the soul and God, that I pray God of his goodness to make him experience it who may think that I am lying.[31]

The second account, that of St. Angela of Foligno, bears even more strikingly on our poem:

> The eyes of her soul were opened," writes the scribe to whom Angela dictated her revelations. "And she saw Love advancing gently towards her; and she saw the beginning, but not the end, for it was continuous. And there was no color to which she could compare this Love; but directly it reached her she beheld it with the eyes of her soul, more clearly than she might do with the eyes of the body, take as towards her the semblance of a sickle. Not that there was any actual and measurable likeness, but this love took the semblance of a sickle, because it first withdrew itself, not giving itself so fully as it had allowed itself to be understood, and she had understood it; the which caused her to yearn for it the more.[32]

The sickle of love which Angela saw "with the eyes of her soul" is of course the famous sickle of *Revelations* 14:14–18, with which the Lord's angels reap the grapes:

> And I looked, and behold a white cloud, and upon the cloud *one* sat like unto the Son of man, having on his head a golden crown, and in his hand a sharp sickle. And another angel came . . . crying with a loud voice to him that sat on the cloud, "'Thrust in thy sickle, and reap; for the harvest of the earth is ripe.'" And he that sat on the cloud thrust in his sickle on the earth, and the earth was reaped.

Angela has simply adopted this metaphor of the sickle to the purposes of her own spiritual eroticism. Now if I'm right—

BOYD: You're losing me, Saettaro. Do you have the slightest evidence that Eliot was familiar with these accounts by Teresa and Angela at the time he wrote this poem, almost ten years before his conversion?

SAETTARO: It's no conjecture, Boyd. In his student years Eliot checked out Evelyn Underhill's *Mysticism* from the Harvard library and made notes on it.[33] The accounts of both Teresa and Angela are cited in their entirety by Underhill. Draw your own conclusions. In 1930 Eliot made his point explicitly:

> . . . in the Spanish mystics there is a strong vein of what would now be called eroticism. I am not in the least disposed to belittle them, but their mode of expression does render them liable to the indignities of Freudian analysis. At any rate, this Spanish mysticism is definitely sensuous or erotic in its mode of expression . . .[34]

May I proceed?

As I see it, Eliot's purpose here is to combine in a single concentrated act not only the lives of these two "lovers" but the different levels of awareness, corresponding to body and soul, profane and sacred, which are invoked by the action. On one side, the victim's agony of physical death; on the other, the equally desperate hunger for life of the sacrificer, and, at a deeper level, the hunger for redemption, for purifying himself of the stain of original sin, which the physical hunger for life conceals. These two hungers are combined, as I said, in a single action. It's the action that is decisive; we see the two tangled bodies becoming, emerging into, themselves; we see them *changing.* The poem's center of gravity clearly lies in the sexual violence of stanzas IV through VI. Whether we like it or not, this is where the poetry is concentrated and the poet's energy has been expended. Eliot's strategy here, I think, is to *ritualize*; to make us see the sacrifice looming in the sexual act; the stabbing knife; the bloodletting; the victim's dying spasm. This is why, I believe, the two human agents seem to dissolve, and the motion which seizes them becomes the syntactical subject:

> The sickle *motion* from the thighs
> Jackknifes upward at the knees
> Then straightens out from heel to hip
> Pushing the framework of the bed
> And clawing at the pillow slip.

What we get in the non-stop unpunctuated rush of discrete motions is the mounting crescendo of a single convulsive spasm. This spasm usurps the copulating couple, confounding face and genitals, fusing them into a single, thrashing *thing*: *la bête à deux dos.* A daimonic force invades them—they're literally possessed, controlled by a primal power moving in and through them, depriving them of individual identity, depersonalizing, and finally, I think, ritualizing them.

The rite completed, they separate into themselves. Into the individual isolation of their private and isolated worlds—an important human point in the poem, I think. We see, on the one hand, Sweeney shaving, all ruddy carnal complacency, like Joyce's "plumb Buck Mulligan"[35]—

AYRES: Or the shaving figure of the apelike artist Kreisler in Wyndham Lewis' *Tarr,* which Eliot, interestingly enough, called "a commentary upon a part of modern civilization . . . our acrobatics animadverted upon adversely, by an orang-outang of genius, Tarzan of the Apes."[36]

SAETTARO: Right, it's this simian Sweeney we *now* see shaving away the ape, his carnality to some degree qualified, as we saw, by his avatars and the purificatory act. Pink as a baby, he found the life, perhaps even the sacred life, he sought in the rite.[37] In the seventh stanza, we see him in the ironic perspective of the quotation from Emerson's "Self-Reliance"—a dark epiphany of Natural Man or Mass Man, *modern* man, projected over past and present as History incarnate. Sweeney's silhouette is also, I suppose, a shadow—a shadow which falls across the bed where the "fallen" woman is lying. It's this shadow, so parenthetically intruded, which precipitates the epileptic seizure of the next stanza. But it's not clear to me why the shadow should have this effect . . .

FLETCHER: I may be able to help you, though I'm unsure too. Anyway, in primitive thought the soul is persistently represented as shadow or reflection. Nobody needs to be told of Eliot's lifelong interest in Frazer's *Golden Bough,* particularly that section entitled *Taboo and the Perils of the Soul,* on which he repeatedly drew. But in the chapter on "The Soul as Shadow or Reflection,"[38] I found this:

> . . . the spiritual dangers I have enumerated are not the only ones which beset the savage. Often he regards his shadow or reflection as his soul, and as such it is necessarily a source of danger to him. For if it is trampled upon, struck, or stabbed, he will feel the injury as if it were done to his person . . . If the shadow is the vital part of a man or animal, it may under certain circumstances be as hazardous to be touched by it as it would be to come into contact with the person or animal. . . . In Shoa any obstinate disorder for which no remedy is known, such as insanity, epilepsy, delirium, hysteria, and St. Vitus' dance, is traced either to possession by a demon or to the shadow of an enemy which has fallen on the sufferer.

There Sweeney *stands,* flushed with the pride of natural man, a huge sun-silhouetted epiphany of the Body, from which *falls,* subtilized and volatilized, the transient body's eternal shadow—the soul. What the soul is in the body, the Spirit is in the world: a darkness and a death which bring light and life:

> Between the desire
> And the spasm
> Between the potency
> And the existence
> Between the essence
> And the descent
> Falls the Shadow

I realize I'm walking on delicate interpretative ground here. And my reading may be resisted because Sweeney's bodily epiphany is so over-whelming, and the signs of spiritual life so faint. But in all the other Sweeney poems and plays, beneath all the irony directed at Natural Man, the poet insists that, by involvement in action, by decision, by suffering the knowledge of good and evil, Sweeney's soul or spiritual life evolves. As Ayres pointed out, Sweeney's hesitation at lines 29–30, razor poised, waiting, suggests the suspense of fateful decision, a suggestion created by the poet's throwing the weight of the sentence on into a new stanza. Poetically, anyway, *something* is stirring. As the anonymous author of the wonderful *Theologia Germanica*[39] declares:

> Now the created soul of man has also two eyes. The one is the power of seeing into eternity, the other of seeing into time and the creatures. . . . But these two eyes of the soul of man cannot perform their work at once; but if the soul shall see with the right eye into eternity, then the left eye must cease and refrain from all its working, and be as though it were dead . . ."

AYRES: I take it you're thinking of one-eyed Polyphemus/Sweeney?

FLETCHER: Right. One-eyed Sweeney/Polyphemus. His one functioning eye has hitherto been, in the language of mystics since St. Augustine, the "eye of the body," the carnal or phallic eye. Now he "crosses the frontier" and the "eye of the soul" begins to open. But it's of course the same eye; the same eye at different stages of awareness, perceiving diverse dimensions of reality, one natural, one spiritual. I'm thinking of course not only of Sweeney/Polyphemus but Eliot's whole gallery of one-eyed men: the monocular Bleistein; the one-eyed merchant in *The Waste Land*; Sir Henry Harcourt-Reilly ("And me bein' the one-eyed Riley"), and on and on. We could, and perhaps should, someday devote a whole session to what I take to be Eliot's Platonic optics. My point for now is simply this: the eye of the soul opens as the body's eye closes. Even Ovid's Polyphemus says, doesn't he, that he too, old cocksman-monster though he is, has one sunlike, *heavenly* eye?

> *unum est in media lumen mihi fronte . . .*
> *. . . Soli tamen unicus orbis.*

But go back to Ariadne. Sweeney's silhouette falls as a fatal shadow on the bed, and the epileptic seizure begins. That seizure is narrated in three swift lines, no more. First the prodromal scream, then the convulsions. This compression is possible because the seizure has already been described. Line 32 ("Curves backward, clutching at her sides") echoes the orgasm at 19 and 20 ("Pushing the framework of the bed/ And clawing at the pillow slip"). The two seizures overlap, dissolving into each other. The physical seizure precedes the spiritual, of which it is an anticipatory "sign," and to which it "corresponds," according to an essentially Platonic dynamic in which physical events or objects reflect the reality of a higher realm of Ideas or Spirit. The "eye of the body" sees real objects but its vision is one-dimensional; it lacks depth, as though what it saw were shadows, silhouettes. The "eye of the soul" sees the substance which casts the shadow, the form concealed in matter or physical reality.

No need to labor the point. For the purpose of the poem what matters is that we see that *spiritual possession* is involved in the epileptic seizure, and that this spiritual event has been triggered by sexual or bodily possession.[40]

So our Ariadne "falls," overwhelmed by an epileptic attack. She falls a victim to Sweeney's lust, and the consequent "death of the body" precipitates the spiritual seizure. Epilepsy, after all, isn't merely the "falling sickness"; it's the great "sacred disease" (*hieros nosos*) of the ancients.[41] "Sacred" for obvious reasons. How else, except by the assault of some dreadful *daimon* or unknown god—a power which felled a man, shattered his control over his bodily functions, twisted his features into hideously inhuman contortions, made him foam and scream, and finally left him senseless and helpless—how, except through the action of some such *daimon* or god, could a human being be so utterly "possessed"?

This sacred disease, then, falls like an invading *daimon* upon the fallen Ariadne, abandoned by her bodily lover, Theseus/Sweeney. Who can this *daimon* be, within the context of *this* myth? Who but Dionysus?

Not of course to the worldly ladies of Mrs. Turner's house. To them as to the secular world at large, spiritual events are routinely demoted to physical events. The attack of epilepsy—the *spiritual* seizure—is accordingly reduced to a manageably ordinary case of hysteria. "Rationalistic writers," observes Underhill, "have seized eagerly on the behavior of mystics, especially the disturbances which accompany the ecstatic trance, and sought to attribute all the abnormal perceptions to hysteria or other disease. They have not hesitated to call St. Paul an epileptic, St. Teresa 'the patron saint of hysterics.' "[42]

Only Doris[43] dimly understands that, for spiritual ills, spiritual remedies are required. Not that she consciously knows what she is doing, any more than Sweeney knows the meaning of his shaving. She belongs, as the poem plainly declares, to the same physical world as Sweeney. Her "broad feet" correspond to his "broad bottom" (as they do to the French waiter's *croupe arrondie* and the "broad-backed hippopotamus"); her "padding" animal footfall matches his "gesture of orang-outang." She's solid flesh and bone, like Sweeney; but she also has an intimation of another world. Dim perhaps, but an intimation all the same. An intimation no less meaningful than the faint stirring of life—the hissing of an ember, the babylike whimper of an ending world—among what Eliot elsewhere called "dead ends."[44]

The poem shies fastidiously from outright religious affirmation. Partly in order to preserve the witty, ironic, secular surface; but also because the poet means to reveal, however glancingly, the appearance of a sacred order in a

profane world and must therefore mask what he intends to reveal. Like
Montale and the *dolcestilnovisti,* Eliot prefers to work with a "sign" (*senhal*)
which hints rather than declares. *Revival* is the essential "sign." You don't,
after all, bring someone smelling-salts unless your purpose is to revive and,
by extension, resurrect. So the ancient miracle recurs. Two worlds, normally disjunct, intersect in a sudden incarnation; the god makes his epiphany in
a fallen world. The god is of course Dionysus, ironically manifest in the
straight brandy and the sal volatile. In and between the lines, the "sign" is
there, at least for those who know the myth (whether from Catullus or Titian[45]
or merely Bullfinch), and who have eyes to see (and ears to hear) the pure
spirit stirring in the "spirits" brought by Doris, the god musically concealed but unmistakably looming and "present" in

> . . . sal volatile
> And a glass of brandy neat.

As I suggested at the outset, the final caesura separating "brandy" from
"neat" has real force and weight. Rightly heard, it imposes a resonant pause,
by which the god's presence is deftly revealed. The poem earns its meaning
through the poet's musical mastery of his form, his ability to exploit to the
full the limited musical potential of these hard, dry, witty quatrains, so
obviously composed in reaction to the earlier lyricism of "Prufrock" and
"Portrait of a Lady."

But I was speaking of Dionysus. Only in the world of the Waste Land—
in the "cracked, brown wilderness," "aux côtes brulantes de Mozambique,"
in "rocks, moss, stonecrop, iron, merds"; only in the fallen world, in the
landscape of "dead ends" is the god's epiphany possible, and the rebirth he
brings. The condition of *new* life is death; in the body's death the life of the
spirit begins. Only when she is without hope, after the "death of the body,"
abandoned by her mortal, physical lover, can the god come to Ariadne. This
is why he is at first mistaken for a god of death, for Death himself. Dionysus, according to Heraclitus,[46] "is the same as Hades." Similarly, the heroine
of Strauss' *Ariadne auf Naxos* greets Dionysus as the lord of death:

> Du bist der Herr über ein dunkles Schiff,
> Das fahrt den dunkeln Pfad.

To die was to be loved by a god, to be ravished away with him, to live with
him in everlasting bliss. This paradox, I believe, explains why the sacrifice—a sacrifice that is, as we have seen, *both* sexual and spiritual—is the
center of gravity of Eliot's poem; the action on which everything pivots. In
its murderous violence is contained, as in all sacrifice, the hunger for larger
life, for contact with the sacred. The emphasis, the same sense of death/
rebirth patterning, underlies, I think the poet's equation, through the word

"anfractuous," of the Cretan Labyrinth with the tortuous rockscape of Naxos and perhaps Mrs. Turner's "house." Here again, according to his customary logic of collapsed time and place, Eliot interweaves past and present, Crete and Naxos. At the heart of the Labyrinth Theseus encountered the monstrous, the brutal orang-outang element of human nature, the Minotaur. In the anfractuosities of Naxos Ariadne meets the same recurrent Minotaur of Sweeney/Theseus' human nature. Through the beast, the god. Through the body, the spirit. Through death, life.

At the center of every labyrinth-myth is this death/rebirth pattern. To enter a labyrinth means symbolically dying, means entering Hades. Hence at the entrance to Vergil's underworld there is a representation of the tale of the Cretan Labyrinth, with its *inextricabilis error* and the ultimate horror at the center. This labyrinth is a map of life and death, of *this* life and another life beyond. The purpose of entering the labyrinth is to enact, or reenact, the great mysteries of existence. Entering means *initiation,* going in. But it also means a beginning or commencement. The initiate in any mystery seeks life, an *initium.* Seeks a return to the sources: the dark womb of earth, the earth's body, from which he was born. He retraces his steps, from man to beast, from manhood to childhood. He is like the seed set in the earth, "buried" in order to be reborn. So the virgin dies in order to become a woman, the body to become a man, the "old Adam" in order to put on "the new man." The body dies in order to become spirit.

Look again at Mrs. Turner. We rightly glossed her name earlier in its secular, sexual sense. But now, in the context of our death/rebirth pattern, she suddenly reveals her other aspect as the agent of conversion or "turning" ("Because I do not hope to turn again . . ."). And now, with this "other" Mrs. Turner[47] in mind, look back to the epigraph (which Eliot has, for his own purposes, very slightly altered),[48] and we see that its main function is, first, to confirm the desolate wasteland world and, second, to suggest, out of the universal desolation, the god suddenly appearing:

Look, look, wenches!

FLETCHER: The hour's getting late, but I think there's still time for a question or two. —Ayres?

AYRES: Early on, Fletcher, you spoke—rather evasively, I thought—of the "classicizing inflation" of the word "anfractuous." I can *hear* the inflation, but I wonder if you aren't surrendering the poem to Boyd's (and Bateson's) criticism. I mean, *why* the inflation? What's gained but a sonorous Greek obscurity? What's the *poetic* point?

SAETTARO: May I answer? I started out, I confess, by assuming that there must be a literary allusion here. Well, I checked the *O.E.D.* but drew a complete blank. "Tortuous"; "winding"; labyrinthine." Most of the instances cited were technical or medical, e.g., "the anfractuosities of the body's circulation," etc. So I concluded that the word was there for reasons of poetic strategy. Eliot's too skilled and conscientious a poet to use a word just because he likes its Greekish sonorities. The strategy is to *compel* the reader—the serious reader, who may not know the word, but who's prepared to make an effort—to look *anfractuous* up. I'd lay odds that everyone here did just that. Eliot, we know, thought that the poet should use words in such a way that the whole history and pressure of the language were present in their use. One effect of involving the reader in this way is to heighten the unfamiliar word and its reference. *Anfractuous* is set off "bracketed" as it were (rather like "polyphiloprogenitive" which so conspicuously begins "Mr. Eliot's Sunday Morning Service"). So the reader has an *earned* sense of Naxos as tortuous rock, a labyrinthine stonescape. The reader's work *weights* the word.

FLETCHER: Exactly. Even if he doesn't know the Latin poems, he gets the effective force of Ovid's *concava saxa,* perhaps even a sense of Catullus' Theseus in the Cretan labyrinth:

> . . . *reflexit*
> *errabunda regens tenui vestigia filo*
> *ne labyrintheis e flexibus egredientem*
> *tecti frustraretur inobservabilis error.*
> [*Feeling his winding way by the fine thread*
> *She'd given him to save him from bewilderment*
> *In the tricky, zig-zag galleries that formed*
> *The labyrinth's inescapable maze.*]
> (trans. Michie)

The effect is to superimpose the Labyrinth of Knossos on the stony maze of desert Naxos. Eliot once again collapses past and present into a single simultaneous event. Theseus' labyrinth melts into Ariadne's mazy Naxos (or the corridors of Mrs. Turner's suburban "house"). Each place has its own distinctive Minotaur or orang-outang. Theseus in the labyrinth confronts the brutal nature in himself as surely as Sweeney or Poe's ape, or as Ariadne confronting *him*. The Minotaur, I mean, is the last of the larval forms inhabiting us, tracked back into the mythical past, almost, we might say, to the age of those "Magdalenian draughtsmen" in their labyrinthine caves. Back to the troglodyte.

BOYD: Ingenious, Fletcher. But Saettaro's original hunch that "anfractuous" conceals a literary allusion was no mistake. Not that I think the allusion in any way invalidates your point. It clearly doesn't; it simply "thickens" things a little. The passage I'm thinking of occurs in the *Emblems* of that very interesting seventeenth-century religious poet, Francis Quarles. Here it is:

>   The world's a lab'rinth, whose enfractuous ways
>   Are all composed of rubs and crooked maeanders:
>   No resting here; he's hurry'd back that stays
>   A thought; and he that goes unguided wanders:
>   Her way is dark, her path untrod, unev'n;
>   So hard's the way from earth, so hard's the way to heaven![49]

I don't suppose Eliot intended his reader to recognize the passage; Quarles is too minor, I imagine, for that. Still, it's clear that Quarles' verse is "saturated" in Catullus' and Vergil's labyrinths, and that Quarles turns the imagery, in a way Eliot would have liked, to his own religious ends. As for Eliot, I assume that anfractuous lay dormant in his memory until the right poetic occasion precipitated its appearance.

AYRES: Bravo, Boyd. I see the pertinence of your own philology is beginning to bring you around. No?

FLETCHER: Before we start twisting Boyd's tail, Ayres, I'd like another word about *anfractuous*. To Boyd's Quarles quotation, let me add Rousseau.[50] Yes, Rousseau. In the seventh of his *Rêveries du promeneur solitaire,* Rousseau describes a memorable outing in a countryside every bit as tortuous as Ariadne's Naxos:

> All my life I remember an excursion I made one day . . . I was alone, I plunged into the labyrinthine enclosures of the mountains [*je m'enfonçai dans les anfractuosités de la montagne*], and from wood to wood, boulder to boulder, I arrived in a retreat so hidden that I've never seen a more savage sight [*un aspect plus sauvage*] in my life. . . . The few openings out of this gloomy enclosure gave onto nothing but sheer rock and horrible precipices. . . . I sat down and began to dream more comfortably, imagining that I was in a place unknown to the whole universe. . . . A flash of pride soon intruded into these reveries. I compared myself to those great travellers who discover an uninhabited island, and I said to myself with self-satisfaction, "No doubt of it, I am the first mortal to have arrived in this place." I saw myself almost as another Columbus. While I was preening myself with this idea, I heard . . . a kind of clanking . . . I got up, broke through a thicket . . . and saw, twenty feet away . . . a stocking-mill.

Let me appease Tom Boyd's doubts by adding that Eliot, in a 1917 review,[51] glances at just this work of Rousseau's. Anyway, I don't think advocacy is much needed. I simply want to point out once again Eliot's uncanny eye for these culturally revealing images or "epiphanies." Here's Rousseau, like a Romantic Columbus—or frontier Theseus/Sweeney—braving the uncharted labyrinth of the primitive (whether within or without) only to find himself seated a few yards away from the very Industrial Revolution which drove him in search of the primitive in the first place. Irony on irony, all obviously apparent to Rousseau. Columbus' America dissolves into industrial Paris (or some small provincial industrial town, like Stendhal's Verrières), just as Ariadne's Naxos dissolves into the labyrinthine corridors of a London boarding-house or bordello. And with the same effect. Not the glorious past confronting the sordid present; but the continuity of human experience beneath all change.

BOYD: But surely it's asking a great deal too much of the reader to expect him to recognize these allusions? I mean, *both* Quarles and Rousseau in *anfractuous*?

FLETCHER: Of course it is. But why should Eliot be rebuked for seeking that impacted concentration of texture which delights Joyce scholars in *Ulysses*? These intensely—no, incredibly—concentrated poems are, despite their apparent slightness of scale, as ambitious as anything Eliot wrote. The slightness of scale, the apparent "cleverness" of this *vers de société* are the form of Eliot's *trompe l'oeil* poetics. The poem outwits its own surface;[52] *that's* what makes these poems witty—their even-handed double vision of things, the way they *disjoin* but also *connect* their own real levity and real seriousness—the opposed but related worlds of body and soul, real and ideal, etc. The one ambition they disdain is, I suggested, the earlier lyricism. Their aim is dry, cool, clear ironic precision, a quality of "intense frigidity" of observation which Eliot admired in de Bosschère,[53] and which he regarded as the source of Villon's power:

> What constitutes the terrible authenticity of Villon's testaments is that he *saw* his feelings, watched them, as coldly as an astronomer watches a comet; and without this cold and scientific observation he could never have given his feelings their permanent intensity.[54]

In these "observer" poems Eliot was watching himself—watching himself see others, as Sweeney, Rousseau, and Polyphemus see themselves—with cold, ferocious intensity.[55] As for the intricacy of allusion, this too, I think, is an effect of the passion for *objective* observation. The objectivity aims at making the object reveal what "scientific" observation often fails to reveal— the spiritual dimension or aura of reality. Only by intense concentration on the immediate object as seen by the "eye of the body" can the poet show us, like a shadow on the fringes of the visual field, the same object as seen by the "eye of the soul," just beginning to open. This is unmistakably Idealist poetry, the poetry of a poet *saturated* in Bradley (i.e., Hegel, despite real and important differences) and Plato. Its optics or theory of perception is that of Plato's Divided Line. And its form—that odd combination of secular and sacred, body and spirit, etc.—is, given the Bradleyan dialectic controlling it, just what we might have expected.

AYRES: Mischievous or not, I'd still like to hear how all this strikes our Doubting Thomas. Boyd?

BOYD: I'm afraid I'm not quite convinced, Mrs. Ayres. Yes, there's a kind of intrication here that I honestly admire in poets like Donne, and a wit not unlike Dryden's or Pope's. The poems are tentacular; like the roots of a locust tree. You start pulling on one root, and before you know it, it's pulling *you*. Before long, you're lost in the webbery of allusion. I'm taken too, I confess, by what seems to my methodical mind the emerging sense of our discussion. The allusions, I admit, are not quite the literary "name-dropping" I've taken them to be, and I'm convinced that the common notion of Eliot as "the poet of fragments" is mistaken. There *is*, I think, as Ayres suggested, an ordered effort to reveal, stratum by stratum, the "changing mind of Europe." But beyond that point I'm still very skeptical.

I'm troubled, I think, by the erudition. I have a feeling that nothing's been engaged but the poet's learning, and that simply isn't enough. I can't find the *poet* because I can't find the *man*. I don't really know what *feelings* are engaged by all this erudition. The poetry's too cold, too labyrinthine, too impersonal.

And there's another problem. And that's the *limit* of these allusions. The echoes are apparently infinite. Polyphemus, Narcissus, Caliban, Buck Mulligan, Dorian Gray, Kreisler, Poe's orang-outang—*where does one draw the line*? What's pertinent? What makes one allusion relevant, another not? And what about the *mirror* all these shaving apemen require? Why's there no mirror in the poem? Or is this simply a poetic ellipsis too subtle for my plodding philology?

And why hasn't anyone—why haven't *you*, Professor Ayres?—mentioned the case of Queequeg in *Moby Dick*? I'm sure you all remember how, in the fourth chapter, Ishmael watches Queequeg's morning ablutions. There they are, Ishmael and Queequeg, that "arm of his tattooed all over with an interminable Cretan labyrinth," locked in "bridegroom clasp," waking to the day. Queequeg stands there naked, except for his beaver hat, and proceeds to put on his boots under the bed. But let me read you the passage:

> But Queequeg, do you see, was *a creature in the transition state*— neither caterpillar nor butterfly. He was just enough civilized to show off his outlandishness in the strangest possible manner. His education was not yet completed . . . Seeing now, that *there were no curtains to the window,* and that the street being very narrow, the house opposite commanded a plain view into the room . . . I begged him . . . to accelerate his toilette somewhat, and particularly to get into his pantaloons. He complied, and then proceeded to wash himself . . . He then donned his waistcoat, and taking up a piece of hard soap on the wash-stand centre-table, dipped it into water *and commenced lathering his face.* I was watching to see where he kept his *razor,* when lo and behold, he takes the harpoon from the bed corner, slips out the long wooden stock, unsheathes the head, whets it a little on his boot, and *striding up to the bit*

of mirror against the wall, begins a vigorous scraping, or rather harpooning of his cheeks . . . The rest of his toilet was soon achieved, and he proudly marched out of the room, wrapped up in his great pilot *monkey* jacket . . .[56]

Well Ayres?

AYRES: *Touchée.* But I'd be less than fair to myself if I told you that the parallel hadn't occurred to me. I dismissed it, maybe wrongly, simply because Eliot, so far as I know, never mentions Melville. Even in his 1953 lecture, "American Literature and the American Language,"[57] Eliot discusses every major American author *except* Melville. It's an astonishing silence; perhaps Professor Bloom's theory of influence applies. But it's extremely puzzling since the Melville allusion's so thematically "right."

FLETCHER: I wonder if our problem isn't one of thinking too much about allusions rather than parallels or *topoi*. Beyond a certain point, the number of them—and therefore the limit, the line to be drawn—doesn't matter. What the poet's after is both unity and diversity. He wants *both* the common denominator—the universal, the generic family likeness—*and* the specifically engaged text (since some texts, like Poe's "Murders in the Rue Morgue" are more specifically invoked than others).

The mirror, I have to say, is essential; that's why it's elliptical. The act of shaving implies the ability to see the face you're shaving; if you don't, you may slit your own throat. A man can no more shave without a mirror than he can breathe without lungs, or read a poem—you'll forgive me, Boyd—without exercise of *intellectual* imagination. Shaving implies a mirror as starlight requires the night. The poem isn't simply an echo-chamber or a collage of fragments. Its aim, I think, is to make *us* see both similarities and differences; to see *con*nection and *dis*connection in the compound images of the shaving animal we've called Sweeney and his avatars. In short, to see the unity *and* diversity, which means seeing diversity-in-unity, and unity-in-diversity. We're dealing, I'm saying, with what Bradley, following Hegel, called a "concrete universal." Read Bradley's *Principles of Logic, Ethical Studies,* or parts of *Appearance and Reality* and you come immediately and inevitably on the essential doctrine of the "concrete universal"—a doctrine as central, I believe, to Eliot's poetry as it was to his critical theory and practice. Bradley's "dialectic" is, in fact, the matrix of Eliot's esthetics and poetics, as Eliot himself, in his strongest statement of Bradley's influence, candidly admitted.[58] The idea of the "objective correlative," the integrated (and its opposite, the "dissociated") sensibility, even the idea of "tradition and the individual talent"—all these derive from Bradley's logic, and the cardinal principle of the "concrete universal." But—here's my point—so does the *poetry,* so does our Sweeney and his fraternity of shaving simians, or Cleopatra-Dido-Fresca-Volupine ("all the women are one woman"), and the whole poetic logic of collapsing times, places, and persons.

This must, I realize, sound a little oracular, and the hour's too late for long elaboration. But here's Bradley's summation:

> What is real is the individual; and this individual, though one and the same, has internal differences. You may hence regard it in two opposite ways. So far as it is one against other individuals, it is particular. So far as it is the same throughout its diversity, it is universal. They are two distinctions we make within it. It has two characters, or aspects, or sides, or moments. And you consider it from whichever side you please, or from the side which happens to be the emphatic or essential side. Thus a man is particular by virtue of his limiting and exclusive relations to other phenomena. He is universal because he is one throughout all his different attributes. You may call him particular, or again universal, because, being individual, he actually is both, and you wish to emphasize one aspect or side of his individuality. The individual is both a concrete particular and a concrete universal; and, as names of the whole from different points of view, these both are names of real existence. . . . The real is individual. The merely universal or merely particular are unreal abstractions. Concrete universal and concrete particular are the individual from different points of view.[59]

For Bradley, the collective—the institution, the body politic, the nation—is, as for Hegel, a concrete universal also, a true individual "organism," in whose context or structure the particular individuals have necessarily to realize themselves:

> It is the life which can live only in and by them, as they are dead unless within it; it is the whole soul which lives so far as the body lives, which makes the body a living body, and which without the body is as unreal an abstraction as the body without it. It is the self-realization of the whole body, because it is one and the same will which lives and acts in the life and action of each. It is the self-realization of each member, because each member cannot find the function, which makes him himself, apart from the whole to which he belongs; to be himself he must go beyond himself, to live his life he must live a life which is not *merely* his own, but which, none the less, on the contrary all the more, is intensely and emphatically his own individuality.

Comment hardly seems needed. Eliot's "tradition" and also his "individual talent" are both concrete universals. Merely set against the second Bradley quotation the words "tradition" and "individual," and it's apparent why "No poet, no artist of any art, has his complete meaning alone. His significance, his appreciation is the appreciation of his relation to the dead poets and artists. You cannot value him alone"; why the work of the tradition-possessing and -possessed individual poet is essential to the modification of tradition; and why the artist's acquisition of a tradition "is a continual surrender of himself as he is at the moment to something which is more valuable . . . a continual self-sacrifice, a continual extinction of personality." He sacrifices himself, not to the tradition, but to the self-realization in his work which renews and reinvigorates the tradition. He makes the tradition *his own.*

AYRES: And later, I assume you're suggesting, he sacrifices himself—i.e., *realizes* himself—in the collective which is incarnate in the church "which lives and acts in the life and action of each"?

FLETCHER: Exactly. As for Sweeney and his simian colleagues, they're all, in their diverse individuality and unity, clearly concrete universals. Each is different—diverse in time, meaning, individuality; and yet they have in common that coming-to-consciousness, that self-realization and *Selbst-Bewusstsein* which, from classical times to the present (above all the Hegel-influenced nineteenth century) is implied in the human face seeing itself—recognizing its humanity—in a mirror. Here, for Hegel and Bradley and Eliot, is *the* critical moment, the peculiarly *human* moment, when man knows himself as no longer wholly animal. He sees the face in the mirror and calls it "I," and in asserting this "I," he asserts the universal "I" as well. He asserts an "I" which as a "we"; he can *say,* because he *sees*: *Lui, c'est moi.* Eliot, following Bradley, seizes upon that fateful instant—remember that suspended razor in stanza eight—when perception and knowledge are still one thing, indivisible, not yet memory. As when Turgenev catches, in Pritchett's words, "the moment between seeing and not seeing": "The moon at last had risen; I did not notice it at first: it was such a tiny crescent." That's the point—the intensely dramatic *instant* of reflective self-consciousness. But Eliot's poem is not one of Hegelian optimism. *Geist* may make its appearance, but the fateful instant is humanly fitful and rudimentary; it's left opaque, inconclusive, or even tragically unresolved. The "I" and even the "other" (Sweeney "knows the female temperament") make their appearance; but there is no individual "other," no concrete "we." Sweeney and Ariadne come together, violently and brutally, only to separate into their private destinies, their different isolation. What Eliot gives us, in short, is not the moment when opposites are reconciled—the happy Hegelian *Aufhebung*—but rather their sad diremption. They *part*:

> As the soul leaves the body torn and bruised,
> As the mind deserts the body it has used.

Body and soul stand humanly opposed, isolated. Theoretically, of course—I mean according to Bradleyan theory—Sweeney's sexual hunger reveals his unhappy finitude; his physical need conceals, like Platonic *eros,* the desire for a spiritual *allo ti*, the "something else" of the soul. The real hungers for the ideal without which it is not real; it hungers, I mean, to be a "concrete universal." And the ideal is incomplete without the real. Ariadne's spiritual seizure is expressed—*necessarily*—in the language of body and senses. And Bradley tells us why:

> Feeling, thought, and volition have all defects which suggest something higher. But in that higher unity no fraction of anything is lost. For each one-sided aspect, to gain itself, blends with that which seemed opposite, and the product of this fusion keeps the riches of all. The one reality, we may say from our human point of view, was present in each aspect in a form which does not satisfy. To work out its full nature it has sunk into these differences. But in each it longs for that absolute self-fruition which comes only when the self bursts its limits and blends with another finite self. The desire of each element for a perfection which implies fusion with others, is not self-contradictory. It is rather an effort to remove a present state of inconsistency, to remain in which would indeed be fixed self-contradiction.[61]

If there is hope here, it is in the dialectic by which these contradictions correct themselves. But in human (and Bradleyan) terms, as our poem suggests, that correction can never be more than partial:

> . . . finite existence and perfection are incompatible . . . the ideal and the real can never be at one. But their disunion is precisely what we mean by imperfection. And thus incompleteness, and unrest, and unsatisfied ideality, are the lot of the finite.[62]

Return, now, from this vantage-point to Boyd's discontent with the poem as a human document. When he tells us that he can't find the poet, the man, that he can't locate the human feelings from which the poem springs, he seems to be complaining that the feelings have been eclipsed by the learning engaged by those feelings. And I think he has *a* point. But I find it hard to read these poems, and this poem in particular, as simply products of poetic drought or anti-lyrical and cerebral exercises. These were years of intense anguish and loneliness for Eliot, surely one of the century's loneliest writers. And the heart of this poem, as well as others, seems to me to lie in precisely those themes and experiences which Eliot found in the prose writers he was at this time reading and meditating upon—Stendhal, Turgenev, Flaubert:

> Stendhal's scenes, some of them, and some of his phrases, read like cutting one's own throat; they are a terrible humiliation to read, in the understanding of human feelings and human illusions of feeling that they force upon the reader. . . . Beyle and Flaubert strip the world; and they were men of far more than common intensity of feeling, of passion. *It is*

this intensity, precisely, and consequent discomfort with the inevitable inadequacy of actual living to the passionate capacity, which drove them to art and to analysis. The surface of existence coagulates into lumps which look like important simple feelings, which the patient analyst disintegrates into more complex and trifling but ultimately, if he goes far enough, into various canalizations of something again *simple, terrible, and unknown.* The Russians point to this thing, and Turgenev seems almost at times to have had some glimpse of it. *Beyle and Flaubert do not point, but they suggest unmistakably the awful separation between potential passion and any actualization possible in life. They indicate also the indestructible barriers between one human being and another. This is a "mysticism" not to be extracted from Balzac, or even from Miss Underhill.*[63]

That seems to me the essence of it. The *feeling* is *there*. It's a poem of *powerfully felt perception.* It's sad, grotesque, and witty. It's *horribly, humiliatingly,* comic.

On the one hand, we have the poem's public or cultural dimension, its engagement through myth and texts of those common or public feelings which for Eliot constituted tradition. The public dimension was what Eliot had in mind when he spoke of the poet's struggle "which alone constitutes life for a poet, to transmute his personal and private agonies into something rich and strange, something universal and impersonal."[64] When Ayres tells us that "*we* are this orang-outang Sweeney," she's talking about this dimension. We could go even further and say that, just as Sweeney and his shaving avatars comes, each in his own way, to consciousness of himself, so we, looking at ourselves in the poem's mirror, see ourselves. In the outsize Sweeney body, with its dark shadow cast across history, and its tenuous spiritual life, we have the image of our own condition in the present; in Dionysus' shy epiphany "between the lines" and the glancing appearance of the sacred order, lies a statement about the life of the spirit now. But if, as I half suspect, the body/soul conflict or perhaps "dialectic" in the poems of this period is based upon a Platonic model by which one ascends through the senses and the world of appearance to the reality "above," then we have a dynamic of hope. "The way up is the way down," says Heraclitus. Which we might colloquially and not inaccurately render as the necessity of going to the bottom, of "bottoming out" in order to rise, of dying to be reborn. As we saw, it's decision and *action* that, for Eliot, count; inaction is, humanly speaking, the refusal to live, the refusal to *become* human. All these considerations, it seems to me, are part of the poem's public, impersonal existence.

Behind this impersonal existence, the poem is, like all of Eliot's poetry, intensely personal. Why, we may reasonably ask, did Eliot choose *this* particular myth (or perhaps, why did it choose *him*)? Why the tale of

Theseus and Ariadne? Because, I suppose, it engaged two strong themes in his poetry. First, the seduction and abandonment (death, whether metaphorical or real) of a young girl. Behind the deserted Ariadne we can (and surely should) see that whole gallery of jilted, abandoned, or murdered Aspatias of Eliot's poetry: the poor little Pipit of "Cooking Egg"; the small girl of "Dans le restaurant" and "Le directeur"; the Dido-like figure of "La figlia che piange"; the Hyacinth Girl; the "injured bride" of "Elegy"[65]; even the *précieuse ridicule* of "Portrait of a Lady." It doesn't matter whether we attach real names, like that of Emily Hale, to these *personae*. Whoever She (or They) were, all that matters is their fate—that they were somehow seduced or abandoned or "destroyed." The point isn't the instrument or even the manner of the death, but the motive. The motive and the fact—the undeniable fact of another's "death." Murder takes many forms. Eliot, it seems to me, recognized the potential violence in himself, even the active violence of volition. The Sweeney he shows *us,* the Sweeney the poem asks us to recognize as a part of *us,* is a part of the poet too.

The second theme is the death of a father. Behind Theseus' father Aegeus, who plunged to his death when he saw the black sail on his son's ship and thought him dead, stands, I suspect, Eliot's own father and the constant echo in the work (strongest perhaps in *The Confidential Clerk* and the constant references to the situation of Alonso and Ferdinand in *The Tempest*) of a son's lifelong "atonement to a dead father." After his first marriage, Eliot and his father never spoke again, and Eliot seems to have believed that his own behavior had precipitated or perhaps hastened his father's death. Hence such lines as

> While I was fishing in the dull canal
> On a winter evening round behind the gashouse
> Musing upon the king my brother's wreck
> And on the king my father's death before him . . .

and

> Full fathom five your Bleistein lies
> Under the flatfish and the squids.[66]

The story of Theseus engages the poet's "private agonies." The poet, by confronting the myth and its associated *Nachleben,* transmutes his private feelings—sacrifices himself as "personality"—and "dissolves" in the mainstream of tradition. The poet's strategy here and elsewhere is to assimilate the personal experience, the private urgency, in the domain of myth. He assimilates, and is assimilated by, the tradition. Or, to use the implicit language of our poem, he "sacrifices" himself to a larger organic order, to which his sacrifice of his individual talent in turn gives life.

BOYD: I'm inclined to agree. In his early (1919) essay on "Hamlet and His Problems," Eliot makes just that point, doesn't he? Shakespeare, he says,

> was occupied with the struggle—which alone constitutes life for a poet—to transmute his personal and private agonies into something rich and strange, something universal and impersonal. The rage of Dante against Florence, or Pistoia, or what not, the deep surge of Shakespeare's general cynicism and disillusionment, are merely gigantic attempts to metamorphose private failures and disappointments.[67]

In this sense, but *only* in this sense, I think, Eliot's later disparagement of *The Waste Land* as expressing merely a private gripe against life, has meaning. The public dimension remains.

FLETCHER: Exactly. Tradition for Eliot simply didn't mean what it's so often been thought to mean—a paradigm of absolute value existing in some timeless dimension. The classical is not the canonical. Eliot, in fact, persistently deprecates the notion of tradition as the canonical, the authoritative *per se*. "Arnold," he remarked, for instance, "gives us often the impression of seeing the masters, whom he quotes, as canonical literature, rather than as masters."[68] Unless assimilated and mastered, tradition is worthless.[69] It has to be *earned*. This is not the stance of a poet whose attitude toward tradition was passively reverent or authoritarian. And it's not based on nostalgia either. What Eliot sought in tradition was, above all else, community and kinship. An exit from private loneliness and suffering into a shared public world. In the poetry of this period, tradition is "the door . . . into the rose-garden."

AYRES: Tradition, in short, as shared experience, shared values; the consortium of past and present, collective and individual; that sense of continuity and common enterprise which for Eliot later came to mean "culture." Tradition was, for its possessor, not a matter of passive inheritance, but active acquisition. If it provided the solace of community, it also imposed responsibilities on the individual.

FLETCHER: Yes. What Eliot wanted above all else was *community*. In tradition he found a sodality which he later found in the Anglican communion. But even in the church, it was not primarily dogmatic authority but community that he sought. Admittedly, his later language upon occasion—the excessively episcopal style, the tiresome insistence on dogma—gave grounds for thinking that his notion of tradition meant dogma and authority. But this is quite untrue of the period in which "Sweeney Erect" was written.

SAETTARO: Eliot needed kinship with the past because he was, I think, one of the loneliest writers of the twentieth century. And he knew it. He was, in his own words, a "metic,"[70] a profoundly displaced and alienated man. He was "a New Englander in the South West, and a South Westerner in New England";[71] a religious man in a secular world; a learned man among pedants and dilettantes. He seems to have thought of himself, with profound pain, as a disinherited son or even parricide; in his first marriage, he clearly "crossed the frontier" that linked him to the everyday world of others. He was an academic dropout at the doctoral level; and not voluntarily, but worse, perforce. He was twice rejected when he volunteered for active duty in the American navy in World War I. He was both exile and expatriate. And in these years he lacked what he envied in both Turgenev and James, the ability to make themselves at home abroad,[72] just as he lacked Pound's gift for turning women into Magdalenes or maenads, friends into disciples, and Hell into "a place for other people, not for oneself and one's friends."

In his poetry the loneliness is tangible, as tangible as pain:

> I have heard the key
> Turn in the door once and turn once only
> We think of the key, each in his prison
> Thinking of the key, each confirms a prison

He was immured within himself almost as solipsistically as in a Bradleyan "finite center," or Ugolino in his tower. Hence the enormous appeal and solace in the friendship and community of the shared experience represented by tradition.

Whether the tradition to which Eliot affiliated himself was *the* tradition, or simply *his* version of *the* tradition, isn't, to my mind, the real issue. Eliot took the risk of actively and intensely engaging the past, even though that engagement might render his work largely inaccessible to readers who lacked that tradition. Where Pound dispersed himself and his energies—the besetting vice of Pound's poetry is, I think, the shallowness concealed by its lyric brilliance—Eliot concentrated his energies. The result was the gnarled, knotty, extremely elliptical, and incredibly dense texture of the quatrain poems, in whose maze the indispensable thread is the poet's craft and musical control. In *The Waste Land* revealed in the *Facsimile Transcript,* Eliot was slowly, I believe, working his way out of the "anfractuous" texture of the quatrains toward a much more open and expansive poetry. And the effect of Pound's radical surgeries were—success notwithstanding—to return Eliot, in the published draft of the poem, to a kind of poetry he had come to find artistically and emotionally confining. But the sense of tradition at work in the quatrain poems and *The Waste Land* is, I think, the same.

AYRES: Let me return to our sense that Eliot's tradition is, in the main, a matter of community and kinship, his exit from alienation and loneliness. I'm inclined to think that Eliot's own formulation in "Tradition and the

Individual Talent"—above all the insistence upon the poet's "impersonality"—is the reason why his idea of tradition is commonly supposed to be authoritarian and canonical. But there are several other versions—preparations for the famous but overly formal version in "Tradition and the Individual Talent"—which reveal a very different angle of vision and a much more genial approach to the relation between the living writer and the past. Here, at length, the most lucid and genial of those documents:

> It is not true that the development of a writer is a function of his development as a man, but it is possible to say that there is a close analogy between the sort of experience which develops a man and the sort of experience which develops a writer. Experience in living may leave the literary embryo still dormant, and the progress of literary development may to a considerable extent take place in a soul left immature in living. But similar types of experience form the nourishment of both. There is a kind of stimulus for a writer which is more important than the stimulus of admiring another writer. Admiration leads most often to imitation; we can seldom remain long unconscious of our imitating another, and the awareness of our debt naturally leads us to hatred of the object imitated. If we stand toward a writer in this other relation of which I speak, we do not imitate him, and though we are likely to be accused of it, we are quite unperturbed by the charge. This relation is a feeling of profound kinship, or rather of a peculiar personal intimacy, with another, probably a dead author. It may overcome us suddenly, on first or after long acquaintance; it is certainly a crisis; and when a young writer is seized with his first passion of this sort he may be changed, metamorphosed almost . . . from a bundle of second-hand sentiments into a person. The imperative intimacy arouses for the first time a real, an unshakeable confidence. That you possess this secret knowledge, this intimacy, with the dead man, that after few or many years or centuries you should have appeared, with this indubitable claim to distinction; who can penetrate at once the thick and dusty circumlocutions about his reputation, can call yourself alone his friend: it is something more than *encouragement* to you. It is a cause of development, like personal relations in life. Like personal intimacies in life, it may and probably will pass, but it will be ineffaceable.

The usefulness of such a passion is various. For one thing, it secures us against forced admiration, from attending to writers simply because they are great. We are not ourselves great enough for that; probably not one man in each generation is great enough to be intimate with Shakespeare. Admiration for the great is only a sort of discipline to keep us in order, a necessary snobbism to make us mind our places. We may not be great lovers; but if we had a genuine affair with a real poet of any degree we have acquired a monitor to avert us when we are not in love. Indirectly, there are other acquisitions: our friendship gives us an introduction to the society in which our friend moved; we learn its origins and its endings; we are broadened. We do not imitate, we are changed; and our work is the work of a changed man; we have not borrowed, we have been wakened, and we become bearers of a tradition.

It's a remarkable statement, humble, warmly human, poetically wise, and it's also, I think, a crucial corrective to the loftier and more Delphic statement in "Tradition and the Individual Talent."

FLETCHER: Thank you, Professor Ayres.

And here, having come full circle, back to the question with which we started, I think we ought to stop. The next voice you hear will be that of Professor Saettaro, two weeks from tonight, discoursing on behalf of "Le directeur."

Notes

1. Cf. "Daedal Harmonies: A Dialogue on Eliot and the Classics," *The Southern Review* 13 (Winter 1977), 1–47.

2. The allusion to Poe's tale, so far as I know, was first observed, but without comment, by Grover Smith, Jr., *The Poetry and Plays of T. S. Eliot* (2nd ed.; Chicago, 1974), p. 47.

3. See F. W. Bateson, "The Poetry of Learning," in Graham Martin, ed., *Eliot in Perspective* (London, 1970), p. 42: "The critical conclusion to which I have been leading is that the 'learning' in Eliot's earlier poems must be seen as an aspect of his Americanism. As scholarship it is wide-ranging, but often superficial and inaccurate. At one level, indeed, the enjoyment that he and Pound found . . . in exploiting their miscellaneous erudition is the same in kind . . . that every American pilgrim of our cathedrals, galleries, and museums experiences. The appearance of literary scholarship parallels the tourist's apparent acquisition of 'culture.' "

In fact, however, in the six or seven examples of Eliot's "pseudo-learning" adduced by Bateson, Eliot is essentially correct and Bateson mostly wrong or inaccurate. Bateson, for instance, chastises Eliot for muddling his allusion to Ruskin in the final line of "Burbank with a Baedeker: Bleistein with a Cigar" ("Time's ruins and the seven laws"), commenting: "If, as seems likely, the seven lamps are Ruskin's *Seven Lamps of Architecture,* an element of satire re-enters. . . . And the pseudo-scholar [Eliot] is again in evidence. . . . The work of Ruskin's that Burbank would have been much more likely to pack with his Baedeker is surely *The Stones of Venice.*"

But it *is* to *The Stones of Venice,* not to *The Seven Lamps of Architecture,* that Eliot is alluding here. Had Bateson taken the scholarly trouble he patronizes Eliot for not taking, and checked his sources, he would have found in *The Stones of Venice* (II, chap. 4, "St. Mark's") Ruskin's detailed account of the Seven Laws according to which St. Mark's was built. Once invested with "authority," scholarly errors have a way of mindlessly persisting. We need not speak of "plagiarizing," as Bateson does of Eliot. But Bateson presumably "borrowed" his mistake from Grover Smith, Jr. (p. 53), who speaks of Burbank meditating "among unSpenserian ruins of time and shattered *lamps* of architecture." And this compounded error now finds its way into works like A. D. Moody's *T. S. Eliot* (Cambridge, England, 1979), p. 61: "Does he [Burbank] realise that Ruskin wrote not of laws but of the spiritual life necessary for an architecture . . . ?"

The pity in all this is not merely that a perfectly accessible allusion has been arrogantly misread, but that the *point* of the allusion—which rounds off the poem and has a great deal more than irony in it—has been lost, with real damage to our understanding. Eliot's allusion, as I see it, is to the *kind* of architecture—"encrusted" architecture, adorned with fragments of older cultures, which are then reworked into a *new* Christian unity—which, for Ruskin, Venice above all represented. Into *this* Venice, as Ruskin takes great pains to show, the pagan cultures of Greece and Tyre, Rome and Byzantium, all flow. And this Ruskinian Venice becomes for Eliot, like London later, the *locus* of that "traditional" world in which past and present are simultaneously present. Ruskin's Venice is in fact the architectural equivalent of the "poem" postulated in "Tradition and the Individual Talent." "Encrustation" is the principle behind the texture of Eliot's poetry in this period, and above all in the richly ornate and text-encrusted poem which invokes Ruskin's Seven Laws defining this very principle of "encrusted architecture."

4. See Eliot's review, "War-paint and Feathers," *Athenaeum* 4668 (Oct. 17, 1919), p. 1036.

5. "A Prediction in Regard to Three English Authors, Writers Who though Masters of Thought, Are Likewise Masters of Art," *Vanity Fair* 21 (Feb. 1924), 29.

6. T. S. Eliot, *Selected Essays* (New York, 1960), p. 135.

7. Ibid., p. 259.

8. *The Use of Poetry and the Use of Criticism* (Cambridge, Mass., 1933), p. 111.

9. "The Dry Salvages."

10. Cf. "Leibniz' Monads and Bradley's Finite Centres" *(The Monist,* Oct. 1916, p. 568): "Leibniz' originality is in direct, not inverse ratio to his erudition." Later, in his essay on Bishop Andrewes *(Selected Essays,* p. 304), Eliot made the same point, observing Andrewes' "erudition had full play, and his erudition is essential to his originality."

11. Fletcher's point is one of considerable antiquity—as is Rousseau's choice of the orang-outang as the earliest form of man. We find it expressed, for instance, as early as 1699, in Edward Tyson's *Orang-Outang, sive Homo Sylvestris,* a book which, via Monboddo and later writers, influenced Rousseau in his *Discours.* "The most perfect of this Order of Beings, the *Orang-Outang,*" observes Tyson, ". . . has the Honour of bearing the nearest Resemblance to Human Nature, tho' all that Species have some Agreement with us in our Features, . . . yet this has the greatest Likeness, not only in his Countenance, but in the Structure of his Body, his Ability to walk upright, as well as on all fours; his Organs of Speech, his ready Apprehension, and his gentle and tender Passions, which are not found in any of the Ape Kind, and in various other Respects."

12. *The Use of Poetry and the Use of Criticism,* p. 78.

13. T. O. Mabbott, ed., *Collected Works of Edgar Allan Poe* (Cambridge, Mass., 1978), II, pp. 521 ff.

14. Jean-Jacques Rousseau, *Oeuvres complètes,* III, ed. R. Derathé et al. (Paris, 1968). Rousseau's discussion of the orang-outang and its relation to man is to be found in Note X of the *Discours, écrits politiques,* pp. 208–214.

For Rousseau's speculations on the orang-outang and the Noble Savage, and his relationship to predecessors like Monboddo, Tyson, the Jesuit Relations, etc., see *The Wild Man Within: An Image in Western Thought from the Renaissance to Romanticism,* ed. E. Dudley and M. E. Novak (Pittsburgh, 1972). In particular, see Novak's contribution, "The Wild Man Comes to Tea," and Geoffrey Symcox's "The Wild Man's Return: The Enclosed Vision of Rousseau's *Discourses.*"

15. Cf. Ronald Schuchard, "T. S. Eliot as an Extension Lecturer, 1916–1919," *Review of English Studies,* N.S. xxv, n. 98 (May 1974), 163–173. In the outline of his Rousseau lecture, Eliot wrote: "Contemporary intellectual movements in France must be understood as in large measure a reaction against the 'romanticist' attitude of the nineteenth century. During the

nineteenth century several conflicting tendencies were manifested, but they may all be traced to a common source. The germs of all these tendencies are found in Rousseau. . . . Romanticism stands for *excess* in any direction. It splits up into two directions: escape from the world of brute fact, the devotion to brute fact." The operative word here, I suggest, is *brute*.

For Eliot's knowledge of *Candide,* cf. "Mr. Leacock Serious," *New Statesman* 7 (July 1916), 404: "The reader of *Candide* or *Pickwick Papers* cannot wholly escape from exercise of intellect or feelings." In his 1916 essay on "Leibniz' Monads and Bradley's Finite Centres" (*The Monist* 26, p. 568), Eliot remarked: " 'Candide' is a classic; Voltaire was a wise man, and not dangerous. Rousseau is not a classic, nor was he a wise man; he has proved an eternal source of mischief and inspiration."

Influenced by Babbit and More, Eliot was already in 1916 meditating on the relation between civilization and the beast—or transcendental ape—in the human heart and soul, as his review of Paul Elmer More's *Aristocracy and Justice* makes quite clear. More's humanism, Eliot observed, "is based upon the belief that Nature is generally unfavourable to man; that nothing is more fragile than civilisation, nothing harder to mend after the slightest fracture. At the bottom of man's heart there is always the beast, resentful of restraints of civilized society, ready to spring out at the instant this restraint relaxes. Nature, even human nature, is impatient of civilisation. . . . As a matter of fact, the human soul—*l'anima semplicetta*—is neither good nor bad; but in order to be good requires *discipline: Onde convenne legge per fren porre . . .*" Cf. "An American Critic," *New Statesman* 7 (July 24, 1916), 284. The conjunction of Dante's *anima semplicetta* here with the Rousseauvian apeman suggests that the idea of Sweeney as Man-in-transition, the ambivalent beast, in declivity or ascent, with his emerging sense of good-and-evil, is already taking shape in the poet's mind.

16. *The Confessions of Jean-Jacques Rousseau,* trans. J. M. Cohen (London, 1953), Bk. IV, p. 148. The note of expulsion from paradise, with the concomitant nostalgia for a lost "home-land" and the conviction of interior emptiness, is extremely strong in Rousseau. For instance, in his famous (third) letter to M. de Malesherbes, Rousseau writes with piercing intensity of just these things: "And yet, in the midst of it all, *the nothingness of my chimeras* sometimes arose before me and saddened me. Even had all my dreams turned to realities, they would not have satisfied me. I should still have imagined, dreamed, desired. I found within myself an inexplicable void which nothing could fill, a certain longing of the heart toward another kind of happiness which I could not even conceive, and of which I yet felt the need." It is hard to imagine Eliot failing to take note of sentiments like these, in so many ways, despite differences, parallel to his own. There is, I suspect, more than detached observation in Eliot's remark that in Romantic poetry there is a pervasive sadness "due to the exploitation of the fact that no human relations are adequate to human desires, but also to the disbelief in any further object for human desires than that which, being human, fails to satisfy them" (*Selected Essays,* p. 379).

Eliot would have known Rousseau's letter to Malesherbes from its citation in Jules LeMaître's *Jean-Jacques Rousseau,* which EJiot listed as one of the required readings for his lecture on Rousseau.

17. See Geoffrey Symcox, "The Wild Man's Return," in *The Wild Man Within.* Symcox attempts to rescue Rousseau's anthropological speculations from a long history of hostile criticism by showing that, while the Noble Savage is well known long before Rousseau, it was Rousseau's achievement to discipline and humanize, largely by interiorizing, the eighteenth-century Wild Man. Rousseau, he claims, "internalized the Wild Man and recognized his presence within himself, a presence which he felt was good and necessary. He came to realize that the Wild Man exists within us all, even though we may prefer to regard ourselves as Noble Savages: below the civilized overlay of reason and balance lies a deeper substratum of feeling inherited from a primitive past. Rousseau's rediscovery of the Wild Man was the uncovering and rehabilitation of the realm of feeling" (p. 234).

18. "Tradition and the Individual Talent," in *Selected Essays*, p. 6.

19. Chorus, Pt. II, *Murder in the Cathedral*, in Eliot, *The Complete Poems and Plays* (New York, 1971), p. 208.

20. See the Myth of Er, *Republic* X 620c: "Far off in the rear he saw the soul of the buffoon Thersites clothing itself in the body of an ape." (The *ther-* of "Thersites" has been derived by Plato from Gk. *ther*—"beast.")

21. For Eliot's early familiarity with Ovid—the *Amores* as well as the *Metamorphoses*—cf. *The Sacred Wood* (London, 1920), pp. 31 and 61.

22. Boyd is, in point of fact, mistaken. There were several notable ancient works dealing with Nausicaa, including a play by Sophocles. But nothing of unusual literary merit has survived.

23. See, for instance, *Cymbeline*, Act II, Scene 4, lines 142 ff.; *Titus Andronicus*, Act II, Scene 1, lines 95 ff.; *Antony and Cleopatra*, Act IV, Scene 12, line 13; etc.

24. *The Little Review* 4 (May 1917), 9.

25. Ernest Crowley, *The Mystic Rose* (rev. ed.; New York, 1927).

26. *Mon coeur mis à nu.*

27. *Selected Essays*, p. 380.

28. The link between murder and defloration is, of course, the issue of *blood*. Thus in the (profoundly Frazer-influenced) writing of Pavese one constantly finds a connection between love-making and violence. In *Il diavolo sulla collina*, for instance, Pieretto observes, "Si fa al amore per ferire, per spargere sangue." ("One makes love in order to wound, to shed blood.")

29. *Sacrifice: Its Nature and Function*, trans. W. D. Halls (Chicago, 1964), pp. 97 ff. Originally published in 1898, under the title *Essai sur la nature et la fonction du sacrifice*. In addition to the passage cited, the following remarks by Hubert and Mauss seem to me to bear upon the Eliot poem:

> The purpose of the . . . rite is to increase the religiosity of the sacrificer. To this end he had to be associated as closely as possible with the victim, because it is thanks to the strength that the act of consecration has built up in the victim that he acquires this desired characteristic. . . . The sinner, just like the criminal, is a sacred being. If he sacrifices, the sacrifice has as its aim, or at least one of its aims, to rid him of his impurity. It is an expiation. But an important fact must be noted: sickness, death and sin are identical from the religious viewpoint (pp. 52–53).

30. Washing and shaving as purgation and "drowning" into new life. Eliot's eye picks it out everywhere in the poetry and prose of this period. Thus in a 1917 review of an early seventeenth-century Christian Utopian tract by Johann Andreae, Eliot seizes upon the feelings of the almost drowned and shipwrecked sailor who sees in the distance—*almen le torre*—the towers of "the happy city." Of the entire book Eliot quotes only the sailor's cry of joy at the prospect of "drowning" into new life by ritual cleansing: "I shall neither evade the bath, nor the razor, nor the brush, that, being washed, scraped, and cleansed, I may be admitted to the pure abodes of truth and goodness." See "A Forgotten Utopia," *New Statesman* 9 (Sept. 1917), 524.

31. *The Life of Saint Teresa of Avila*, trans. David Lewis (London, 1911), pp. 266–267. The passage is also cited by Evelyn Underhill in *Mysticism* (London, 1911), p. 92, a book which Eliot intensely admired and which, according to Lyndall Gordon (*Eliot's Early Years*, New York, 1977), he read during the student years at Harvard: "During Eliot's last years at Harvard he made a study of the lives of saints and mystics, St. Theresa, Dame Julian of Norwich, Mme. Guyon, Walter Hilton, St. John of the Cross, Jacob Böhme, and St. Bernard. . . . Eliot made copious notes from Evelyn Underhill's book, *Mysticism*" (p. 60).

32. Cited by Underhill, p. 343. See preceding note.

33. See Gordon, p. 142.

34. "Thinking in Verse: A Survey of Early Seventeenth Century Poetry," *The Listener* 3 (March 12, 1930), 443.

35. The parallel is too striking to be coincidental. For essential thematic reasons Joyce chooses to begin *Ulysses* with the image of the shaving animal and the concomitant idea of self-consciousness. In an unmistakably ritual way, body and soul, beast and god, starkly confront each other:

> Stately, plump Buck Mulligan came from the stairhead, bearing a bowl of lather on which a mirror and razor lay crossed. A yellow dressing gown, ungirdled, was sustained gently behind him by the mild morning air. He held the bowl aloft and intoned:—*Introibo ad altare Dei* . . . Laughing again, he brought the mirror away from Stephen's peering eyes. —The rage of Caliban at not seeing his face in a mirror, he said. If only Wilde were alive to see you . . .

Caliban's mirror comes, of course, not from Shakespeare, but from the preface to *The Picture of Dorian Gray*: "The nineteenth century dislike of realism is the rage of Caliban seeing his own face in the glass. The nineteenth century dislike of romanticism is the rage of Caliban not seeing his own face in the glass." But the aesthetic polarity of realism/romanticism conceals the platonic polarity of body/soul, real/ideal, beast/god contained in the contrast of Dorian's mirror and the picture. In the mirror he sees the young god as a pure Narcissus, the human soul in its divine purity; in the changing and increasingly monstrous portrait he sees a "satyr" and a "devil" (chap. 13), and shudderingly sees himself in Gautier's Lacenaire—the "cold yellow hand *du supplice mal lavé* . . . with its *doigts de faune*." Wilde's emphasis, unlike that of Joyce and Eliot, is, it seems to me, wholly decadent in its insistence on *necessary* declivity.

36. The parallels, again, are too striking to be written off as coincidence. Lewis' character Kreisler is in fact an artistic Sweeney, a troglodyte expatriate painter in Paris. "From his window . . . Kreisler's eye was fixed blankly on a spot thirty feet above the scene of the Hobson-Tarr dialogue. He was shaving himself, one eye fixed on Paris. . . . Kreisler's room looked like some funeral vault . . . placarded with nude and archaic images. . . . But cafés were the luminous caverns where he could be said, most generally, to dwell. . . . Kreisler, measured by chairs or doors, was of immoderate physical humanity. He was of that select section, corporally, that exceed the mean. [His body] was in Rome or in Paris. It had an air of possession everywhere . . . he had only to look at a woman for her to become pregnant." This "efficient chimpanzee" looks at his model Bertha Luntken and sees "arms like bananas." He physically and sexually assaults her. As for her, "she has a nice healthy penchant for self-immolation. . . . She is apt to lie down on the altar at the wrong moment—even to take all sorts of unrelated things for altars." Waking at eight in the morning ("Kreisler's windows had been incandescent with steady saffron rays"), she struggles out of bed and shrieks at him: "Oh Schwein! Schwein! Ich hass es—ich hass dich! Schwein! Schurke!" "Kreisler stood at the window . . . still swamped and strung with violence . . ." Then follows the passage which Eliot, in his 1918 review ("Tarr," *The Egoist* 5, Sept. 1918, 105) cites verbatim—Bertha perceiving this "double" Kreisler:

> She saw side by side, and unconnected, the silent figure drawing her and the other one full of blindness and violence. Then there were two other figures, one getting up from the chair, yawning, and the present lazy one at the window—four in all, that she could not bring together somehow, each in a complete compartment of time of its own.

The passage cited juxtaposes, in a way that reveals the meaning and technique of "Sweeney Erect" (and, even more clearly, "Sweeney Among the Nightingales"), the apparently disconnected images of civilized artist and Neanderthal apeman. In the same review Eliot concludes that the artist "is more *primitive*, as well as more civilized, than his contemporaries, his experience is deeper than civilization, and he only uses the phenomena of civilization in expressing it. Primitive instincts and the acquired habits of ages are confounded in the ordinary man. In the work of Mr. Lewis we recognize the thought of the modern and the energy of the cave-man." For the same idea cf. "War-Paint and Feathers" (*Athenaeum* 4668, Oct. 17, 1919, 1036) and of course Eliot's remarks in "Tradition and the Individual Talent" about the artist as the possessor of a tradition in which nothing is superannuated, not even "the rock drawing of the Magdalenian draughtsman."

37. See the passage cited in Note 28.

38. Frazer, *The Golden Bough*, pp. 78–83.

39. Ed. J. Bernhart (New York, 1949). Reprint, with new Introduction and Notes, of the 1854 translation by Susanna Winkworth, as revised by Willard Trask. Cf. chap. vii, pp. 123–124.

40. From ancient to modern times it was widely believed, presumably for reasons of homology, that there was direct causal link between sexual intercourse and epilepsy. For discussion of the history of epilepsy, see Owsei Temkin, *The Falling Sickness* (Baltimore, 1945), passim. Epilepsy, according to Temkin, "was thought to occur more often in men than in women and . . . sexual life in general was connected with it in many ways. The epileptic attack was compared to the sexual act, and both Hippocrates and Democritus were credited with the saying that 'coitus is a slight epileptic attack'" (p. 30). . . . "In Antiquity the influence of sexual intercourse upon epilepsy had been widely discussed. During the Middle Ages and the Renaissance the opinion prevailed that sexual excesses were harmful for epileptics. . . . From the second half of the 18th century, this point of view was strongly emphasized" (pp. 220–221).

In Bk. II of his *Confessions*, for instance, Rousseau describes his first sexual encounter (a homosexual one) and comments, "I could not understand what was the matter with the wretch. I thought he had been attacked by epilepsy or some madness more terrible. . . . I have never seen another man in such a condition, but if we men look like that when we are with women, they must certainly be bewitched not to feel disgusted with us."

41. Cf. Temkin, p. 6: "The very variety of explanations proffered by the ancients shows that they themselves could only speculate about the true meaning of the name epilepsy. But their suggestions at least reveal some of the popular beliefs surrounding epilepsy. The disease might have been called sacred because a deity had sent it, or because a demon had been thought to enter the patient. . . . Furthermore, it might have acquired its name because its cure was not human but divine. *At the bottom of all the alleged reasons lies the basic belief that the disease is an infliction or possession by a higher power for sin, and that its cure must be supernatural.*"

42. Underhill, *Mysticism*, p. 58.

43. Doris enters "towelled from the bath" not merely because Eliot wants her ritually pure, cleansed for the sacrament of the god's epiphany, but because she is, as early as Homer and Hesiod, a Nereid or sea-nymph. In Ovid's tale of Acis and Galatea (*Metamorphoses* 13, 742), she appears as wife of Nereus and mother of Galatea.

44. Chorus from *The Rock*. Eliot, *Complete Poems and Plays*, p. 107.

45. Titian's great painting "Bacchus and Ariadne" hangs in the National Gallery in London, where Eliot would have seen it. With it he would also have seen Titian's other great mythological rendering of "Perseus and Andromeda," to which the final stanza of the suppressed "Ode" presumably alludes.

46. See G. T. W. Patrick, *Heraclitus of Ephesus on Nature* (Baltimore, 1889), p. 52. This text and commentary on Heraclitus was, according to Lyndall Gordon's Appendix (p. 141), among the books checked out of the Harvard library by Eliot during his student years. The full quotation reads: "For were it not Dionysus to whom they institute a procession and sing songs in honor of the pudenda, it would be the most shameful action. But Dionysus, in whose honor they rave in Bacchic frenzy, and Hades, are the same." On which Patrick comments: ". . . since Dionysus and Pluto are the same, the rites are really a symbolism expressing the power of life

over death and the indestructibility of life even in death. These vile phallus songs are in fact songs of triumph of life over death . . . Although far-fetched, this is a possible interpretation of this obscure passage."

47. Cf. *O.E.D.* under "turning" for examples. Eliot's use of "turning" in this sense was extremely early in his career. Just after leaving Harvard, Eliot wrote an (unpublished) religious poem entitled "After the Turning" (cf. Gordon, p. 54). It is worth noting how, thanks to Eliot's metrical skill, stanza IX is made to straddle stanza X; in this way, the poet assigns both accent and tonal stress—i.e., musical meaning—to the "Turn-" of "Mrs. Turner."

48. Instead of the "Look, look, wenches" in the last line of Eliot's epigraph, Beaumont and Fletcher have "See, see, wenches / A miserable life of this poor picture" (Act II, Scene 2, lines 77–78). The effect of the change is to suggest between the lines or beyond the frame, the sudden epiphany of the god. The reader, like the wenches, is enjoined to *look*. These quatrain poems are not, *pace* Kermode, "puzzles without epiphanies."

49. *Emblems*, in *The Complete Works in Prose and Verse of Francis Quarles*, ed. Grosart (London, 1881), p. 80.

50. An allusion whose identification I owe to the detective eye of Richard Macksey.

51. In a review of Diderot's *Early Philosophical Works*. *New Statesman* 8 (March 17, 1917), 572–573. Diderot, observes Eliot, expresses a sentiment, a feeling, not unknown— "one which was beginning to be heard more loudly in the eighteenth century. It is heard from the *promeneur solitaire*."

52. An observation I owe to Robert Kent.

53. Cf. "Reflections on Contemporary Poetry," *Egoist* 4 (Oct. 1917), 133.

54. "Modern Tendencies in Poetry," *Shama'a* 1 (April 1920).

55. See, for instance, Eliot's comments on Donne, who gives what few other writers of his period do—"the sense of the artist as an Eye, curiously, patiently watching himself as a man." "The Preacher as Artist," *Athenaeum* 4674 (Nov. 28, 1919).

56. The next chapter begins with a description of the whalers at breakfast: "They were nearly all whalemen: chief mates, and second mates, and third mates, and sea carpenters, and sea coopers, and sea blacksmiths, and harpooners, and ship keepers; a brown and brawny company, with bosky beards: an unshorn, shaggy set, all wearing monkey jackets . . ." For bringing this parallel forcefully to my attention, I am indebted to my Melvillian friend, Herbert Golder.

57. *To Criticize the Critic* (New York, 1965), pp. 43–60.

58. Cf. "A Commentary," *Criterion* 3 (Oct. 1924), 2: "Few will ever take the pains to study the consummate art of Bradley's style, the finest philosophic style in our language, in which acute intellect and passionate feeling preserve a classic balance: only those who will surrender patient years to the understanding of his meaning. But upon those few, both living and unborn, his writings perform that mysterious and complete operation which transmutes not one department of thought only, but the whole intellectual and emotional tone."

59. F. H. Bradley, *Principles of Logic* (rev. ed.; 1922), pp. 188 ff.

60. See "My Station and Its Duties," in *Ethical Studies* (London, 1976), pp. 162–163.

61. *Appearance and Reality* (2nd ed.; Oxford, 1897), p. 161.

62. Ibid., p. 217.

63. Cf. "Beyle and Balzac," *Athenaeum* 4648 (May 30, 1919), 393.

64. "Shakespeare and the Stoicism of Seneca" (1927), *Selected Essays*, p. 117.

65. Cf. *Facsimile Transcript of The Waste Land* (New York, 1971), p. 117.

66. Ibid., p. 121.

67. *Selected Essays* (New York, 1932), p. 117.

68. *The Sacred Wood* (London, 1920), footnote to p. xvi.

69. Eliot cites J. B. Yeats to this effect, approvingly: "Only old ideas," which are "part and parcel of the personality," are "of use to the poet." Cf. "The Letters of J. B. Yeats," *The Egoist* IV, 6 (July 1917), 90.

In another essay of the same period Eliot speaks disparagingly of the passive and reverential attitude toward unexamined "tradition": "All the ideas, beliefs, modes of feeling and behavior which we have not time or inclination to investigate for ourselves we take second-hand and sometimes call 'tradition.'" This statement is in turn footnoted by an even more condemnatory and ironic comment: "For an authoritative condemnation of theories attaching extreme importance to tradition as a criterion of truth, see Pope Gregory XVI's encyclical *Singulari nos . . .* and the Vatican Council canon of 1870, *Si quis dixerit . . . anathema sit.*" "Reflections on Contemporary Poetry (III)," *The Egoist* IV, 10 (Nov. 1917), 151.

70. During the forties Eliot was a member of "The Moot," a group of distinguished intellectuals in London who met regularly to discuss major problems of culture and society. Eliot's contribution was signed "Metoikos"—i.e., "metic" or "resident alien."

71. See Edgar Ansel Mowrer, *This American World,* with a preface by T. S. Eliot (London, 1928), p. xiii.

72. See "In Memory of Henry James," *The Egoist* V, 1 (Jan. 1918), 1–2.

73. "Reflections on Contemporary Poetry," *The Egoist* VI, 3(July 1919), 39.

PART THREE

Psychology and Authority

In *The Idea of a Christian Society* Eliot touched upon a suggestion with which most contributors to this anthology would perhaps agree even if they disagreed with Eliot's conservative politics. "Out of Liberalism itself comes philosophies which deny it." Eliot had in mind not only the skeptical temper of modern liberalism that questions all beliefs and faiths, and thereby grants to every individual the right to dispute authority, but also an increasing *etatisme* that more and more had made planning and control, not freedom and autonomy, the hallmark of contemporary political thought. Eliot also discussed several other ideas relevant to the three papers that follow: the order and unity that authority promises and the chaos and alienation that society produces, the inability of modern man to subordinate himself to any system of authority that calls for some sacrifice of the desires of the ego, and the family as the fundamental channel for the transmission of culture. "When I speak of the family, I have in mind a bond which embraces a longer period of time than this," Eliot complained of the current "vanities and pretensions of genealogy" and the "sentimentalisized" vision of the family based on little more than the "personal affection between the members of it." "I have in mind . . . a piety towards the dead, however obscure, and a solicitude for the unborn, however remote. Unless this reverence for past and future is cultivated in the home, it can never be more than a verbal convention in the community." It was the traditionally sacred "idea" of the family to which Eliot desired to reinstill reverence, and it is that idea that is today in such disarray due not only to the tensions in contemporary society but also to the status of psychology in general and of Freudianism in particular.

Like Hegel, Freud has spawned opposing schools of thought regarding the problem of authority. Just as there were right and left Hegelians in the 1830s so there have been conservative and radical Freudians in the twentieth century. In the case of Freud the source of the division on the question of authority can be traced to his own writings. Ample references can be found in Freud's texts to suggest both positions. Whether the issue at hand is the family, personality structure, or the state, coherent arguments can be made that Freud is a radical or a conservative.

The immediate impact of Freud's thought on European culture was certainly revolutionary. Psychoanalysis was taken as a challenge to traditional attitudes about childhood sexuality, the autonomy of the ego, the source of conscience, the relation of the mind to the body, the validity of religious experience, the nature of "slips," dreams, and other common experiences. The prospect of a psychoanalytic critique of social and cultural authority was quickly recognized by many young socialist theorists. As early as the late 1920s, Erich Fromm and Wilhelm Reich developed Freudian critiques of authority in the family to supplement their Marxist positions. This early Freudo-Marxism looked to the psychoanalytic theory of the instincts as a source of radical thought. The patriarchal father was denounced as a repressive force whose authority was the cause of neurosis, sexual inhibitions, and even the rise of fascism.

In *Eros and Civilization* (1955) and other essays Herbert Marcuse advanced considerably the line of Freudo-Marxist thought. He argued that, while some degree of instinctual repression was necessary for the existence of civilization, capitalist society produced "surplus repression," a degree of sensual renunciation only required to maintain the irrationality of the contemporary mode of production. Marcuse modified Freud's notion of a "reality principle" that guides the ego in its effort to gratify instinctual drives. Under capitalism, a specific reality principle, "the performance principle," akin to the work ethic, exacted its heavy toll on the lives of individuals by demanding inordinate efforts at repression. What Freud saw as the increasing discomfort of men and women with civilized life Marcuse viewed as the tragic unhappiness induced by the capitalist mode of production. Psychoanalysis was the basis for a generalized antiauthoritarian theory.

In the 1960s Marcuse confronted a culture that apparently had given up the work ethic in favor of hedonistic consumerism. Freudo-Marxism now had to explain not the repressions of the compulsive personality but the free, easy gratifications of the impulsive consumer. The new consumerism, Marcuse contended, did not signify a genuine sexual liberation but a phenomenon he termed "repressive desublimation" in which the instincts were released in a relatively uninhibited fashion but were nonetheless canalized according to social imperatives. The cultural system of late capitalism induced a flow of the instincts while shaping their direction toward ends that benefited the growing capacity of the economy "to deliver the goods."

In the first essay in this section, Russell Jacoby, following in Marcuse's footsteps, offers another Freudo-Marxist explanation of contemporary culture. The Freudian concept of narcissism provides the key for Jacoby to the analysis of the "me generation" of the 1970s. Parents today, he argues, are no longer willing to sacrifice for their children at the expense of their careers and leisure pursuits, a charge that falls more heavily on women who had traditionally stayed at home with the kids than on men who never "sacrificed" much anyway. Modern parents, he continues, are cold and indifferent to their children, avoiding the thankless tasks of child care in favor of tennis lessons, hot tubs, and professional careers. As a result, a new configuration of authority confronts children, one that bears little resemblance to the rigid patriarchy of Freud's Viennese bourgeoisie. In the new family context children internalize their parents to a lesser degree than before and, consequently, grow up with "damaged superegos." In the end the new generation recapitulates the previous one, becoming "narcissists" who are adjusted to the society and incapable of resisting the demands of the state. In the culture of narcissism, to invoke the phrase of Christopher Lasch, human relations are reduced to affectless instrumentality as the ethic of sacrifice and hard work becomes a thing of the past.

Jacoby is rightly concerned that his radical analysis may be taken as a conservative eulogy to a past patriarchy. Remorse for the passing of the heroic, individualist bourgeois—a theme characteristic of the Frankfurt School from which Jacoby's thought derives—leads to an overhasty condemnation of recent cultural trends. For it is not at all clear that mothers who pursue careers that bring them a degree of happiness or fulfillment are worse parents than mothers who "sacrificed" themselves for their children, submerging their own needs to those of their families, while making certain that their children knew it. Who is to say that the narcissistic disorders of today are more damaging or more widespread than the hysterical neuroses of yesteryear? It appears as though Freudo-Marxism has become, in the hands of Jacoby and

Lasch, the last defense of patriarchal authority against the assault of the feminist movement.

The second essay in this section by Jessica Benjamin tries to preserve the antiauthoritarian impulse of Freudo-Marxism by relying not on the concept of narcissism but on the object relations school of psychoanalysis. This little-known branch of Freudianism derives from the British analytic school of Winnicott and Bowlby. The intellectual thrust of the object relations school is to diminish somewhat the primacy of the intrapsychic dimension as well as the instinct theory of Freud in favor of a more interpersonal view of the psyche. Nevertheless, this tendency of psychoanalysis does not go so far as the so-called cultural school of Sullivan, Horney, and Fromm in departing from the initiatives of Freud. It occupies a position somewhere in the middle, between the original psychoanalytic tradition and those who do away with the influence of the instincts in favor of social determinants.

"Individuality, as we have known it, is male," Benjamin asserts, thus setting herself in opposition to the Freudo-Marxist tradition. The outcome of the Oedipus complex, according to Benjamin, is not the freedom and autonomy posited by Marcuse and now by Jacoby, but a false differentiation of the ego that is well suited to patriarchal capitalism. The assumption of Freud and the left Freudians is that the child confronts a choice between fusion with the mother, which leads to narcissism, and identification with the father, which leads to the differentiation of the self. Benjamin rejects this polarity for several reasons. First, differentiation in the Freudian sense appears as the imposition of the father's external authority. Benjamin thinks that human beings naturally seek such autonomy. Second, the Freudian model is biased against the nurturant maternal figure who stands opposed to the claims of civilization. Benjamin argues convincingly that a more satisfying notion of individuation would include a nurturing component. Third, Freudians assume arbitrarily that the differentiating and nurturing figures must be embodied in separate parental figures and that these must fall respectively to the father and mother. Again, Benjamin is no doubt correct in questioning this hallmark of patriarchal thought.

Benjamin's conclusion is not that differentiation or autonomy must be abandoned in favor of some romantic vision of tribal consciousness, but that a superior form of autonomy can be postulated on the basis of a nonpatriarchal family arrangement, and that this new form of autonomous personality structure can realize the ideal of mutual recognition first posited by Hegel. Such autonomy would imply that others are treated as subjects, not as instrumental objects of a manipulating ego. Benjamin raises here a powerful feminist argument that, although it leaves many questions unanswered, promises to provoke significant dialogue in the future. For one thing, it offers an alternate perspective on current cultural developments to that of the narcissist thesis.

The papers by Jacoby and Benjamin may give the impression that Freud's theory lends itself to the cause of radicalism. But such is hardly the case. On many grounds one can legitimately argue that psychoanalysis supports the case for authority in society both in the family and the state. After all, in *Civilization and Its Discontents* Freud set out to show that culture was unthinkable without high levels of psychic repression, indeed, that happiness was incompatible with civilization and that superior forms of culture were proportionate to psychic malaise, anxiety, guilt, and instinctual frustration. He also maintained that the prerequisite for personality formation was a strong, external authority that set sharp limits for the ego. Finally, and perhaps most tellingly, he supported the claims of political authority by demonstrating that social groups of any kind could only be formed by the submission of their members to a clear leader. The psychological basis of groups was both the identification of each member's ego with that of others and the substitution of the member's superego by the figure of the leader. Democratic groups, according to Freud in *Mass Psychology and the Analysis of the Ego,* were at best a hopeless illusion and at worst an overture to barbarism. If these arguments were not enough, Freud turned repeatedly to the question of Marxism only to denounce communist ideals as a fantasy that overlooked basic features of psychic structure.

A basis for a conservative theory of authority was thus firmly laid in Freud's writings. The third essay in this section, written by Philip Rieff, explores this aspect of psychoanalytic thought. Rieff, himself a conservative traditionalist, believes that culture is based on discriminations between choices or values and that these institute a system of authority in every society. Authority, which Rieff thinks is always with us, divides into three types: interdictive, remissive, and transgressive. In a healthy culture, there is a balance among them that, in effect, constitutes a sacred order. According to Rieff, Freud attempted to account for the force of authority with his concept of the superego, an attempt which ultimately fails. The controversial argument that Rieff makes in this essay is that psychoanalysis falls into a preponderantly remissive mode of authority, thereby confirming what is the great disaster of contemporary culture.

It makes no difference to Rieff that Freud regretted the "emotional poverty of groups" in America, which was caused by a lack of authoritative leadership. Freud's apparent respect for authority figures such as Moses does somewhat mollify Rieff's hostility to psychoanalysis. For Rieff, Freud is the leading thinker in the birth of modern therapeutic culture, a culture that is dangerously impoverished due to its weak interdictive mode of authority. Rieff warns that "the high culture of the American present constitutes a general lowering, an identification downward, in the hierarchy of stipulations, the expansions of what is remissive into transgressions, by which modern culture appears to be assuming its uniquely characterless character." Although Rieff grants little analytic value to the concept of narcissism, his conclusions about the bleak future of American culture are similar to those of Jacoby. In different ways each of these three essays offers severe criticisms of contemporary society and in particular its treatment of the problem of authority.

7

The Politics of Narcissism

Russell Jacoby

To characterize society by anything but the most accepted and conventional labels—modern, industrial, capitalist—runs several risks. The complexity of society, if not its incoherence, may damn to irrelevance any single designation. No term can bridge Beverly Hills and the South Bronx, stockbrokers and migrant workers. In addition, the pressures of academic life discourage original and accessible vocabularies. Suspicion falls on those who desert cautious fact collecting, timid conclusions, and arcane language. To the domesticated specialists, to seek a more general audience, to be read—even to be readable—connotes a weakening of standards and scholarship.

For these reasons the American public has rarely been graced with social analyses that are popular and original but not irresponsible. Those who have advanced such theories have typically been academic outsiders, from Thorstein Veblen to C. W. Mills. And even those proffered by insiders have been few and far between. Yet public and intellectual life would be poorer without such efforts. Terms like the affluent society, end of ideology, leisure class, organizational man, one-dimensional society, lonely crowd, and so on, have provoked valuable discussion. Their vulnerability to empirical criticism is not the only test; these terms have drawn attention of a wider public to critical social issues.

To this vocabulary, narcissism can today be added. Largely due to Christopher Lasch's *Culture of Narcissism*, it has joined the other labels of contemporary society. To be sure, it also shares their weaknesses: too vague, general, abstract. Yet its strength is inseparable from its weakness. For an instant, by its very audacious generalizing, it has illuminated the social landscape. The popular response is hardly proof of its truth, but it does indicate that the concept of narcissism touched a raw nerve of public life.

Of course, to situate narcissism within the general crises of society may kill its meaning. The continuing crises may suffocate it. Today we are drenched in crises. We have perpetual crises in foreign affairs, housing, education, and energy sources; we have crises of inflation, medical care and costs, public transportation, affirmative action, family disorganization, child abuse, occupational safety; this hardly exhausts the list. Moreover, these crises only provide the background for daily and personal life.

This life itself is increasingly composed of emergencies and crises squeezed together by a vise of carnage and violence. Distant bombings, starvation, and miseries are part of the nightly TV fare. No resident of any large American city, no reader of the daily press can avoid the numerous and horrifying accounts of the local murders, shootings, dismemberments, and accidents. To dwell on these reports is to risk numbness. Exponents of growth and self-realization notwithstanding, to flourish, even to function in this society, requires a shell of coldness.

"Narcissism" does not escape the general fate; as a cry and a crisis it may simply add to the din. Even rescued from the barrage, it is not immune to criticism. As a social category, narcissism suffers from the danger of personalizing the impersonal. Political and economic power is sublimated into individual pathology, as if the traits of a character, and not the economy were the evil.

Moreover, a conservative, if not reactionary, atmosphere clings to the critique of narcissism. It hints of past and better times when people were less self-obsessed. It alludes to an epoch when a patriarch ruled a sound and healthy family, and this family turned out morally and psychically tough egos. The decay of the patriarchal family signaled the onset of the new narcissism: so goes the argument. In brief, the critique of narcissism is suspected of secreting a love of authority. It honors patriarchal authority and bemoans its decline. The term "permissive" society similarly suggests an affection for obedience and families and societies that did not spare the rod or gallows.

Yet social theories that sever all links to conservatism risk blindness to present and past. In different terms, theories that have interpreted history as one-way streets of progress have themselves deteriorated into public relations for the contemporary individual, family, or culture. Edward Shorter's *The Making of the Modern Family* closes basking in the vision of the "free-floating couple" with "relatives hovering in the background, friendly smiles on their faces."[1] Modernization theories, and this includes varieties of Marxism, are cleansed of the taint of conservatism by washing out their color and substance. The cheerleaders of the future know the cheerless past only by the trophies of the winners.

Psychoanalysis, the theoretical sources of the critique of narcissism, also provokes the charge of conservatism. While Freud was hardly a political radical, the allegation is largely inspired by the theories and practices of later psychoanalysts. That Freud was unimpressed by historical change may be due less to his yearnings for the past than to his premonitions of the future as more of the same. To burden the theory with the deceit of social change is to aid the deceivers, not the revolt.

In any case, psychoanalysis did register changes that the psyche underwent, as the popularity of narcissism in contemporary psychoanalytic literature testifies.[2] Toward the end of Freud's career, psychoanalysts commented that "classic" patients no longer were appearing in their doors. The "original" patients of Freud had been afflicted with distinct neurotic symptoms, such as hysteria or hand-washing fetishes. The newer patients suffered more diffuse symptoms and complaints. Wilhelm Reich, describing this phenomenon, introduced the terms character analysis and character disorder. Where analysts had once seen neurotic *symptoms*, they now saw neurotic *characters*. Character disorders suggested less a specific impairment than general patterns and behaviors.

The practical and theoretical consequences of character disorders were far ranging. The patient felt the neurotic symptom as a "foreign body," and feeling ill sought medical or psychological relief.[3] The patient with a character disorder did not suffer from a discrete symptom; hardly feeling ill, he or she was not motivated to seek relief or insight into the disorder.

What makes the patient with a character disorder a patient at all? In fact, this, as well as the related question—when is analysis terminated?—reveals the inner limits of psychoanalysis. The theory of the individual becomes a theory of society. The psychoanalytic theory of narcissism is entangled in the same web. Narcissism is a character disorder, often surfacing with such vague symptoms as "emptiness" and "futility." Moreover, the narcissistic patient is often not dysfunctional but well adjusted. Otto Kernberg comments that the narcissistic patient who is successful in professional life often appears to himself and others as perfectly normal.[4] This confesses, without admitting, that the character disorder is not an individual but social disorder.

If psychoanalysts registered the relative decrease of the "classic" symptoms of neurotic compulsions and the relative increase of character disorders, few speculated on the reasons for this change in traffic. Otto Fenichel, an exception, reasoned that classic neurosis was formed under the impact of simple repressions and prohibitions. A social environment of strict taboos bred clear-cut sexual neuroses. A liberalization of morality and sexual ethics during the twentieth century transformed the raising of children. An inconsistent, looser, and shifting series of sexual commandments and taboos no longer yielded well-defined neurotic compulsions.[5]

Contemporary psychoanalytic theorists confirm that narcissism does not derive from specific childhood traumas. No fantasy (or reality) of an uncle who has seduced or raped the mother before the eyes of the child lies at the root of narcissism. Rather, an entire upbringing and atmosphere is involved.

According to Heinz Kohut, the most common etiology of narcissism is the personality of the parents; they themselves are narcissistic. With their children, they are cold, distant, and uninterested. Narcissistic parents breed narcissistic children.[6]

A liberalized sexual code and behavior restructures the psyche. The end of chaperoned dating and courtship, approval of premarital sexuality, availability of automobiles for sexual encounters, and diffusion of birth-control technology all weaken sexual prohibitions. That this liberalization cannot be judged unalloyed progress is due to the impact of social authority on the erotic experience. Yet the dangers of falling into a cranky conservatism must be faced. If the banners for a sexual revolution are sagging, the bumper stickers for family revival are worse. It cannot be maintained that the liberalization of sexual codes yields cheap thrills while traditional prohibition produced deep, satisfying relations.

Marcuse's concept of "repressive desublimation" sought to do justice to the antagonistic reality of sexual liberalization: a simultaneous release of sexual energies—desublimation—and a contraction of its mode. Sexuality was integrated into late capitalism. The idea that sexuality is used to sell every possible commodity hardly captures the reality. Sexuality more than adorns the commodity; the commodity adorns denatured sexuality. Sexuality is explicit and encouraged and loses its explosive and individual dimension. It can no longer be separated from cigarettes, beer, and shampoo. Capitalism seduces the sexuality it shackles with the sweet talk of a life without chains.

Repressive desublimation may shed light on the narcissistic character. The psychoanalytic discussions of narcissism regularly refer to the damaged superego. While both fact and fantasy comprise the superego, the fact of distant, cold, and inconsistent parents takes a toll. The process of idealization of parental authority, required for the superego, is impaired. Kohut states:

> The environment which used to be experienced as threateningly close is now experienced more and more as threateningly distant; where children were formerly *overly* stimulated by the emotional life (including the erotic) of their parents, they are now often *under* stimulated.[7]

Deprived of parents to idealize, the child, according to Kohut, grows up with a damaged superego.

If Kohut is accurate, the small hothouse of the family, an incubator for neuroses, is traded in for air-conditioned condos, homes of narcissistic individuals. Kernberg states that a "composite picture" of the narcissistic patient shows "consistently a parent figure, usually the mother or mother surrogate, who functions well on the surface, . . . but with a degree of callousness, indifference, and non-verbalized spiteful aggression."[8]

Yet many questions that have dogged discussions of narcissism remain unresolved. Is there a decline of authority per se ("permissiveness") or a deflection of authority? Is the "classic" bourgeois family with a strong patriarch associated with resilient egos and critical intelligence? Can or should this family form be defended? Is the newer, fragmented family composed of passive and accepting individuals?

The Frankfurt School has often been accused of romanticizing and desiring to return to the classic bourgeois family, which is in essence their own. It is indubitable that calls to shore up the family smack of down-home religion and hatred for uptown living. The left, and especially the utopian left, has historically advocated the reconstruction, not restoration of the family. Yet this is a fact, not an argument. It would not be the first time that the left critique has lagged behind the developments of capitalism and that the blueprints for a socialist future were nothing but photocopies of the capitalist past. The reorganization of the family as a program of the future may confuse the acceleration of the past with emancipation.

In any case, the critics of narcissism and dwindling parental authority, or at least the Frankfurt School, do not urge the restoration of past forms of authority. Their analysis distinguished between authority and authoritarianism. This is no quibble. If this distinction is lost, the social psychology of fascism and the social configuration of narcissism blur. Their *Autorität und die Familie* (1936) and *Authoritarian Personality* (1950) dissected authoritarianism in the family. The later work correlated personality traits with a predisposition toward fascism. These traits included a rigid conformity, an inability to tolerate ambiguity, a barely repressed hostility and aggression, and so on. The parents of authoritarian personalities tended to be rigid disciplinarians. They demanded of their children total and unquestioned obedience and submission.[9]

Is this what the Frankfurt School wants to restore? Obviously not. Here there is no abdicated authority but total, traumatic, unbending authority. Max Horkheimer himself cites a relatively unknown text of Marx that illuminated the problem. Marx in 1846 wrote a short article called "Peuchet: On Suicide," essentially a long extract from the memoirs of Jacques Peuchet, keeper of the archives of the Parisian police. Peuchet recorded in loving detail the tale of a young couple from the "lower mercantile classes," honest, decent, hard-working people, who were engaged to be married. After all arrangements for the marriage were completed, a dinner celebration was held at the family of the bridegroom. The bride stayed the night. When she returned home the next morning, her parents heaped abuse on her. Their

fury knew no bounds; neighbors joined in attacking the daughter. Utterly
humiliated, she fled and threw herself into the Seine. Marx commented:

> The most cowardly, unresisting people become implacable as soon as
> they *can exercise their absolute parental authority. The abuse of this
> authority* is, as it were, a *crude compensation* for all the submissiveness
> and dependence to which they abuse themselves willy-nilly in bourgeois
> society.[10]

Authority here is the power of the powerless; those who submit daily in
the larger society take their revenge on their children. In home and hearth
they are dictators, brooking no dissent. They do to the weak what has been
done to them.

This vignette and Marx's comments tally with the description and analyses of the authoritarian personality. Brutal parental authority consoles the
brutalized. No regret for the passing of this family of authority (if it in fact
has passed) flutters through the Frankfurt School or the critique of narcissism. The obverse is true. The Frankfurt School has indicted family authoritarianism as the crucible of fascist and authoritarian character structure. The
ego of the child, crushed by unyielding and vengeful authority, gravitates
toward political authoritarianism.[11] Total hatred for authority is transmuted
by pain into total identification. If narcissism is the successor to the authoritarian personality, society has advanced.

Yet narcissism may not be the successor to authoritarianism but to another
social psychological form. Class may be the missing and elusive ingredient.
What lurks behind the critique of narcissism is the authority of the "classic"
bourgeois family; this family and the authoritarian family diverge in their
social composition. It does not seem fortuitous that Marx's example is
drawn from the "lower mercantile classes" and that the authoritarian personality and the sources of fascism are associated with marginal or threatened
social groupings (which, however, are in no way numerically insignificant).[12]

The bourgeois family in its "classic" phase was not marginal or threatened
but secure and independent. The issue is, not its numerical frequency, but
its unique configuration of authority and affection. Authority was severe but
not brutal or inconsistent. Total submission was not the goal, nor was the
family lacking in warmth.[13] This is not to say there were no victims; there
were, especially women. These victims furnished the patients for psychoanalysis.

The bourgeois family, it seems likely, developed into the narcissistic
family; the class composition remains roughly the same. The case reports of
narcissistic patients allow fleeting views of family life. These do not show
parents who, after long, grueling days of waiting on tables or driving cabs,

come home to bark at their too many children, but parents who are relatively successful, whose energies are directed toward themselves and their careers, and who tend to be enlightened but also cold to the few children at home.

That narcissism may be circumscribed by class does not, of course, dispose of it. The bourgeoisie makes society in its own image. The impact of narcissism in society may be measured by the attitude toward children. A new ethic is taking shape, and this ethic exposes the commodity structure of narcissism. More and more couples decide against, or perpetually delay, having children. This decision marks a departure from the ideal (and imperative) of a family with children.

Childless couples are not the most visible among those working the hardest for the least wages. Here, a case could be made for the rationality of no children; they drain scarce psychic and economic resources. Rather, childlessness has surfaced among young, relatively wealthy professionals. These individuals, it might seem, are richest in the psychic and economic resources to bestow on children. Yet the reverse seems true; they are unable or unwilling to afford the psychic energy, affection, and attention that children require.

If these sociological impressions are accurate, the terrain where psychological narcissism speaks the language of the commodity can be charted. The most advanced social groups—affluent young professionals—expose most sharply the advanced tendencies of capitalism. Narcissism is conventionally designated as hedonistic, the pursuit of self-gratification. The description misses its inner structure: the hedonism of narcissism is parsimonious. It does not squander its energies in the mad pursuit of pleasure but doles them out while scanning interest rates and stock reports.

Hedonism is not an invariant beyond and outside society, but it bears the imprint of history and class.[14] Not the dissolute hedonism of the surplus aristocracy but resolute hedonism marks the ambitious professionals; hedonism becomes calculated and calculating, healthy and approved, as well as profitable. As the psychic household of the individual is remodeled into a financial counseling service, children receive a poor rating; they are high risks, requiring too much initial investment and too few guaranteed returns. The exchange principle, capitalism's own weapon, is used by the bourgeoisie to prune its own family. Hedonism devours itself.

The bourgeoisie organized society around an already primordial principle—that of exchange. An eye for an eye was renovated into equal exchange of value. As Marx knew, the principle of exchange value revolutionized the world and, within a class society, razed distinctions of birth, talent, blood, and tradition. Money was the universal language, and, regardless of other virtues, those who manage to obtain it wield power.

Within an exchange economy, the family sticks out as an irrational blot.

Based on blood and love and hate, it crassly violates the rationalizing drive of exchange value. Its relationships are not simply reciprocal. The relationships of parents to each other, to their parents, to their children, and so on, are not two-way streets. Love and attention are not returned in equal measures. Love relations are compounded and complicated not simply by antagonisms and hatreds but by excesses that cannot be parcelled out in neat packages. An infant cannot return the love and attention bestowed on it.

The exact development of the family remains disputed, yet it can be argued that the family has ineluctably surrendered to the law of exchange. Exchange value has not simply knocked at the door but migrated into bedroom, nursery, and sickroom. This means that the family casts off unequal relationships. All relations are appraised with an eye on the psychic bank account; spending must balance earnings. Consequently, the family contracts, eliminating the old and other kin. Requiring more care and attention than they can return, they are herded off to the state agencies and institutions. Psychic bankruptcy is avoided by retrenching, cutting off losing investments: the old, children, the sick, and so on.

Neither narcissism nor the family can be considered apart from the tendencies of capitalism. Both express in different terms the subordination to the exchange principle. Both accept the same currency. Children are deemed an increasingly unwise investment. For the professional, children are judged a drain and obstacle to career and pleasures. Pets, autos, jogging, and tennis lessons offer more reliable compensation for the same expenditure. The "fatherless" and "kinless" society devolves into the "childless" society. Alvin Toffler, the professional seer, anticipates that children will play an insignificant role in the future society. Love relations that cannot be commodified are treated as if they were the threats they actually are.

The loosening of the ties between parents and children bespeaks a fundamental shift in emotional life. Once an ethic of sacrifice bound parents to children. For many groups in America this ethic constituted a religion: work, sacrifice, and self-denial for the sake of the children. It also testified to a belief in a better future. Sacrifice glued together parents and children, and parents and parents, and parents and their parents.

It is no secret that sacrifice has fallen on dog days. At best it is obsolete, honored but hardly practiced (and well captured in Mary Gordon's *Final Payments*). Sacrifice, not simply with regard to children, but with regard to all people and commitments, erodes. Like the family, sacrifice is invaded by exchange value. By definition, sacrifice is a one-way, not two-way, relationship. More is given, bestowed, or invested than received. To the narcissistic, sacrifice is a con job, a loss with no benefits. Self-effacement, in the name of sacrifice, is a burden that the self threatened with effacement can no longer endure.

The corrosion of sacrifice did not originate in the deep recesses of the psyche but in the excesses of the economy. For decades capitalism has been shoring itself up by intensifying consumption. The imperative to buy and enjoy displaced the religion of saving and sacrifice. A deliberate attack on the "puritanism in consumption" dates at least from the 1920s.[15] Advanced capitalism required a programmed hedonism as much as earlier capitalism needed Calvinism and sacrifice.

To ease overproduction and underconsumption capitalism extended credit toward itself and its consumers. If the public and private debts bail out the economy, they also yield inflation, the unassailable argument against saving and sacrifice. To bank on the future is to risk bankruptcy. Through every pore the message is drilled in to spend and enjoy in the here and now.

Talk of the erosion of sacrifice, like the critique of narcissism, seems to regret the passing of an era, to long for the return of honest sacrifice. Let there be no doubt; the nonrational moment of sacrifice has oiled all irrational movements and institutions. Its kinship with domination cannot be mistaken. That the big as well as the petty despots, the preachers and presidents, dictators and kaisers, kings and generals have all celebrated sacrifice and defamed hedonism is hardly an accident. Citizens and subjects were berated and often compelled to sacrifice their happiness, and sometimes their lives, to keep the larger institutions wheezing along. Dressed up as patriotism and duty, sacrifice coerced the weak to surrender quietly.

For this reason, the corrosion of sacrifice—parents to children, wife to husband, citizens to state—is hardly pure regression. Narcissism harbors a protest in the name of individual health and happiness against irrational sacrifice. Where the dead weight of sacrifice crushes, this cannot be minimized. Nor should it be uncritically celebrated. Narcissism is historically specific, dissimilar in southern Italy and the upper-east side of New York City.[16] The protest of narcissism within advanced capitalism is shot through with the society it rejects; it affirms and buttresses the commodity market. Its mode of protest is private, its substance the exchange principle of capitalism. If sacrifice recalls precapitalist life, narcissism beckons a step closer the stock market of human relations.

Notes

1. Edward Shorter, *The Making of the Modern Family* (New York, 1977), p. 280.

2. See Christopher Lasch, *The Culture of Narcissism: American Life in an Age of Diminishing Expectations* (New York, 1979), pp. 87 ff.

3. Wilhelm Reich, "On Character Analysis" (1928), in *The Psychoanalytic Reader*, ed. R. Fliess (New York, 1973), p. 109.

4. Otto Kernberg, *Borderline Conditions and Pathological Narcissism* (New York, 1975), p. 254.

5. Otto Fenichel, *Psychoanalytic Theory of Neurosis* (New York, 1945), pp. 463–464.

6. Heinz Kohut, *The Analysis of the Self* (New York, 1972), pp. 65 ff.

7. Heinz Kohut, *The Restoration of the Self* (New York, 1977), p. 271.

8. Kernberg, *Borderline Conditions*, p. 235.

9. Else-Frenkel-Brunswik, "Intolerance of Ambiguity as an Emotional and Perceptual Personality Variable," in her *Selected Papers, Psychological Issues,* monograph 31 (New York, 1974), pp. 67 ff. Frenkel-Brunswik was a collaborator of the *Authoritarian Personality*.

10. Karl Marx, "Peuchet: On Suicide" (1846), in Marx and Engels, *Collected Works,* IV (New York and Moscow, 1975), 605.

11. T. W. Adorno et al., *The Authoritarian Personality* (New York, 1950 and 1969), pp. 372 ff.

12. The social and class base of fascism obviously cannot be discussed in a sentence or two; it has provoked a large debate. See Reinhard Kühnl, *Formen bürgerlicher Herrschaft: Liberalismus-Faschismus* (Reinbek bei Hamburg, 1971); Thomas Childers, "The Social Bases of the National Socialist Vote," *Journal of Contemporary History* 11, no. 4 (Oct. 1976): 17–42; and Anson G. Rabinbach, "Towards a Marxist Theory of Fascism and National Socialism," *New German Critique* 3 (Fall 1974): 127–153.

13. Cf. Mark Poster, *Critical Theory of the Family* (New York, 1978), pp. 166 ff., and generally Lawrence Stone, *The Family, Sex and Marriage in England, 1500–1800* (New York, 1977).

14. See Herbert Marcuse, "On Hedonism," in *Negations* (Boston, 1968).

15. Stuart Ewen, *Captains of Consciousness* (New York, 1976), p. 57.

16. See, for instance, Anne Parsons, "Paternal and Maternal Authority in the Neapolitian Family," in her *Belief, Magic and Anomie* (New York, 1969).

8

The Oedipal Riddle: Authority, Autonomy, and the New Narcissism

Jessica Benjamin

The decline in paternal authority is a recurrent theme in the discussion of the changing nature of authority today. The nostalgia for the strong father, master in his house and autonomous agent of his own enterprise, may not only be an expression of antifeminist backlash. It is also the expression of individual helplessness in the face of a society that offers diminishing opportunities for individual self-determination. Increasingly bureaucratic, hierarchical, and depersonalized forces, which appear from the outside to be disorganized, arbitrary, and uncontrollable, shape the fate of the "little man." Whether he falls prey to the denunciations of "big government," or more accurately perceives the work of large corporations, the arena of effective political self-determination is increasingly narrow. In short, the rationalization of society, the persistent organization of social life around abstract principles of profit or manageability rather than human need, must be taken seriously. Even if the waning of paternal authority be viewed as a positive (albeit prematurely celebrated) outcome.

Puzzling in the laments for authority is the positive relationship assumed between strong parental or paternal authority and strong, responsible individuals who do not bow passively to social forces. Why should the obvious lack of active democracy, the apathy of individuals before overwhelming threats to their social existence and physical survival, be equated with a lack of authority? Why are we called upon to discuss the crisis of authority's legitimacy when there is so little resistance to political domination in our society? Or, to be more moderate and precise, why is the notion of a crisis in authority/leadership so closely associated with the idea of a crisis in our form of individuality?

Most recently and most powerfully, Christopher Lasch has articulated this necessary relationship between authority and individuality in his books *The Culture of Narcissism* and *Haven in a Heartless World*.[1] Lasch's account draws on forty years of psychoanalytically oriented social criticism beginning with the works of the Frankfurt School.[2] He has captured the public imagination with his claim that the cultural prototype of our times is the New Narcissist. Ruthlessly self-seeking and self-improved, lacking in a sense of responsibility toward other or society, the New Narcissist is a caricature of self-interested individualism. Lasch explains that the New Narcissism is the product of parents who could or did not exercise authority. The failure of parental authority is, in turn, attributed to the weakening of their autonomy and individual decisiveness by the interference of experts, social agencies, and prescriptive literature. The disenfranchised parent, no longer trusting her or his ability to rule at home, is counterpart to the man in the gray flannel suit, who does not control or take responsibility for his work because he is only a cog in the bureaucratic wheel. By contrast, the model figure who unifies authority and autonomy is described as something like the nineteenth-century father who runs his own business and his family with a just but firm hand.

To understand the criticism of the New Narcissist we must understand this exemplary figure he has ostensibly superseded—Oedipal Man. First identified, named, and explained by Freud, the oedipal drama was shown to reproduce on the psychological level that fusion of autonomy and authority uniquely suited to the epoch of liberal capitalism. In theory, at least, the personality of the normal little boy—and boys alone were the prototype for this theory—who was to become the responsible man of yesteryear, was formed by what Freud called the Oedipus complex. In the Oedipus complex the triangular relationship between parents and child was crystallized. The (male) child loves his mother and wishes to possess her, hates his father and wishes to replace/murder him. Induced by fear of the father and the threat of castration, the child renounces his dependency upon the mother and internalizes the paternal authority that has demanded this of him. The father's insistence on renunciation is thus also an insistence that the child become autonomous. Henceforth, the boy's superego will perform the paternal function within his own psyche, proclaiming autonomy at the price of sexual renunciation and his former childish dependency.[3] These desires, which the child once proclaimed quite openly—"I'm going to marry you when I grow up, Mommy,"—now go underground and are repressed. With them go also the once natural forms of tenderness and vulnerability, the cuddling and tears that are not for "big boys." The successful resolution of the Oedipus complex meant the transition from approval or fear of external authority to self-regulation by the superego; authority was replaced by independent conscience, prohibition by self-control.

Lasch bases his critique on the growing observation by analysts that the Oedipus complex no longer decisively organizes psychic life nor underlies the most prevalent psychic disturbances. The hysterics or obsessives of Freud's day are infrequent visitors to therapeutic consulting rooms; contemporary psychoanalysts treat individuals whose problems date from preoedi-pal conflicts, so-called narcissistic disturbances. Lack of meaningful related-ness, a sense of inner emptiness, in short a vague and general malaise rather than a specific neurosis—these frequently described symptoms of contem-porary patients seem to correspond to the critics' observations about the superficiality, emptiness, and self-preoccupation of narcissistic culture.

The theory of narcissism and the current focus on preoedipal conflicts have added a new wrinkle to the old psychoanalytic view of authority and the oedipal model. Classical psychoanalytic theory sees the child as begin-ning in a stage of primary narcissism in which he feels entirely fused or one with the mother. Self and other are as yet entirely undifferentiated in the child's mind. The primary psychological task of this early developmental phase is considered to be differentiation: recognizing the distinct existence of others apart from the self and so of realizing the self as an ongoing entity with age-appropriate autonomy. Until differentiation occurs, the uncon-ditional and unfailing support of the parent is experienced as part of the self. Consequently, the self feels *omnipotent.*[4] Feelings of omnipotence and gran-diosity are components of early narcissistic experience that must be modified by the process of differentiation. Recent theories of narcissism have estab-lished a kind of parallel to Freud's earlier argument that the superego was necessary to replace the fear of external authority and provide inner judg-ment. The current argument sees the superego as necessary to insure that the child does not regress to infantile dependency, the need for an ideal omnipo-tent parent, or to grandiosity, the loss of the distinction between self and other—secondary, or pathological, narcissism. The superego is also seen as necessary to regulate inner feelings of self-worth and self-esteem that other-wise remain wholly at the mercy of others.[5] In short, internalization is now seen as the inner structure that prevents the pendulum swing from grandiosity to worthlessness in the individual's self-representation—the twin aspects of narcissistic disturbance.

Interestingly enough, Lasch chooses to emphasize the view that sees narcissistic disorders not as a lack of inner structure but the development of pathological structure, not a lack of superego but "an alteration of its con-tents." The use of grandiose self- and object-images is seen as a defense against inner aggression far more primitive than that provided by the oedipal superego.

> It is important to distinguish between those representations (of author-ity) which derive from archaic, preoedipal impressions and those resting on later impressions and therefore reflecting a more realistic assessment of parental powers. . . .
> As authority figures in modern society lose their "credibility," the superego in individuals increasingly derives from the child's primitive

fantasies about his parents—fantasies charged with sadistic rage—rather than from internalized ego ideals formed by later experience with loved and respected models of social conduct.[6]

Lasch thus sees not a "decline of the superego" but the "development of a harsh, punitive superego that derives most of its psychic energy, in the absence of authoritative social prohibitions, from the destructive, aggressive impulses within the id." This development he attributes above all to "the growth of bureaucracy," the erosion of "all forms of patriarchal authority" and the consequent weakening of "the social superego formerly represented by fathers, teachers, and preachers."[7]

The feelings and conflicts of preoedipal or Narcissistic Man seem to bespeak less individuation and autonomy and greater vulnerability to one's own or others' claims to omnipotence than the dilemmas of Oedipal Man. Missing the oedipal legacy of superego and conscience, individuals remain disposed to all forms of dependency and unable to exercise adult responsibility. The child's attitudes remain alive in the adult: passive, yet defiant, dependent on others and helpless before their own impulses, they are easily bent to the will of powerful others. The positive view of paternal authority is actually an attempt to explain the apathy and passivity so widespread today. What could be more compelling than the argument that the waning of authority has left individuals at the mercy of their most primitive, archaic, unconscious impulses, left them unable to take on mature relationships, public responsibility, and independent activity.

In the broadest sense, Lasch and others are engaged in a critique of the effects of rationalization in late capitalism. Rationalization means that impersonal, abstract ways of transmitting values of behavior, exercising authority, and insuring conformity, have replaced familial communal culture. Relationships of exchange—commodities—have increasingly occupied the area of daily life that used to be carried on by cooperative, concrete relationships between individuals. Capitalist enterprise, no longer confined to industry, subordinates all activities of everyday life to the production of profit. Rationalization means also that authority is no longer located in identifiable personal or symbolic institutions and bonds between people. It is now naturalized, or reified, as a function of the social organization that takes on an aura of immutability. In the wake of these developments, no doubt, earlier forms of personalized authority—for example, paternal authority—are easily idealized and used to critique the present.[8]

My purpose is not to dispute the destructiveness of societal rationalization but simply the ideal that is being used to pose the problem. I question whether the oedipal model, with its affirmative view of paternal authority as a *sina qua non* of autonomy, is an ideal or universal path of development to individuality. This is not to say that the theory of the Oedipus complex is simply wrong or irrelevant. In those aspects that pertain to the affirmation of childhood sexuality and the power of the unconscious imagery that expresses it, the theory remains central to much clinical endeavor. This phenomenological relevance stands apart from the (increasingly generalized, schematized) use of the oedipal model of socialization since Freud's time, which assumes that internalization of authority is necessary to differentiation. It is this model that I propose to investigate, not as a universal, but as an *ideal type* of socialization in our culture. I propose to explain what the Oedipus complex and its waning can tell us about gender domination in our society. I assume that the oedipal model probably reflects quite accurately the way that individuality has been developed in our culture, but this development can no longer be accepted as the only possibility of human development. The apparent crisis of this pattern of socialization suggests that we should question rather than defend this form of individuality and its connection to authority.

The crux of both the earlier oedipal model and its contemporary reformulations seems to be the notion that unless some form of authority is internalized, the individual will remain dependent on others for what she/he ought to embody in the self. Here lies the oedipal riddle: why is authority central to developing autonomy? Why must differentiation be linked to domination, the growth of an autonomous self to the acceptance of authority over the self? How can internal assimilation of paternal power possibly be a route to individual autonomy? Freud answered the question by referring to a natural, universal characteristic of human beings. He argued that no pleasure or gratification once experienced is ever willingly given up. The child must be forced to give up the maternal love object by its fear and respect for the father. More generally, Freud maintained that the instincts were fundamentally conservative, pushing us to return to earlier states, and that the ego only develops under pressure of the outside world.[9] Freud spoke of dependency in the sense of "dependent upon the approval of external authority" and saw the intervention of authority as the agent to dispel this dependency. For later theorists it was only a step to the generalization that human beings do not willingly differentiate. Thus Lasch maintains that "men do not wish to be free."[10] The emergence of the autonomous self in all aspects can, by this logic, be attributed to the intervention of the father and the oedipal resolution. Paternal authority is seen as the source of differentiation.

If we are not to rest with this contention, we must first examine more closely the basis on which the Oedipus complex continues to be given its importance. The oedipal conflict has been seen as the culmination of the preoedipal struggle to differentiate and to relinquish infantile omnipotence.

The oedipal wish to make the mother one's own exclusive love object has been interpreted as a later expression of the same longing for fusion and return to omnipotence. Chasseguet-Smirgel has suggested we might view "the wish to be big like father and to thus possess mother . . . [as resulting] from nostalgia for primary fusion, when the infant enjoyed fullness and perfection."[11] Possession of the loved one (in the sexual imagination) is a more developed version of, or substitute for, the lost sense of oneness with her. However, actual fulfillment of the incest wish would mean return to oneness, or death of the self. It is this danger of complete narcissistic regression, or death of the self, that the superego protects against by prohibiting incest.[12]

But the superego itself represents a transformation of early narcissism, growing out of the earliest ego ideal. The origins of the superego, Freud thought, lay in the early identification with the omnipotent parental object in the period when self and object were one. "Man has shown himself incapable of giving up a satisfaction he once enjoyed. He is not willing to forgo the narcissistic perfection of his childhood . . . he seeks to recover it in the new form of an ego ideal. What he projects before him as his ideal is the substitute for the lost narcissism of childhood in which he was his own ideal."[13] It is the superego, heir to the early longing for perfection and omnipotence, that modifies and insures renunciation of the longing.

There is an ambiguity at the heart of this formulation that is the marrow of the difficulty in the affirmative view of authority. The superego is both part of the problem and part of the solution, a contradiction that Freud was more aware of than many of his successors. In his lengthy disquisition on the need for authority in *Civilization and Its Discontents* Freud develops this contradiction in terms of the superego's role in curbing aggression. The expression of aggression, he suggests, provides "an extraordinarily high degree of narcissistic enjoyment, owing to it presenting the ego with a fulfillment of the latter's old wishes for omnipotence. The instinct of destruction, moderated and tamed . . . provide[s] the ego with the satisfaction of its vital needs and with control over nature."[14] But the superego grows out of internalization. It is fueled by the "same harsh aggressiveness" which it turns against the ego in its efforts to curb this satisfaction of "the omnipotence wish."[15]

Thus in both Freud's formulations on the origins of the superego, whether pertaining to the desire for perfection or the pleasure of aggression, it never escapes the taint of omnipotence. The superego is a sublimation, not a cure for omnipotence, using the grandiosity and aggression of early narcissism to fuel its demands for self-control. Herein lies the irony: the very authority that keeps omnipotence in check derives from this same fantasy of omnipotence its ultimate force in the psyche. The superego works only because it inspires the fear and promises the perfection of the earliest authority. Its ambiguous nature is rooted in its origin because what we experience or wish to experience as omnipotence is really the state of our greatest dependency.

Perhaps it is not too far-fetched to compare Freud's model to the reflections on self-interest and the state of nature entertained by the early theorists of liberalism. The state of nature was a myth of the absolute freedom to pursue self-interest, in which the only limit to one's own pursuit was the unbridled self-assertion of every other individual. Thus it was argued that the institution of rational limits by legitimate (consensual or not) governmental authority was the only hope of preserving some of the independence that was hypothetically part of man's [sic] natural state. The rational character of authority was due to its obligation to preserve what is realistically possible in the way of freedom at the price of some absolute, naturally endowed autonomy and also to the appeal to self-interest: only with the acceptance of some limit to absolute self-interest, only with some reasoned willingness to curtail immediate self-assertion, are the conditions for the expression of self-interest insured. Rationality, then, is fueled by self-interest even as it is also used to curb self-interest. By limiting self-interest, rationality actualizes it.

Analogously, the superego has the double function of protecting and limiting the absolute claims of the self. It is both fueled by narcissism and serves to curb it. As Freud conceived it, the superego was the internalization of two seemingly opposite injunctions (and here as nowhere else does the male derivation of this theory become apparent): the father's command, "you may not be like me," means that the superego forbids incestuous fusion with the mother. The command, "you must be like me," enforces the distinction between the mother, who is object of love, and father, who is object of identification.[16] The mother, love-object, now represents lost dependency; the father, object of identification, now functions as the ideal of future autonomy. One is no longer permitted to identify with the mother because this is also a form of fusion, even more primitive than possession of her. So both commands have the function of forbidding fusion and dependency. The identification with the mother, being feminine like her, is now experienced as dangerous regression, dedifferentiation. The superego seems to forbid omnipotence or fusion in all aspects—being one with, being like, or possessing the source of perfection. Yet it does not do so completely. For it promises gratification in the future: if you are good and realistic and independent now, if you defer gratification and control yourself, you may one day possess and control someone like mother. It is this premise that makes for the specifically *rational* character of paternal authority. In Weber's sense, rationality is based upon the appeal to self-interest. The child wants to destroy authority but instead identifies with and internalizes it. The power, or threat behind the promise—like the carrot and the stick—is gradually lost to consciousness. Bowing to reality by submitting to paternal authority has this dual element of prohibition and promise of fulfillment. In the case of the wish for omnipotence this promise turns out to be fatal.

Here it must be added that this promise foreshadows the structure of the future relationship between adult men and women, the outline of gender domination. The power of the oedipal paradigm derives from its ability to explain simultaneously the development of gender identity and the development of individual selfhood. It is highly significant that it does this by collapsing individuality and masculinity. The oedipal father represents our peculiar form of individuality; his authority represents the only alternative to remaining undifferentiated; his freedom up till now is the only freedom. He teaches us the lesson that she who nurtures us does not free us, that he who frees us does not nurture us, but rather rules us. As we shall see later, this constellation is the basis for gender domination in our culture.

Equally significant about this constellation is the split or polarity that it institutionalizes between two essential needs, nurturance and freedom. Acceptance of the oedipal resolution means accepting this polarity. *Either* we differentiate or remain dependent; *either* we bow to reality or we remain infantile; *either* we deny our needs or we are enslaved by them. The Oedipus complex institutionalizes and reifies, gives social form and assigns gender to this polarity. The superego redefines the utopian longing to recover the unity of these needs as the prohibited and dangerous regression to total dependency and loss of self. The necessity of the superego is intimately bound up with this split between nurturance and freedom as well as with the human reluctance to differentiate.

We are now much closer to the heart of the question of why human beings require authority, the oedipal riddle. On the basis of the foregoing discussion of the Oedipus complex, the superego, and its origins in the experience of narcissism, several more specific sets of questions emerge. First, there is the question of the necessity of paternal authority and its internal form, the superego, in preventing regression or enforcing differentiation. We must ask why dependency should retain its exclusive allure even after we are no longer helpless? Why is the mirroring of autonomy not sufficient to anchor autonomy? In short, don't human beings want to differentiate? The second set of questions has to do with the splitting between autonomy and dependency, between nurturance and freedom, that is enjoined by the oedipal superego. We must ask why identification and object love must be directed to opposing parents in the Oedipus complex. Why does independence or individuality consist of rejecting identification with one parent? And why is this split projected along gender lines? Finally, there is the paradox that the superego emerges from the same impulses it is needed to control. We must inquire into the consequence of giving up omnipotence by projecting it onto a realistic external authority and then internalizing it in modified form. Is the dependency that is hidden in the illusion of omnipotence not the well-kept secret of the superego? Is this method of control any less dangerous than the regression it is supposed to prevent? Is rational authority less dangerous, its claim to power smaller than the naked domination it is supposed to replace?

As psychoanalysts have explored the early conflicts around differentiation and the early fate of our normal narcissistic needs to develop self-esteem, a perspective different from that afforded by the oedipal model has developed. Increasingly, clinical theory and practice emphasize the early dyadic experience of differentiation in the development of psychic structure and deemphasize drives or intrapsychic factors. The analysis of preoedipal experience, which focuses on the mother and the maternal-child dyad, has allowed many psychoanalysts who began with Freud to move beyond some of his categories. Both from within and close to traditional psychoanalysis, as well as from outside it, positions have emerged that challenge the view of human beings as essentially conservative, unwilling to give up old satisfactions for new. Indeed, they challenge the primacy of oedipal experience in individual development.[17]

This perspective is evident in the work on narcissism by Heinz Kohut, who has developed what he calls a psychology of the self.[18] Kohut understands the narcissistic dilemma primarily in terms of a failure to receive positive responses to one's early narcissistic strivings. The more satisfied the early strivings for self-display and autonomy, he believes, the less likely the self-image will remain grandiose. In the preoedipal phase there are two types of experiences needed: to merge with another person's cohesive self and to be mirrored by an audience in one's autonomous performance. Given essentially positive experiences, the child can react to minor losses by developing a sense of self and providing these functions for itself (optimal frustrations). Appropriate gratification would allow narcissism to develop naturally from fantasies of omnipotence to real autonomy. Kohut questions whether the Oedipus complex is truly a ubiquitous experience, whether it is not a failure of parental responsiveness to the child's assertiveness that calls forth the sexual and hostile attitudes known as oedipal.[19] It is also noteworthy that Kohut distinguishes between two different kinds of object relationships: the idealizing one that permits reliable dependency and the mirroring one that encourages autonomy. It is these functions that become split and set up as either/or in the oedipal constellation.

This perspective suggests a new answer to the first set of questions as to whether the development of autonomy might not be voluntary, dependent upon the *responsiveness*, but not the *authority* of the parent. According to

Freud's view of the drives, this could never be the case, for the very nature of the libido directed toward others is asocial. Object relations theory, an offshoot of orthodox psychoanalysis, has for some time maintained a different view of the drives. It has argued that the primary drive, or libido, seeks not release of tension or pleasure but the object as another person. Subsequent research in ethology and human infancy bears out the perspective that humans are motivated by an impulse toward attachment to specific persons from the beginning of life.[20] This attachment is not based simply upon physiological need or dependency, as Freud thought, but it is an essentially social impulse. Attachment develops through the active participation of both child and parent. It is an impulse that pushes toward a deepening awareness of the other's independent existence, the culmination of which is mutual *recognition*.

Recognition of the other's independent existence, a vital aspect of differentiation, goes hand in hand with the assertion of one's own independence. The ability to recognize significant others and to initiate and regulate social interaction begins to develop by the fourth month of life.[21] In addition to its early capacity for sociability the infant shows a disposition to assert itself, to explore and master the environment as well.[22] It might be possible to posit two fundamental capacities that, in our culture at least, shape human development: the strivings toward the *other* for connection, attachment, closeness; and the strivings toward assertion of *self* for activity, mastery, and exploration.* These two capacities define a human nature that strives to become independent and differentiate self from other, as well as to remain connected to and protected by a sense of oneness with a loved and trusted companion. These strivings, or capacities, are intertwined from the beginning of life, and both constitute the process of successful differentiation, even as they both contribute to successful attachment.

Assuming such innate dispositions, the vehicle of differentiation appears to be not prohibition and injunction by authority but recognition by a loved other: appropriate mirroring of autonomous activity and secure confirmation of connection and closeness. Is this perhaps an overly optimistic, "oversocialized" view of human nature? I don't think so. In my view the notion of such primary strivings—I shall call them object and activity strivings—

---

*While the terminology I use to describe these two tendencies may be somewhat arbitrary, the intention behind them should be clear. The joy of the infant who has just climbed a ladder and stands crowing at the top and the rejoicing to see the loved parent return home are distinct experiences that refer to self-assertion and attachment, respectively. These two capacities cannot develop independently of one another, though our conventional usage implies that they can by making independence the opposite of dependency. It has therefore been suggested that we think not in terms of dependency but of attachment, the loving bond that can be as strong on the part of an independent person as a dependent one, if not stronger.[23]

opens the way for profound conflict. This notion helps to explain those conflicts that define psychological life in our culture—between autonomy and mutuality, nurturance and freedom. The two tendencies easily, if not inevitably, assume an antithetical relationship to one another. I think the splitting of object and activity strivings is the key to that split between two kinds of objects in the Oedipus complex—between the ideal object of attachment and the mirror of exploration and between the objects of love and identification. This polarity becomes the greatest obstacle to differentiation, although it appears in our culture as a necessary path to it. To conceptualize this polarity, we must imagine a possible unity that the oedipal model has pulled apart. Ideally, as the study of preoedipal experience suggests, both capacities need to be recognized and responded to in the same relationship. We must now consider how these strivings become divided and opposed to one another. The answer lies in what I call the paradox of recognition.

Human beings require recognition to develop a sense of their own agency. Autonomous selfhood develops, and it is later confirmed chiefly by the sense of being able to affect others with one's acts. Ultimately, such confirmation also allows us to develop an appreciation of the other's subjectivity, to recognize another person. Such recognition of the other is as much the culmination of true differentiation as is autonomy. Developing the awareness of self and the awareness of the other are really parts of the same process. Paradoxically, the need for recognition means that we are dependent upon another person to acknowledge our independence. In our very attempt to establish independence from the other person, we are dependent on that person to confirm or recognize our independence. It is this paradox that governs our first relationship, the relationship between infant and primary parent (object attachment). The child is in the position of having to (metaphorically) destroy the authority of the one it loves and depends on in order to be independent. Because it is so difficult to endure this paradox, the impulse to split these vital needs easily takes over. This paradox is the key to how the needs for autonomy and for recognition become split and opposed, as well as to the connection between domination and differentiation.

This theoretical construct corresponds remarkably to the findings of Mahler, Pine, and Bergman in their observation of infants and their mothers.[24] The paradox of recognition corresponds to the dynamic that they term the rapprochement crisis. In the rapprochement phase the toddler insists that the mother "share" in all his/her newfound discoveries and performances and seeks validation for his/her self-assertion. Although more independent, he/she is not as content as earlier to discover the world without this constant affirmation. The child's contradictory wish is to be (and be recognized as) "separate, grand and omnipotent on the one hand, and to have mother magically fulfill their wishes, without their having to recognize that help was actually coming from the outside, on the other."[25]

The most important attempt to explain these interconnections, the first articulation of this paradox, was Hegel's discussion of the struggle for recognition.[26] The struggle for recognition becomes a struggle to the death—as if only by risking death (of the self) can one's autonomy (the self) be established. Each self struggles to achieve its selfhood in the eyes of the other. So each is caught between the need to negate the other and the need to be recognized by the other as an equal. Hegel asserted that in order to exist for oneself one had to exist for another, that each person must affect one another through one's acts. In order to be recognized by someone, one must recognize him or her in return. Hegel's point is that absolute independence is not possible (for self-conscious beings) because mutuality is a condition of independence. Recognition of the other person's independence means accepting one's own dependency rather than denying it: the person whom we need to recognize us is outside our control. Should we obtain control over the other, the other would no longer be an independent subject capable of conferring recognition upon us. However, as human beings do not wish to "give up" their absolute independence, they often do attempt to obtain power over the other person as if by doing so they could solve this dilemma of the need for recognition. The struggle for recognition culminates in the relationship of domination, master and slave.*

Hegel's interpretation of the problem suggests that the refusal to relinquish omnipotence occurs not because we cling to dependency but because it is too painful to acknowledge it. While Hegel, like Freud, believes that human beings do not voluntarily give up omnipotence, he confronts the ego with the intrinsic necessity of giving up independence in order to obtain it. The intervention of authority—the acceptance of domination—is not necessary to achieve independence, however. Rather, caught between the inherently social nature of selfhood (self-consciousness) and the desire for absolute independence, the ego creates domination. Because of this conflict, one self subjugates another. Indeed each self struggles to be the subjugator, for the first time, as it were. Hegel's metaphor of the struggle for recognition is, not a justification of authority, but an explanation of its origins as domina-

*In his discussion of Hegel in *Authority*, Richard Sennett attributes to me the notion that the master-slave relationship is "best thought of in terms of the pleasure which power gives." This in no way represents my argument, which is precisely that recognition is a goal in itself and power a derivative of the desire for recognition. My point is more adequately presented in his statement that recognition means self-confirmation: "If you take account of my needs and desires in the way you act, then they are real and I am real."[27]

tion (*Herrschaft*). Domination is a substitute for or escape from differentiation, from recognizing another's independent existence.

Domination is a substitute for differentiation not only for the subjugator but also for the dominated. This gives us an added perspective on the acceptance of domination, internalization of authority. Here, so beautifully put by George Eliot, is an illustration of the oedipal resolution: "I will accept your (the father's) power if you will let me become like you." She wrote, "We are all of us born in moral stupidity, taking the world as an udder to feed our supreme selves: Dorothea had early begun to emerge from that stupidity, but yet it had been easier for her to imagine how she would . . . become wise and strong in his strength and wisdom, than to conceive with that distinctness which is no longer reflection but feeling that he had an equivalent centre of self, when the lights and shadows must always fall with a certain difference."[28] It is easier to immerse ourselves in the power of the father rather than to become autonomous on our own, to accept his principle of difference rather than our difference from him. Yet it is the very opposite of that feeling by which we know the other to be truly different from ourselves.

True differentiation involves not only the awareness of the separation between self and other but the appreciation of the other's independent existence as an equivalent center. Properly speaking, *recognition is the activity of the object striving and the activity striving is realized through the recognition by the object*. The most vital aspect of differentiation is the ability to see the other person as an independent subject—someone who is both similar to and different from, connected to but separate from the self. True differentiation means accepting dependency not as dangerous regression but as enjoyable connection. It lies not in the splitting of autonomy and recognition but in accepting the tension of their paradoxical relationships. It means tolerating the ambivalence of being connected to and separate from another without the defense of imagining oneself becoming like some all-powerful other. Only by giving up the aspiration to complete control can both self and other be experienced as vibrantly distinct, as in the feeling that "I am I and you are you."

As I have stated elsewhere, the struggle for recognition entails a dialectical tension.[29] If one person completely controls another, the other ceases to exist as a person who can recognize him or her. If the other does not offer that sense of uncontrollability but appears to succumb entirely to the first person's power, then this other will no longer appear as a person. So in the earliest struggle for recognition, the mother must at some point actually remove herself from the child's sense of control, of omnipotence. She must establish her existence as another subject, as a person, that the child too can have a sense of selfhood. If the mother herself is not able to tolerate this degree of differentiation from her child, to inflict this pain upon her or him, or if she is able to do so only by asserting her own total control over the child, the child's narcissism will either be unrealistically inflated or wounded. The outcome of the early experience of differentiation from the mother-child dyad (for this dyad is the usual context in our society) depends upon the mother's responses in the first years of life, not upon later paternal intervention.

So far I have argued that human beings do wish to differentiate, to become autonomous, but that autonomy itself is an ambiguous phenomenon. It cannot be realized as absolute independence, but only in conjunction with what, in our culture, is often defined as its opposite: mutual recognition. Mutuality is often experienced as intolerable because it involves acknowledging dependency. To the extent that such dependency is perceived as a threat to autonomy, the individual must protect her/himself by identifying with someone she/he imagines to be truly strong and independent. The process of escaping differentiation by this use of authority parallels the attempt in which domination, or control over the other, substitutes for mutual recognition.

The superego can be seen not as a necessary agency to insure differentiation but as a mechanism of these "false" forms of differentiation. By forcing the repudiation of dependency, the superego reflects the authority it derives from, an authority that also keeps secret his dependency and appears ideally autonomous. In other words, a one-sided or false differentiation is promoted by the solution in which one subject tries to repudiate his/her own dependence and insure the submission of the other. This sort of independence, which is not based on the mutual reciprocal appreciation of distinctness, is promoted by the internalization of the father as an ideal of absolute autonomy.

This form of false differentiation can, I believe, be seen as institutionalized in the Oedipus complex and perpetuated in oedipal socialization. Man/father achieves absolute autonomy because woman/mother represents dependency. Individuality, then, is constituted by what is male, by the permanent assignment of man to the role of subject, through the father's assertion and insistence on complete independence. Originally it is through this denial of subjectivity to women that men lose the mirror of their subjectivity. Recognition occurs not through the love relationship but only in the competitive struggle with other men. Man's domination of woman has found expression in the oedipal relationships in which the split between male and female is reproduced in each generation. Let us examine more closely how this process of splitting between love and identification, nurturance and freedom, is embodied in the Oedipus complex; how the form of individuality we are familiar with grows out of these splits.

The oedipal father is the enforcer not of true differentiation but of splitting and polarity. In our model of the preoedipal experience, the tension between recognition and autonomy occurs in relation to one figure, traditionally the mother. In the oedipal model, identification, that is, validation for autonomy, is projected onto the father; love, recognition by the other, is projected onto the mother. Each partner becomes the object of one striving, and the price of autonomy is, of course, relinquishing the love object, and so, repression of the object striving itself. Thus the father demands not only that the two tendencies be split, but that the object striving be subordinated to the activity striving, that autonomy develop at the expense of mutual recognition. He denies the contradictory unity of the differentiation, which includes the assertion of self *and* the recognition of the other.

The splitting of this unity does not begin at the oedipal level. But it is consolidated and institutionalized in terms of gender at this point. The contradiction begins in the preoedipal experience of differentiation and gender identity, based on the paradox of recognition: the felt tension between dependency and autonomy, attachment and separation. The classical preoedipal model has failed to wholly grasp this tension. To a large extent it has been construed teleologically in terms of the oedipal model, as if the oedipal conflicts represented a graduation from the earlier stage. Consequently, differentiation is conceived from the beginning largely in terms of independence and separation rather than in terms of the positive capacity to appreciate the mother's subjectivity.[30] The ability to recognize her selfhood is confounded with sexual renunciation, giving up the hope of possessing her. But, of course, recognition means more than this. Similarly, in the classical preoedipal model, self-assertion and activity are seen only as separations from, not as connections to, other subjects. In actual fact, a baby's assertiveness develops as much through trying to affect the parent as through detaching itself from the parent.

In this sense we could say that the classical preoedipal model sees differentiation through the lens of male experience. For it stresses separation from rather than recognition of the mother. And the denial of identification with the mother is the great imperative of male differentiation in both phases. The little boy is to think he is, or must be, nothing like the one he loves and who loves/nurtures him. This repudiation of identity also functions as a denial of dependency. It is an attempt to differentiate by dominating or objectifying the other person. Unconsciously, denying the mother's subjectivity and the need to identify with her confirms the sense of omnipotence— in this case of self over object. Furthermore, not merely the identification with the mother but identification as a mode of relating is repudiated. The two elements of recognition, identification and distinguishing self from other, are split. One no longer feels both the *same* as and *different* from the other—one only feels different. Similarly, one feels not connected and separate but only separate. The capacity for identifying with, feeling like, is henceforth feminine, an aspect of the forbidden narcissistic fusion. Female children, whom Freud saw as remaining narcissistic, could develop the capacity for identification—but, in his view, at the expense of their autonomy, conscience, and ability for object love.[31] The girl's narcissism is only partially fulfilled—her need for mirroring of activity and autonomy is denied.

Since the mother is deprived of subjectivity for men—and this fact of woman's domination seems the most probable origin of this pattern of differentiation—the identification with her would mean a loss of subjectivity. Activity, differencing, and nonidentification are equated with the father and with individuality (subjectivity) in itself. But also, object love without identification does turn the mother into an object—she is only different, The Other. Since boys are forced to achieve their individuality by repudiating dependency and the identification with the mother, they become fit for the stalemate of one-sided or false differentiation. Since girls are denied identification with the father, who stands for difference and separation, they are unable to achieve the accepted form of autonomy. Each gender is able to represent only one aspect of the self-other relationship; each gender plays a part in a polarized whole. One is independent, the other dependent; one master, the other slave.

Neither gender can appreciate difference, for each is forbidden the identification with the different parent. Hence, identification with someone who is, in part, different is virtually an unknown feeling. One can only imagine identifying with someone essentially like oneself, someone who is in the same category. Identification then assumes an all or nothing quality—it threatens dedifferentiation, the regression to loss of identity. It is not developed as one part of the object striving for recognition, the part that feels likeness within difference. Furthermore, only identification with the father's activity, with the father as activity principle, is considered to be a form of differentiation. The process of recognition, the coming of activity and object strivings that makes up true differentiation, is totally devalued and repressed. To differentiate under the aegis of the oedipal father is to do so one-sidely and falsely. The oedipal father has become an embodiment of this form of differentiation—of one side, the principle of difference over likeness, activity over object love, object love over identification. He represents and enforces the principle of polarity—the conflict of opposites—as the context for individual development.

Thus far I have described an ideal type of differentiation and its consequences for our system of gender and our type of individuality. It is important to bear in mind that the oedipal model is an ideal type and that the contradictions and polarities that arise from oedipal socialization are far less clear in "real life." This conceptual scheme does shed light upon the intimacy of the connection between autonomy and authority in our culture. As Freud developed it, the oedipal model purported to speak for nature rather than for history: it assumed the inevitability of domination and gender difference. This inevitability and immutability no longer seem so self-evident. According to the model, we must have someone outside the first dyad to recognize our difference from the mother, to free us. This seems quite reasonable and does not conflict with the idea that humans have as much desire for independence as for fusion. It simply means that our drive for independence must be recognized, finding resonance in a person other than the one from whom we are becoming independent. But why should this person be essentially different from the first? Why not simply two (or many) mothers? What is not convincing in the oedipal father's intervention in the dyad is not only the element of authority but also the element of polarity, opposition. To provide recognition of the child's independence, the father need not enforce the principle of difference, embody the repudiation of dependency, deny the mother's common subjectivity. He need not have been a less nurturant or nonparticipating parent in the child's earliest life. These aspects of his role are a function not of the inevitable course of differentiation but of institutionalized gender domination.

Similarly, the mother's inability to model autonomy is also a function of her debasement in the present gender system. The metaphor of the Oedipus complex is the point at which the child struggles with and accepts that he is not the center of his mother's life. The father sets this limit. In fact, true differentiation requires that the child perceive its mother as an equivalent center not only because she belongs to father (or, in the modern version, loves father). Rather, the child must be able to gradually experience this nurturing relationship as a relationship between persons, a relationship that has limits. The mother sets a limit to one's own narcissism not only by loving another but by feeling and acting as a person who cannot be totally controlled by anyone. The mother who is not infantilized, shut out of the public world, dependent on her husband for her existence is more likely to experience herself as a person in her own right. Feminists have therefore argued that both parents should have an equal role in raising children and both have a foot in the world of adults. But this demand covers a far broader terrain than the rearing of children. It implies a challenge to the entire sexual division of labor, as well as to the separation of domestic/personal and productive/public spheres in our society. And this separation has been absolutely intrinsic to the growth of capitalism. It is this separation that, on the societal level, embodies the split between activity and recognition—the former is depersonalized and the latter is privatized. To women as mothers is assigned the Promethean task of raising individuals who can harmoniously balance what society pulls asunder. The family must bear the entirety of the individual's needs for recognition, needs that our small, child-centered families tend to cultivate intensely.[32]

The sweep of changes implied by dual-parenting, then, is enormous. Nor should we imagine that such changes in our culture and social structure would put an end to human ambivalence. Rather they would mean that the relief and pleasure, as well as the pain of being a separate person, are experienced together. This ambivalence would not be resolved defensively: by denying the need for nurturance and dependency, by attributing these needs only to babies and not to adult individuals, by controlling the other person so as to conceal one's feeling of dependency. Differentiation would not occur through the principle of polarity but through sustaining the unity of opposites in tension.

The analysis of the Oedipus complex as a polarization of drives that ought to remain interdependent raises a number of highly important, if presently insoluble, issues. What is the historical relationship between the rule of the father and the polarity within our culture, between nurturance and freedom? Is some form of authority inevitable because human beings are incapable of maintaining these drives in tension (as Hegel analysis might indicate), of enduring mutual recognition? The argument in favor of paternal authority is that without the father's rational authority the mother would permit endless fusion, blur all differences, keep us in a swamp of undifferentiated narcissistic bliss.[33] Such a view of the other can clearly be seen as a *result* of the gender polarity. This is how women-mothers appear once domination is institutionalized. This view of maternal love is also an expression of the revulsion and distortion that repression confers upon a forbidden wish, in this case a wish for fusion. The view of regression to narcissistic fusion as dangerous, requiring the vigilant prevention of the superego, is equally likely to be the result, rather than the origin of repression. While regression appears as an absolute, a journey away from civilization with no return, a more flexible ego might find it an excursion. One may wonder whether the regressive wish of men to remain dependent is not the wish for what is denied them. Analogously, one might find in the secret heart of women just the opposite, the longing for the activity and independence that have been the lot of men. Does not each sex crave what the other is permitted to express, the other pole of selfhood? In short, to what extent have the sexual division of labor and gender domination created what appears to us as natural forms of individuality, indeed, polarity itself?

The real dissolution of the Oedipus complex would make some of these speculations more real. Were we truly able in one fell swoop to wipe out centuries of socialization and confront the conflicts of earliest differentiation without institutionalized gender polarity, we might answer these questions. As it is, we can only wonder whether human beings are capable, no doubt with great anxiety, of suffering true differentiation. Our present state seems to offer less than such a total decline of the Oedipus complex. The change decried by Lasch and others as the end of oedipal socialization is something more like a loosening of it. This loosening reflects the lack of the powerful, idealized paternal authority of yesteryear, a far more intense generational conflict, the growth of a child-centered, emotionally intense family culture. While these factors have significantly changed the psychological relationship to authority, it is hardly clear that they have led to a decline in individuality or a failure of differentiation. They have led to a heightening of the contradiction between assertive activity and emotion connection. As Joel Kovel has so aptly put it, "In capitalism an enhanced individuality encounters a deadened public world." Public life "is nowhere enriched . . . to the level of demand created by the development of the personal sphere."[34] In fact, we are raising children with more individuality into a world where there are fewer opportunities to be author of one's acts or be recognized as such.

The depersonalization of authority and the less authoritarian role of parents have led to a new perspective on fathering, male identity, and the very nature of normal individuality. In the words of one psychoanalyst, "Modern life, both moved by and moving psychoanalysis, is redrawing the outlines and shifting the standards of normality" to include what were previously considered archaic[35] (and, I might add, female). Psychoanalytic work with patients Freud would have rejected (borderline, psychotic, preoedipal patients), of whom presumably far more come to clinical attention, has led to a questioning of the exclusion of "empathy and identification from normality." It has led to a respect for the "quest for irrational nondifferentiation of subject and object" as containing its own truth which challenges our received order of objectivity, rationality, and reality.[36] For many psychoanalysts, then, the opposite conclusion from Lasch's is emerging, that is, a questioning of the old ideal of individuality rather than the impulse to restore it.

These psychological changes do not necessarily mean that men no longer control society. The association of the male gender with the qualities and the practice of rationality and autonomy has not changed despite the diminishing opportunities for public exercise of individual powers. However, the image and practice of male individuality have suffered certain shocks. The superego's best kept secret, the father's dependency on the woman he controls, is out of the bag. As the dependent woman is no longer so reliable, this image of the father is no longer so convincing—indeed we might ask to what extent such changes have revealed self-esteem as a major clinical issue. The one-sidedness of male individuality, its inability to provide a solution to the tension between the needs for autonomy and oneness, has also been exposed. Further, the paradox between autonomy and authority has been intensified. The combination of affirmative and destructive attitudes toward authority on which autonomy was based is difficult to maintain when each previous generation of authority appears less rational to the new one. Thus, despite the persistence of our one-sided form of individuality, we are witnessing great dissatisfaction as previously hidden contradictions rise to the surface.

The crisis of authority exposes more clearly the paradoxes that were always inherent in the link between authority and autonomy, domination and differentiation. The final paradox to be considered is the use of an authority based on the ideal of omnipotence to control omnipotence. Thus far I have investigated two aspects of the oedipal riddle. First, I have asked whether the oedipal solution—the path to differentiation through domination—is necessary because otherwise human beings would refuse to give up the fantasy of omnipotence. To this I have answered that the human strivings for recognition and autonomy do not make this solution necessary but that their potential for conflict may explain why this form of development occurs. Second, I have addressed the psychological consequences of this solution, the kind of differentiation that oedipal socialization allows. I argued that the Oedipus complex embodies the polarity of gender and through it leads to a polarization of human capacities. These capacities would, in true differentiation, be united with one another—mutuality and autonomy, nurturance and freedom, identification and separation—in a creative tension. Breaking this tension, oedipal socialization promotes a false differentiation, a one-sided individuality that is identified solely with those capacities attributed to the male or father.

According to the oedipal model, the nature of the narcissistic bond with the mother necessitates the role played interpersonally by father and internally by superego. Either we seek to retain her as the omnipotent object we once experienced her to be—in that case we do not really separate from her, or we seek to become as we imagined her, omnipotent ourselves, as the only viable notion of how to be independent. "Mother does not need me, she is perfect; I will become perfect, cease to need *her*." This is the fantasy image of a person who cannot be affected by us, the unmoved mover, who need not recognize or be recognized by us. In Freud's view the very act of trying to establish independence derives from our aspiration to such omnipotence. Only the brutal head-on collision with the other shatters this fantasy. Seemingly, it is up to the father to be this other—he demands the renunciation of fusion with the mother, but he does not replace it with permission to fuse with him. Furthermore, he is supposed to represent a less omnipotent authority as a model of autonomy. That is, he is perceived neither as object or omnipotent ideal but as a rational, if authoritative, subject. What becomes of this fantasy of omnipotence and perfection after the oedipal collision with the father? Does this form of differentiation truly succeed in containing human aspirations to omnipotence, narcissistic longings for regression; or does it not, by repressing them, allow their reappearance in a more dangerous form?

I will argue that the aspiration to power—the attempt to deny dependency by controlling the other—is the result of this repression, and not the inevitable form in which narcissistic longings are expressed. It converts the struggle for recognition to a struggle for control over the other, over woman, over nature. The oedipal version of autonomy means that the mother's subjectivity must be denied and her nurturance rejected. It has often been stated that, as a body symbol, the phallus stands for the opposition to and differencing from the mother, the attempt to replace her (imagined) omnipotence with one's own.[37] Equally important are the mental and cultural myths that embody the repudiation of the mother and aspiration to her omnipotence. Thus oedipal socialization culminates in a deep sense that individuality is the accomplishment of autonomous activity at the price of mutual recognition. More generally, the principle of polarity, of either/or, becomes a normal way of experiencing the world. The image of human subjectivity is "purified" of the other (female) pole of human experience. A subject is no longer one who recognizes others, who nurtures others, who identifies with others. *He* is above all defined by his opposition to a world of objects, nature, woman, all that is other. The elements of mind that correspond to the male stance in differentiation reflect the emphasis of difference over sameness, separation over identification, as well as the depersonalization of the other. These are the elements of mind that correspond to a rationality that is objective, controlling, analytic, antiemotional.

The world orientation that emerges through the male posture in differentiation corresponds, then, to a peculiar form of rationality. While I cannot develop this contention at length here, I have elsewhere proposed that this rationality should be understood as male rationality because it is psychologically rooted in the male rejection of the mother, her nurturance, and her existence as a subject. The depersonalizing or objectifying attitude and the instrumental attitude toward others are reflected in this rationality. I have also suggested the parallel between male rationality and what Weber called instrumental rationality, *Zweck rationalitaet*, which he saw as the dominant type of rationality in modern society.[38] Instrumental or goal rationality means the orientation of activity to product rather than to process, or to human values and needs. It is oriented to control, calculability, and impersonal objectivity. In Weber's view it is this principle of Occidental rationality that allowed capitalism to develop and triumph in the West. I believe it is not unfounded to suggest that instrumental rationality is the generalization of the male pole in the psychosocial division of labor. And because the male position is the dominant position, this rationality was and is hegemonic in our culture. It can be viewed as an ideology that is born of women's subordination and that serves to perpetuate it.

The process of societal rationalization, as discussed earlier, means the replacement of personal forms of social intercourse by impersonal, abstract, bureaucratic institutions. It means the replacement of personal authorship, determination of goals and values, by impersonal social forces that seemingly have no author whatsoever. But the triumph of instrumental rationality, however much it undermines the visible forms of paternal authority, is actually the exaggerated and extreme form of male domination, the generalization of male rationality. The waning of paternal authority, and hence of the Oedipus complex itself, does not so much change the basic structure of domination as reveal it more clearly.

Speaking very schematically, the progress of rationalization means that rationality can no longer be contained within the personal, paternal forms that gave it life. It is now institutionalized in ways that challenge the more personal aspects of male subjectivity, the sense of rational individual authorship. The most dangerous upshot of this development is not that the loss of the internalized father allows the recurrence of the most primitive, regressive form of narcissism. Nor is it the erosion of personal, community, and kinship ties that allows the problem of exploiting others for one's self-esteem to emerge as an analytic problem and source of suffering (instead of being tolerated as the socially sanctioned way of treating one's wife or one's children). The most serious consequence of the dominance of instrumental rationality is most assuredly the destruction of nature. This "taming of the destructive instinct" has its own nemesis. It is in the technological rationality that has taken nature as its object to be exploited and controlled that the nemesis of male domination is most frighteningly apparent. The aspiration to omnipotence is nowhere more clearly evident than in the rape of nature. For while the oedipal father may prohibit the blissful union with mother and mother nature, he does promise control, possession, and the subordination of her as object. The use of such authority, individuality, and rationality as the oedipal father embodies to hold omnipotence in check only creates an ideology and practice of control that is far more destructive.

The notion of narcissistic omnipotence is ambiguous, connoting both the desire to be one with the world (eros) and the desire to be all there is (aggression). Omnipotence, which is always a fantasy rather than an experience, refers either to the pole of absolute merging or of absolute separation/ self-sufficiency. As absolutes, both represent death of the self. As polarities, they are expressed through gender division, the irreconcilability of the urges toward oneness and separateness.

In the course of this essay I have used the term omnipotence in both ways, as a fantasy or aspiration to perfection, to be one and all, as well as to be fused with the mother or the world. In so doing, I have slanted the issue of narcissism away from the reference to pathological ways of protecting self-esteem and toward the primary bond with the mother and differentiation from this bond. This slant probably reflects my bias that issues of self-esteem and power, and indeed ego, must be referred to issues of the fundamental need for the other, the object striving. So, for example, the patent efforts of men to control women must be understood foremost in the context of the ultimate need/desire for oneness with the beloved source of love, secondarily as a fear or revulsion against such fusion. The fantasy of omnipotence, in my view, refers first to this image of perfection in oneness. It is only later, as the paradox of recognition develops, that dependency is repudiated. From this perspective I have asked what happens when the quest for omnipotence is suppressed by an idealized figure whose power derives from that same omnipotence idealization—the superego that grows from the earliest ego ideal, the father who replaces the mother. I would suggest that, in the course of development, longings for perfect selfhood change from a preoccupation with love to a preoccupation with power and control. This probably occurs under the impact of loss, frustration, and feelings of help-lessness. The qualitative change from the search for recognition to the search for power is crucial to understanding how narcissistic longings are modified in oedipal socialization into a quest for control and power. It is this transformation that, in retrospect, makes the struggle for recognition come to resemble the struggle to destroy or subjugate the other. The attempt to replace the mother's omnipotence with one's own becomes a quest for control, not for bliss. This transformation in desire is consolidated as I have so far charted it, through identification with the oedipal father—his individuality, his rationality.

The theme of control over destiny is, of course, the subtext of the original Oedipus myth. The outcome of the myth is entirely opposite to the outcome that the Oedipus complex, in its ideal form, is supposed to produce. The very destiny from which he sought to escape and the very thing he sought to control overtake the oedipal father. I am referring here to the father of Oedipus, Laius, who sought to prevent his prophesied death at the hands of his son by setting him out to die. In this act he insured that everything he feared would take place. Oedipus survives unaware of his true parentage, returns to his place of origin, where he unknowingly murders his father and commits incest with his mother. Whether the act was committed knowingly or not, the main point is that such control of destiny as the father imagines is not really possible. It is highly significant that, contrary to Freud's usage of the myth, the problem begins with the father, who is seeking to avoid what in some sense is the fate of all fathers—to die and be superseded by their sons. The maternal principle, represented in the myth by the malevolent sphinx, triumphs in the end by bringing chaos, disorder, and death. The riddle of the sphinx, which only Oedipus solves, reminds us that we begin and end our lives in helplessness: what walks first on four legs, then two, then on three. Attempts to control events otherwise end in the vengeful return of the repressed, the intolerable experience of helplessness.

The myth of Western history shows that the attempt to control nature and woman-as-nature has been unparalleled in its destructiveness. The belief that internalization of rational authority protects us from our inner drive for omnipotence seems to parallel the misguided efforts of Laius to save his kingdom. In the attempt to control, to repress, the disaster one imagined is actually set in motion. Internalization is, after all, the reproduction of the guilty desire to replace authority by becoming it. Internalization is the translation of the desire to merge with an all-powerful other and/or submit to his authority into a desire to be such a person. The image of adult independence as such all-powerful control is one version of omnipotence. The persistence of this urge to be one with such an authority is equally dangerous whether expressed as conformity (submission to external power) or internalization (identification with that power). In reality individuals often swing from one stance to the other, as the contradictory imperatives to be one of a kind and be like everyone else simultaneously suggests.

Internalization proceeds by turning the force of omnipotence against ourselves; we may not be able to control the world, but we can at least control our own omnipotence. We may not be able to be truly independent of all other creatures, but at least we can control and objectify them so as to appear completely autonomous. Nor is internalization of authority the only source of human reason and morality, although certainly these capacities must be practiced and recognized to develop. It is important not to confound the internalized principles of paternal morality and guilt with the inner wellsprings of sociability and autonomy, to confuse the injunctions of the superego with our innate capacity to respect others and ourselves, which develops with the experience of mutual recognition. It is important to distinguish these abilities from the respect for individuality, which appears in our culture as power, self-control, the machismo of the lone wolf. The defense against omnipotence as fusion is fueled by the narcissistic wish embodied in our image of autonomy—to be one and all alone.

In *The Dialectic of Enlightenment* Max Horkheimer and Theodor Adorno proposed that the reasoning ego always contained this narcissistic kernel that finally culminates in the rationality of control. They argued that the omnipotence of thought adheres not, as Freud said, to magical primitive thinking, which respects the independence of nature. It adheres to Western science, which inherited Adam's fiefdom, dominion over every living thing. The voice of the realistic rational superego, which is thought to curb the limitless strivings for narcissistic grandeur, to chasten the sense that I am the world and the world is mine, in short to cut off omnipotence in the bud—this reasonable internal father seems to be invested with scarcely less omnipotence than we once attributed to mother or wished for ourselves. Where could one find a better spokesman for the oedipal voice of reason than in the man who wrote of his resolution with more than a hint of self-congratulation: "My third maxim was to try to conquer myself rather than fortune, and to change my desires rather than the order of the world, and generally to accustom myself to believing that there is nothing entirely in our power except our thoughts . . . and this alone seemed to me to be sufficient to prevent me from desiring anything in the future that I could not obtain."[39]

No doubt Descartes thought himself modest, claiming only himself and his thoughts for the sphere of omnipotence. Freud knew better—yet he could not but also succumb to the same ideal of autonomy and the same Faustian imperialism toward nature that it implied: "Where id was, there ego shall be . . . it is a work of culture not unlike the work of reclaiming the Zuider Zee."[40] Contemporary psychoanalysis often permits a more critical awareness of the trouble caused by this arrogant ego, its exclusion of the irrational, the subjective, the empathetic. Reason may conquer nature, but how can reason alone, especially the rationality of control, help us to find a way into the world of other subjects?

I have been trying to suggest that the authority of reason has collapsed because it carries the secret wish for omnipotence within it, as well as the exalted position we once attributed to less reasonable hopes. Reason has become materialized in the social world, not as reason, but as rationality—as the domination of impersonal, abstract bonds and of exchange value over the living web of social ties. I have argued that the psychology of our rational culture was transmitted by the internalization of paternal authority. This process has been accurately reflected and scientifically codified as the oedipal model. Thus the oedipal model seems to reflect the truth of our culture, the fatal polarity between autonomy and recognition, nurturance and freedom, subject and object. If it is true that the father, or the paternal principle, is no longer the vehicle of this rational autonomy; if his authority is now embodied in impersonal institutions; if autonomy and rationality are, as psychological traits, increasingly degendered and distributed among men and women; if maternal nurturance and recognition are also rationalized and limited—this reflects not the triumph of archaic impulses but of the rationality of control.

It is not hard to understand those who fear that now nurturance and maternal love have become infected with the ruthless rationality of the public sphere, that private life has been increasingly invaded by institutions of mass culture. The degree to which the image of acceptable manhood has become macho and more nurturant, to which independence and activity have become acceptable postures for women may seem to them small by comparison with the overwhelming destructiveness of our social systems. The immediate gains of the disruption of the private sphere caused by the waning of paternal authority may seem small to some. The painful effects of unstable families are perhaps more visible than the emancipatory effects. The long-range goals of androgyny, of parenting based on mutuality, equality, true differentiation, must seem wholly utopian in the context of our overwhelming instrumental culture and rationalized society.

Yet there are some grounds for some optimisim. The salience of oedipal conflicts may have decreased both because of the changes in parental authority and because of the emergent expression of needs for "preoedipal" experience—formerly "archaic" or female. True, the repudiation of the need for dependency and recognition, once embodied in the oedipal father, seems alive and well throughout our culture. He was heir to our narcissism, preserving it in the particular form of rational paternal individualism, and if he is no longer needed, it is because his legacy has achieved such enduring impersonal form. If this means that rational individualism no longer "works" psychologically, revealing its roots as a defense against helplessness and the ambivalence of differentiation, then we are faced with the alternative of reviving more primitive defenses (pathological narcissism) or of considering the possibility of a more terrifying state than we have yet been able to endure. But at least we are in a position to begin thinking about reunifying aspects of human life that have been split, preserved as antagonisms, in the gender system. We are in a position to think about the dangerous, destructive consequences of investing our omnipotence in rationality—a rationality that seeks to control the world, to dominate nature, to be as powerful as the imaginary omnipotent mother. We are in a position to face our narcissism, to find more constructive ways to nourish it, to satisfy our utopian longings for self-knowledge and perfection.

If we do not disclaim Narcissus in ourselves, it is because, as Marcuse wrote, his image is that "of the Great Refusal: refusal to accept separation from the libidinous object (or subject). The refusal aims at liberation—at the reunion of what has become separated."[41] I like to think of this liberation as the joy of being known. I like to think of this reunion as preserving the tension between the parts of ourselves that have become polarized into woman and man, mother and child, self and other, as the reunion of true differentiation and recognition, of the vibrant aliveness that says, "I am I and you are you."

Notes

1. Christopher Lasch, *Haven in a Heartless World: The Family Revisited* (New York: Basic Books, 1977), and *The Culture of Narcissism: American Life in an Age of Diminishing Expectations* (New York: W. W. Norton, 1979).

2. Most of the fundamental themes of Lasch's critique of narcissism were anticipated by the writings of the Frankfurt critical theorists: on the decline of paternal authority, Max Horkheimer and Theodor Adorno, *The Dialectic of Enlightenment* (New York: Seabury, 1972); Max Horkheimer, "Authority and the Family Today," in *The Family: Its Function and Destiny*, ed. Ruth Anshen (New York: Harper Brothers, 1949), pp. 359–374; on the use of psychoanalysis for social theory, Theodor Adorno, "Sociology and Psychology," *New Left Review* 46–47 (1967–1968): 67–81, 79–91; on the decline of the Oedipus complex, Herbert Marcuse, *Eros and Civilization* (Boston: Beacon Press, 1955), and "The Obsolescence of the Freudian Concept of Man," in *Five Lectures* (Boston: Beacon Press, 1970), pp. 44–61. Their position was further developed by Alexander Mitscherlich in *Society Without the Father* (New York: Harcourt Brace and World, 1969). Most recently, the idea of the decline of the individual has been presented by Russell Jacoby in *Social Amnesia* (Boston: Beacon Press, 1975). For a critical discussion of these important and early contributions to understanding the familial and psychic changes brought about in late capitalism, see my "The End of Internalization: Adorno's Social Psychology," *Telos* 32 (Summer 1977): 42–64, and my "Authority and the Family Revisited: Or, A World Without Fathers?", *New German Critique* 13 (Winter 1978): 35–58.

3. See Sigmund Freud, *The Ego and the Id* (New York: W. W. Norton, 1962), pp. 18–29. While Freud's interpretation of the Oedipus complex and its resolution pointed to the renunciation of the love object, or the desire for incest, not to dependency as such, I have sometimes made this transposition because I think it is appropriate to the sense of the oedipal model as it is used by Lasch and others. It signifies the contrast between early preoedipal and post-oedipal relations to the object. However, it should be noted that in this context dependency means, not "the need for the other," but the use of the other to provide something one ought to be able to provide for oneself.

4. The most comprehensive formulation of a psychoanalytic theory of early differentiation can be found in Margaret Mahler, Fred Pine, and Anni Bergman, *The Psychological Birth of the Human Infant* (New York: Basic Books, 1975). Many researchers on infancy would dispute the claim that infants initially perceive the mother as part of the self. The attribution of narcissism and omnipotence feelings to infants is seen as an adultopmorphism (see Emanuel Peterfreund, "Some Critical Comments on Psychoanalytic Conceptualizations of Infancy," *International Journal of Psychoanalysis* 59 [1978]: 427–441). While I agree with this criticism, I am interested here in criticizing psychoanalytic theory on its own terms, developing an "immanent critique."

5. The first view is expressed by Kernberg as follows: "The developmental state of the superego (particularly the ego ideal) and the nature of the predominant outcome of the oedipal conflicts . . . influence the degree to which any object relation is 'anaclitic'; that is, the degree to which there is a regression or fixation to normal infantile characteristics in which the dependent needs color both the self and the object investment." Otto Kernberg, *Borderline*

Conditions and Pathological Narcissism (New York: Jason Aronson, 1975), p. 324. The second view, expressed by Robert D. Stolorow in "Toward a Functional Definition of Narcissism," *International Journal of Psychoanalysis* 56 (1975): 179–185, is closer to the other seminal work on narcissism, Heinz Kohut's *The Analysis of the Self* (New York: International Universities Press, 1971). This view emphasizes the need for inner structures. In his most recent work, *The Restoration of the Self* (New York: International Universities Press, 1977), Kohut attributes scarcely any role to the superego.

6. Lasch, *The Culture of Narcissism,* pp. 11–12.

7. Ibid., p. 11. Lasch consistently attributes aggression to id impulses, and when they are out of control, it is because the parents' failure to punish only makes the superego more punitive and harsh. So he cites the father who mildly remarks in *Something Happened* that his daughter provokes him because she wants him to punish her. Viewed with a clinical eye, the scene reveals the daughter's provocation as an attempt to get her withdrawn father to engage and interact with her; she correctly, though not consciously, perceives his refusal as a passive aggressive form of punishment for demanding anything of him and for disturbing his withdrawal.

8. I have developed the theme of rationalization and decline of paternal authority in "Authority and the Family Revisited," where I use the term "instrumental culture" to describe the pervasiveness of depersonalized, product-oriented modes of interaction from which even the domestic sphere is no longer exempt.

9. It is difficult to assign such a determinate meaning to a concept as ambiguously and complexly developed as Freud's concept of the ego. A helpful discussion is provided by J. Laplanche and J. B. Pontalis in *The Language of Psychoanalysis* (New York: W. W. Norton, 1973).

10. "Contrary to Weinstein and Platt, men do not 'wish to be free.' They wish to remain dependent; only the renunciation of the mother and the internalization of the father's authority forces them to overcome this dependence." Thus Lasch in "The Emotions of Family Life," *New York Review of Books* 22, no. 19: 39.

11. J. Chasseguet-Smirgel, "Some Thoughts on the Ego Ideal," *The Psychoanalytic Quarterly* 45 (July 1976): 357.

12. Ibid., p. 349.

13. Sigmund Freud, "On Narcissism: An Introduction" (1914), in *General Psychological Theory,* ed. Philip Rieff (New York: Collier, 1963) p. 74.

14. Sigmund Freud, *Civilization and Its Discontents,* ed. and trans. James Strachey (New York: W. W. Norton, 1962), p. 68.

15. Ibid., p. 70.

16. Freud, *The Ego and the Id,* p. 24. Freud also states here that each individual develops an "inverted complex," an object-love for the same-sex parent and identification with the cross-sex parent. What is probably most significant is the maintenance of a barrier between identification and object-love.

17. Outside of classical psychoanalysis, the interpersonal school exemplified by Harry S. Sullivan early provided a notion of development in which oedipal issues were not primary. From within, the increasing emphasis on the preoedipal dyad in object relations theory (see Harry Guntrip, *Personality Structure and Human Interaction* [New York: International Universities Press, 1961]) offered a different set of assumptions about human nature. Most recently, Kohut's *Restoration of the Self* reorients the center of analytic treatment away from oedipal issues.

18. Kohut, *The Analysis of the Self.*

19. Kohut's recent work, *The Restoration of the Self,* questions whether the Oedipus complex as we know it is not the result of "empathy failures" on the parental side, of the environment's

failure to respond to the child's "whole self." He asks if "it is only the self of the child whose primary affectionate and competitive assertiveness is not responded to that is then dominated by unassimilated lust and hostility?" p. 247.

20. Attachment theory was chiefly formulated by John Bowlby. See *Attachment and Loss: Vol. 1 Attachment* (London: Hogarth, 1969).

21. Daniel Stern, *The First Relationship* (Cambridge, Mass.: Harvard University Press, 1977), p. 1.

22. Mary D. Salter Ainsworth has developed Bowlby's work to explain development in terms of a "more inclusive concept of a balance between exploratory and attachment behaviour." See Ainsworth, S. Bell, and D. Stayton, "Individual Differences in the Strange-Situation Behavior of One-Year-Olds," in *The Origins of Human Social Relations: Proceedings*, ed. H. R. Schaffer (London: Academic Press, 1971), p. 18. One of the earliest formulations that stresses the activity impulse of infants is Ernst Schachtel's *Metamorphosis* (New York: Basic Books, 1959). Research psychologists in the last decade have documented the active differentiating side of infant life, especially her/his search for experiences of contingency that confirm the sense of efficacy. See Susan Goldberg, "Social Competence in Infancy: A Model of Parent-Infant Interaction," *Merrill-Palmer Quarterly* 23, no. 3 (1977): 163–177.

23. Mary D. Salter Ainsworth, "Object Relations, Dependency and Attachment," *Child Development* 40 (1969): 969–1025.

24. Mahler, Pine, and Bergman, *The Psychological Birth of the Human Infant*, esp. pp. 76–108.

25. Ibid., p. 95.

26. G. W. F. Hegel, "The Independence and Dependence of Self-Consciousness: Master and Slave," chap. 4 A., *The Phenomenology of Spirit* (Hamburg: Felix Meiner, 1952), pp. 141–50. I have developed this analysis of the relationship between the need for recognition and domination at greater length in "The Bonds of Love: Erotic Domination and Rational Violence," *Feminist Studies* 6, no. 1 (Spring 1980): 144–174.

27. Richard Sennett, *Authority* (New York: Alfred Knopf, 1980), p. 127.

28. George Eliot, *Middlemarch*.

29. Benjamin, "Bonds of Love."

30. Feminist writers have seen recognition of the first other as crucial to differentiation, for they are aware of the relationship between non-recognition of mothers and domination of women. See Nancy Chodorow, *The Reproduction of Mothering: Psychoanalysis and the Sociology of Gender* (Berkeley: University of California Press, 1978), and Dorothy Dinnerstein, *The Mermaid and the Minotaur: Sexual Arrangements and Human Malaise* (New York: Harper and Row, 1976). Chodorow has made the important point that the emphasis of separation over relation in the differentiation process reflects a male bias, in "Difference, Relation and Gender in Psychoanalytic Perspective," *Socialist Review* 9, no. 4 (July–Aug. 1979): 51–70. This viewpoint is perhaps most compatible with Ainsworth's position ("Object Relations, Dependency, and Attachment"), which is critical of Mahler for stressing "hatching" over attachment. But it should be noted that Mahler (*The Psychological Birth of the Human Infant*) does not overlook the infant's developing awareness of the mother as a separate person, rather she places it in the questionable context of breaking out of a state of complete unawareness.

31. Stephanie Engel has provided an analysis of the way in which femininity, narcissism, and identificatory relatedness are associated and rejected, in "Femininity as Tragedy: Reexamining the 'New Narcissism,'" *Socialist Review* 10, no. 5 (Sept.–Oct. 1980): 77–104.

32. Joel Kovel suggests in his forthcoming book that as the family becomes more like a greenhouse, cultivating an individuality that has no place in the public sphere, women in particular become the locus of conflicting demands for individual independence and restful domesticity.

33. Dinnerstein, *The Mermaid and the Minotaur*, suggests that the mother's omnipotence is

the source of the turn to the father's more limited, rational authority. In so placing the locus of the problem in the mother's exclusive power over the child, she does, I suspect, confirm one major rationalization for male domination. Like de Beauvoir, she seems to share some of the negative view of dedifferentiation or merging as a danger rather than a repudiated and therefore distorted impulse.

34. Joel Kovel, unpublished.

35. Hans W. Loewald, "The Waning of the Oedipus Complex," *Journal of the American Psychoanalytic Association* 27, no. 4 (1979): 773.

36. Ibid., pp. 772–773.

37. The work of Jacques Lacan has generated the most attention to the function of the phallus as that which creates difference. See Gayle Rubin, "The Traffic in Women: Notes on the 'Political Economy' of Sex," in *Toward an Anthropology of Women*, ed. Rayna Reiter (New York: Monthly Review, 1975), pp. 157–210, and Chodorow, "Difference, Relation and Gender."

38. See my "Authority and the Family Revisited" and "The Bonds of Love."

39. Rene Descartes, *Discourse on Method and the Meditations* (1637) (Middlesex, Eng.: Penguin, 1968), p. 47.

40. Sigmund Freud, *New Introductory Lectures on Psychoanalysis*, ed. and trans. James Strachey (New York: W. W. Norton, 1965), p. 80.

41. Marcuse, *Eros and Civilization*, p. 154.

9

By What Authority?
Post-Freudian Reflections on
the Repression of the Repressive as
Modern Culture

Philip Rieff

For the last time, psychology.—Kafka, *Diaries*

In face of the metaphysical, even if you should have no other word for
it than simply death, all political concerns dwindle into nothingness.
—Huizinga, "Conditions for a Recovery of Civilization"

There is a memorable change in the face of authority in an otherwise poor
play by Shaw, *The Devil's Disciple,* the first of his three plays for Puritans—showing them up, as he thought. Richard, the disciple who has
pledged himself to the "devil," as he calls himself, must end, as he does, a
minister of the living God while the official minister, Anderson, finds himself, at the end, a soldier—a man of power. Early in the play, Richard
sounds the great and attractive prophecy of the therapeutic, at his solicitous
worst: "No child shall cry."[1]

Imagine a world in which no child cries. Where would be his joy if he
were incapable, even so young, of sorrow? As a source of civilizing sorrow,
as a refining device of realistic melancholy, some decently irrational *Cannot*
must be felt at their fingertips by all ages among wanton boys and girls; if
they are to become civilized, then, very early in life, all must feel the
offense, even before they think of doing something so harmless as pulling
the wings off a fly. If it be true, then guilt is the civilizing emotion. False
guilt follows another path, as we shall see. Throughout this essay, I shall
deal with this essential and suprarational—if not irrational—dynamic of
Cannot, inseparable as I think it to be from the dynamics of *distaste/taste* or
sense/sensibility. I intend to argue that true guilt is the distinguishing thing,
as between higher authority and lower.

From authority itself there is no escape. A "crisis" of authority derives not least from some more or less intellectually elaborate failure to understand that authority, higher and lower, is immortal and unalterable in its form. In that form, unchangeably vertical, however ingeniously the big children of modernity may try to level it, every lowering act produces the pain or fear humans experience as true guilt; every raising act produces a saving sense, as of being redeemed from guilt or of a remission from pain or fear.

A certain inversion now characterizes our common and received sense of what is lowering and what is raising in the form of authority. No culture can survive a widespread treatment of this common and received sense as if it were false and unworthy of enlightened minds. This essay proposes, without hope, a counter-enlightenment. Our great enlightenment, the slow work of the centuries since the Renaissance, has ended catastrophically, in our own time, not in the failure of authority, as is widely believed among the late enlightened themselves; rather, the catastrophe of our enlightenment lies in the success of its lowering movements.

Gulag and Dachau, torture and terror, are the dry-eyed children of our enlightenments. Some of our greatest talents are the last officers of our enlightenment and coeval with its dying genius. Nietzsche is the first fully self-conscious theorist of authority in modernity. I reckon Picasso the greatest painter of modernity and Joyce its chief storyteller. Not for the first time, and for more than reasons of familiarity, I shall work through certain facets of Freud, from whom I have taken certain hints toward a portrait of the true and yet always masked face of authority.

Imagine an authority that will not fail and cannot disappear. What, then, of its crises? I imagine that we mortals can only enact, and re-enact the raising or lowering possibilities of action stipulated in the social organization of our received culture. Any reference to a "crisis of authority" in contemporary American culture would refer to those strange pleasures that may be taken in lowering acts, or thoughts, within a vertical order of possibilities in their primacy. From that primacy culture delimits its operative acts.

Works of art, acts of thought, all sensibility and expression, are even more illuminative than they are operative acts. Hands may be washed as an illuminative gesture; they may be washed operatively. Both acts tend to merge; by that mergence, authority is carried in its culture. There can be no culture without authority as the mergence of illuminative and operative acts. From illuminative acts, which ordain the direction of operative acts, life takes its meanings and culture its energies. An act, in culture, can only become operative in the vertical. Try as we may, we cannot live horizontally in the vertical world of culture; so to prostrate oneself would be to live beyond the range of authority; such a life—such a culture without an authority that is either raising or lowering, and both—is impossible.

One way to imagine an impossible culture is to imagine the primacy of possibility, rather than its repression, as precisely that rebus we call "culture." I propose that what Freud named "primal repression" is the unrelievable pressure, in any and all cultures, against the primacy of possibility. That primacy cannot happen even in our wildest imaginings. Chaos is itself an order. Within a vertical of specifically operative acts become illuminative, the most disorderly acts take their positions in an order that is sacred. Those positions, in sacred order, must be, wherever they are, raising or lowering; or that complex of both I shall call "remissive."

Authority is that about sacred order which will not brook its levelings, however brilliantly they may be conceived. The very effort at leveling sacred order must be sensed as guilt. Pain is the objectification of guilt even at the possibility of a move downward in the vertical along which cultures express themselves as closures of possibility. The primacy of possibility is a negational inference of secondary realities in sacred order. A raising act, I shall call *interdictory*. A lowering act, I shall call *transgressive*. Mixed acts, what is not done, yet done, I have already called *remissive*. Much of our lives are spent in a remissive flux. The order of that flux is unchanging—I daresay, sacred.

Cultures give readings of sacred order; these readings are their arts and sciences. In this both natural and supranatural capacity, every man, born as he is into a culture, is both artist and scientist. Man is a reading animal, to the sacred manner born. Every effort to unlearn the sacred manner, even the most ingenious, must fail. Even our highest conceivable illiteracy is itself an achievement of those complex motifs by which, in our thoughts as well as actions, we are no longer able to read our endless rise and fall along that vertical of illuminative acts inseparable from every operative act. In the face of the metaphysical, "to be" is to suffer, more or less gladly, generally less than more, our raisings and lowerings within a vertical of possibilities otherwise not even to be entertained by the secondary imagination in safely distorted and distanced images. As we cannot cease to be fearful, but only resist knowing what we are fearful about, so we cannot lower ourselves permanently into the transgressive depths of authority. Fear prevents this free fall. Fear is the original respect in which we receive the fact that sacred order is evident even in our disorders. That we cannot kill authority is the beginning of wisdom. A fearful recognition of authority, even at its lowest, may also be the end and purpose of wisdom. Without timely readings of timeless order, no authority can put on even its briefest dress, to play hide-and-seek with freedom, conjuring such nervous tics of self-justification as would make an angel weep.[2]

What Freud psychologized as "primal repression" can be seen, less darkly, as that mindfulness that denies entry into consciousness of any and all lowering possibilities. Before such closed mindfulness, the true name of what Freud recognized negationally as the repressive unconscious, every fear in lowering position, persists both active and unaltered.[3] Equally active and unaltered: possibilities high enough to need no negations. Mind is not necessarily a reformed whore. I see no reason to call every risen possibility by its Freudian name, "sublimation." What is sacred does not rise out of what is profane. Interdicts do not derive from their transgressions; that theory is sheer gnosticism and so rings true to the modern mind. But its truth is challenged by the fact that enactable possibilities, including sexual acts, are not spiritualized. What is spiritual is always present, in our shifting obediences to the hierarchy of repressive imperatives from among which we are free to choose both what we are not to be and be, in our irreducibly complex responsibilities as enactors of sacred order.

Artful Self in Sacred Order

In its shifts within the vertical, self is an artful dodger; that would appear to go best without saying. Yet precisely what is self-evident, being sacred, occurs in constant repetitions. Repetition is authority in its form, making clear, in endless variations of such knowledge experienced, that self cannot endure a world imagined entirely profane, possibility undenied to consciousness. Authority is the achievement of rank order out of a primacy of possibilities so slow to change that primary possibility itself can only be inferred from secondary imaginings of it. Those secondary imaginings, generally named "Culture," direct humans in the manner and matter of what to deny to themselves. By these teachings of denial, the more commanding in their characteristic indirections—distortions and distancings—self has contained its own artfulness. Freud's rebus for these distortions and distancings, self in its unalterable artfulness, is negationally named "repression." In the equal and opposite rebus "sublimation," he supplied the negation of the negation. Sublimation is to repression as secular is to sacred order. It is the preferred term of modernity for those indirections by which artful self sounds out its directions, in painfully and slowly achieved addresses to the complexity of sacred order. Sublimations, themselves unconscious, by Freudian definition, will not be divorced from repression. Both occur with whatever cleverities of denial the mind contrives to conceal the worshipful element in the addresses that are self, more or less articulate, in sacred order. "Sublimation" is a concealing word, in face of what is sublime, for the prevalent doctrine of faithlessness, which is different from bad faith.

Theologies are but one form of address to sacred order; and by no stretch of the imagination always the most illuminative. Indeed, as Nietzsche thought, theologies reek of bad faith. Read aright, as a modernist reading instrument of sacred order, in which readings can be given only in negational language, Freudian doctrine reveals itself in the paradox of a faithless address to sacred order. That order is a dream from above. All the other dreams Freud interpreted were dreams from below.

It is widely acknowledged that Freud, like Weber, claimed to be religiously unmusical. But this is only to say that both Freud and Weber took their unconscious vows of faithlessness so early in life that neither could recognize himself for what he was: an intellectualizing rebel in sacred order, substituting for the specific commands of faith in life those terrible abstractions of command that pass for psychology or sociology. Beyond bad faith lies faithlessness. Freud's faithlessness is announced in the matter of his interpretation of dreams as possible only if they come from the bottom up and never from the top down: "If I cannot bend the Higher Powers, I will move the Infernal Regions." Freud never came closer to recognizing the downward direction of his movement in sacred order.

Though elsewhere I shall choose to work through Nietzsche, Kafka, Joyce, Picasso, Wilde, and other inversionists of obedience in sacred order, here Freud's works have been again chosen because none have had greater or more popular authority in the modernist culture to which the others also belong. That greater authority, downward, has come of popular, often caricaturing, imitations of Freud's resistances in sacred order. It is Freud's negationally sacred manner, far more than the apparently sexual matter of his doctrine, that accounts for his appeal to the classes re-educated in lowering versions of that manner. If that appeal is now ending, as I reckon, then the indirections of authority may be again turned around. We may be at the end of modernist inversions of sacred order. We can only have faith and wait; and see. Meanwhile, in the act of waiting, essays such as this are nothing more than wordy versions of proverbial wisdom successfully forgotten by the cultivated classes. All the intellectualizings that follow have been said far better and briefly in Proverbs 27:20: "The nether world and Destruction are never satisfied; so the eyes of men are never satisfied."

The Culture of the Never Satisfied

To be cultivated is to know, at least by indirection, through the artfulness of our recognitions, what it is to be obedient, and what is not, in those stipulations of sacred order that constitute authority in every culture. Authority must be deeply cultivated and long prepared. Every *Not*, if it is operative, needs settling enough in time to be conveyed, mainly through casuistries of excusing or critical reasons, across the generations by teaching classes that are sanctioned more by their propriety than property. Propriety is always subject to a certain nervousness about being breached. Authority is bound to take its toll in nerves. To live within the limiting dynamics of authority is to measure up to the prohibitions and permissions from which the metamorphic range of *illuminative/operative* acts derive. These metamorphoses stipulate, as they moralize, social reality. To live amorally may be possible to the Machiavellian or Nietzschean imagination, but that imagination can never satisfy the requirements of real life. In real life, nothing is neutral and moral indifference a pose.

Everything real is real because it exists within limits, a verticality at once illuminative and operative. Is handwashing obsessive or worshipful, symbolic or functional? A handful of dust takes direction in sacred order from its complex of illuminative and operative relations in the risings and lowerings we call "experience." A place, or we ourselves, can be more or less clean. Polluted or cleansed, brought down or up: there is fright at living in either extremity, interdictory and transgressive, of sacred order. Our fears, expressed in unconsidered rejections, first teach us what is acceptable, what heart's ease there may be in laughter and tears before thought. Every child must cry. Freud first named this fright, at the primacy of possibility, interior "flight."

There is an interior flight that leads self deeper into sacred order. It is this flight, necessary and inescapable, that now goes by its popular nickname, the apparatus of pain Freud named "repression." Daring as he was, Freud dared make little more than negational sense of repression. He admitted it into his theory on condition that it become, and never cease to be, his crucial problem. The illuminative facet of repression was itself repressed by the operative. Before this gatekeeping *Not* Freud sat all the main part of his intellectual life, without being able to know how cleverly he had recognized sacred order. That cleverity had to be negational. It follows that in Freud's unconscious denial of it, sacred order is like a woman who can never say no; her virtue is her complete want of virtue. With her, everything is possible and nothing is true. With Freud, the repressive, unadmitted as predicate of repression proper, imagines itself a little freer at last of its own limits.

To admit the repressive would have confronted Freud with the most frightful theoretical necessity: "of postulating a third *Ucs.*, which is not repressed."[4] That third unconscious, predicate of the second, raised a possibility superior to Freud's lowering second: that of making the "characteristic of being unconscious lose significance."[5] In the repressive repressed we may find the combination that unlocks again the meaning of authority. The repressive thus rendered by Freud, unrecognizable in its imperative as sacred order, becomes that very general rule, about the degree of distortion and remoteness from the primacy of possibility achieved by linked repressions proper, that Freud himself could not see.[6] Distanced from sacred order, tastes and distastes, addictions and abhorrences, become inexplicable or historical in their determining origins. Culture becomes the history of otherwise inexplicable splittings into oppositional modes of that primacy of possibility that aims only at its own expression.

Repression is to psychoanalysis as unknown gods are to pagan theologies. Repressive splittings make of every cultural expression an illuminative act that refers to Freud's own radical dualism more than it refers to the distancing arts of obedience and disobedience in sacred order. "Ambivalence," along with "ambiguity," becomes the code word, favored in modernity, for a faithlessness that forbids knowledge of sacred order. Freud's repression of the repressive allowed this forbidden knowledge to play upon its enactors. "Repression" became Freud's word for what culture must include: deeply forbidden knowledge; that which is, at once, known and unknowable. These intellectualizing and paradoxical resistances to the repressive predicate of repressions show the brilliance of the one kind of knowledge forbidden to us: of sacred order, for which Art and/or the Science of Society are the chief substitutes. What we modernists fear to know, we admit back into our Arts and Sciences on condition of Its denial. Where It is, there the Sacred once was. Freud's ingenious repressions of the repressive serve continuously, and in an intensely stipulative manner, against admitting sacred order back into a modern consciousness pregnant from the father of these repressions. The repressive father unacknowledged, except as "primal repression," modern sensibility has been achieved at the cost of a critical insensibility. The sacred is denied even as the arts of its address are celebrated as ends in themselves—as Art or Science, but more as Art. Rather than Science, Art is our repository of faithlessness. How much more easily Freud is accepted nowadays as Artist rather than Scientist; and rightly so. Our culture feeds on its doubly critical addresses: to a sacred order that is allowed to exist only for purposes of lowering everything high in it. Critical intellect becomes something "criminal," as Freud was not the first or last to remark.

Our endlessly critical culture is ending, I reckon, in its movements of inversion. To lower the interdictory motifs, to raise the transgressive: in sum, this is the function of that criticism for which our humanists and other enlighteners held such high hope. To come nearer understanding modernist movements of inversion, authority celebrated in its lowering modes, we must first recognize its love affair with death as the interdict of interdicts that modernism would abolish as meaningless. In his negational language of the "death instinct," Freud framed his most completely up-to-date resistance to the eternal yesterday that is sacred order. Authority must be eternally past, in every culture, however unstable. The sense of the past may be in it. Compared to others less negational in their traditions of acknowledgment, our culture may be rightly considered more unstable. But all cultures are unstable precisely in their vitality: all are moving balances of abhorrences and idealizations, one the predicate of the other. Repression is best imagined in its mobilities rather than, as popularly conceived, in its immobilities. If the repressive in culture is not constantly renewed and attached to fresh possibilities, then authority will lower, and so destroy, itself. It is in this repressive mode, raising and lowering the threshold of possibility in its denials, that cultures constitute unstable responses in sacred order to it.

The acutely unstable character of contemporary culture may be seen in its egalitarian attack on the hierarchy of repressively ordered balances by which it, like any other culture, must be constituted. In order to approach the last possibility within reach of the modernist imagination, what, for want of better coinage, I call an "anticulture," I shall have to introduce a long exegetical section on the extremist negational language through which the dominant mind of Freud conveyed its own raising and lowering addresses, arguably the most powerfully delivered and influential in this century.

Sacred Order as Death Instinct

What does it mean to say, as Freud did, that the "unknown,"[7] is timeless, knowing no before and after? Ignorance of temporality may be no excuse for misunderstanding death, which will not brook understanding. The mystery of the timeless unknown forced Freud's theory onto a path at once strange and familiar in the Western tradition of rationalizing the unrepressed repressive.

The great fable in the *Gorgias* (523a), on judgment and condemnation, of the naked and dead, is but one in a tradition on the meaning of death that includes Kafka's "In The Penal Colony." Freud's allegories on death are far more abstract, far more distorted and distanced from their "internal excitations." But Freud's quantifying images have appealed to the positivist age of Science, now ending, more than the images of Plato or Kafka. His art of address to the sacred, like all art, is a delicate balancing of too much or too little. Too much: then these "excitations" are experienced as "unpleasure." Too little: then these "excitations" are experienced as ended, beyond pleasure. In these intensifications and diminutions of the possible in its primacy, Freud tried to quantify the beginnings of what has been better called "primary imagination."[8]

The familiar Feuerbachian negational equivalent of "primary imagination" is "projection." Projection is a "defense mechanism" in the service of the pleasure principle. It is the "tendency to treat" excitations "as though they were acting, not from the inside," as the active energy that is unconsciousness as such, "but from the outside, so that it may be possible to bring the *shield against stimuli . . .* into operation as a means of defense against" excitations. Defense against the primacy of possibility is "the origin of *projection,* which is destined to play such a large part in the causation of pathological processes."[9] Brought under this curse of "pathological processes," Freud's one-eyed vision of what is interdictory, as projection, is a criticism, aiming to become therapy, of every interdictory presence, all finally merged into his most terrible abstraction, the "death instinct."

"We describe as 'traumatic' any excitations from outside which are powerful enough to reach through the protective shield."[10] The concept of "trauma" is linked to a failure of "an otherwise efficacious barrier against stimuli." It is "disturbance" in the "functioning of the organism's energy" that sets in "motion every possible defensive measure." Interdictory presences reappear as "defensive measures," against disturbing motions of what would be at rest, but for the vital trauma. Life is pain. Everything in life, if it is to become pleasure, must dance upon the point of pain. It is as if children will be spared their tears in fire. So far Freud goes with Shaw; and that is quite far enough in the modernist language of destructive dualism. Like Shaw and other modernists, Freud tried desperately to reconcile pain and pleasure as operative acts, with nothing inscribed on either side of that same Manichean coin.

Mental strife, illness as it is known in the Manichean realm, is a crack in the shield of faith. "The specific unpleasure of physical pain is probably the result of the protective shield having been broken through in a limited area."[11] Against this "invasion," how "shall we expect the mind to react?" The psychophysical metaphors of war carry their own meaning. "An 'anti-cathexis' [that is, repression] on a grand scale is set up, for whose benefit all the other psychical systems are impoverished, so that the remaining psychical functions are extensively paralyzed or reduced."[12] Dualist abstractions displace the warring gods of the higher and nether worlds. "The higher the system's own quiescent cathexis, the greater seems to be its binding force." On the other hand, "the lower its cathexis . . . the more violent must be the consequences of such a breach in the protective shield against stimuli."[13] Freud celebrates both gods and believes in neither. To the question how we are to be, without our repressions, Freud maintains the silence of utter incredulity. Without his protective and projective shields, man cannot live an instant; with them, man must live at odds with the pleasure principle and never be reconciled to reality, which is bad enough to satisfy the most radically dualist temper.

In *Beyond the Pleasure Principle,* Freud admits a "certain indefiniteness" in his metapsychology because he knows "nothing of the nature of the . . . process that takes place in the elements of the psychical systems." He never made up his mind.[14] The metaphors that conceal his being of two minds reveal the death instinct as his second god term. "We may suspect that the binding of the energy that streams into a mental apparatus consists in its change from a freely flowing into a quiescent state."[15] Trapped in his own allegories, which represent what they are not, Freud could only respond, to that which commands response, by obscuring that to which it responded: he refers to (1) "preparedness for anxiety," and (2) "hypercathexis of the receptive systems" as constituting the "last line of defense of the shield against stimuli."

In Freud's negational understanding of sacred order, "preparedness for anxiety" conceals and admits *guilt/knowledge*. That Freud saw the meaning of anxiety emerges in his discussion of anxiety and punishment dreams as "they fulfill the wish of the sense of guilt which is the reaction to the repudiated impulse." The wish disguises the aspiration of *guilt/knowledge* itself, in the very "repudiation" to which Freud refers. The dream can no longer be merely a harmless remissive occasion; the "purpose of dreams" cannot be, in the way Freud had thought, a simple inner "fulfillment of wishes."[16] Indeed, "wish-fulfillments" are Freud's stipulation, I suggest, of what Nietzsche better understood as "will to power." That will is hierarchical and the will of all wills is, in Freud's supreme negation of sacred order, the death instinct. It follows that, even in dreams from below, every mind must, sooner or later, "obey the compulsion to repeat." Dreams express, in images that would be a very different illuminative act but for the body's inactivity, the interdictory supreme over its lowering. We dream in the horizontal, under the protection of the repressive imperative that makes of sleep the most familiar surrogate of death.

Repetition of our involuntary responses in sacred order, to it, can be read in the play of children toward the meaning of authority. "Each fresh repetition seems to strengthen the mastery they are in search of."[17] This mastery is ours, in repetition, only if we are mastered: *mastery* means something that, done, cannot be done better in another way. Other ways become wrong. At play, children know what is right. "They are inexorable in their insistence that the repetition shall be an identical one." But "repetition, the re-experiencing of something identical, is in itself a source of pleasure" that takes the organism beyond pleasure to what commands it to repeat itself. The "predicate of being 'instinctual'" must be subject to another predicate: the "compulsion to repeat." What is this compulsion? It is an *"urge inherent in organic life to restore an earlier state of things"*—in short, the authority of the past.[18] Freud has arrived at his penultimate version of the interdictory: "the *conservative* nature of living substance."[19]

Like repression, authority, in order to live, can only conserve its attaching obediences by multiplying them. The ultimate conservative attachment can be made only by a return, "by circuitous and ever more complicated detours" to "an old state." Finally, Freud arrives at the highest and final truth, a truth "that knows no exception": "Everything living dies for internal reasons . . . '*the aim of all life is death.*'"[20] Authority dictates its own end in its aim. Every "organism wishes to die only in its own fashion. These guardians of life, too, were originally myrmidons of death."[21] So Freud joined the company of Plato and Augustine, Tolstoy and Kafka. Death imagery has been central to every great theory of authority. What is there in life to "repeat"? There is "to repeat the performance to which they owe their existence."[22] This is the language of *guilt/knowledge.* Upon this *guilt/knowledge* all that is "most precious on human civilization . . . is based."[23] In death, and the guilty knowledge of death, the repressive strives for its own complete form. But death has its lover. In sexuality, that which is repressed never ceases to strive for complete satisfaction.

In Chapter 6 of *Beyond the Pleasure Principle,* Freud turns to eros, that which lures the ego or death instincts out of their own repetitive form.[24] Eros, too, gives the "appearance of immortality."[25] With that appearance humans have tried to comfort themselves in face of the apparent unnaturalness of death.

Who believes that his own death is "natural"? An opposing "immortal" part of life, the reproductive, is itself a repetition—a "perpetual attempting and achieving [of] a renewal of life." So obviously near a then fashionable address to sacred order, Freud "cannot remain blind to" the fact that he has "unwittingly steered our course into the harbour of Schopenhauer's philosophy. For [Schopenhauer] death is the 'true result and to that extent purpose of life.' "[26] Teaching some purpose of life takes no part in psychoanalytic theory. Yet, in a living culture, that is the chief thing taught; and Freud knew a culture cannot survive without a minority, perfected in its repressions, to guide itself and the majority toward that chief thing. A repressed repressive class constitutes the guiding class in every culture. Then, and only then, can "what appears in a *minority* of . . . individuals as an untiring impulse toward further perfection . . . *easily* be understood as a result of the instinctual repression upon which is based all that is most precious in human civilization."[27] The tension of life and its unyielding purpose never ends; a repressive class, the guiding minority in a culture, must allow for that ineliminable condition and limit of its teaching. "Repressed instinct never ceases to strive for complete satisfaction, which would consist in the *repetition* of a primary experience of satisfaction. No substitutive or reactive formations, no variety of sublimations, will suffice to remove the repressed instinct's persisting tension."[28] Virtuosi of instinctual repression, understanding their condition, as Freud thought he did, see "no alternative but to advance in the direction in which growth is still free—though with no prospect of bringing the process to a conclusion or of being able to reach the goal" of a perfection that, if achieved, would end the tension that is life itself.

"Be ye perfect" states the aim of life with a clarity and certitude so frightening, as a truth so remote, that it becomes hidden, heavily dressed, like Kafka's officer, in symbols of what it represents. In this respect, Freud's "death instinct" is a true symbol: it *is* what it represents. Kafka's apparatus, in the penal colony that is sacred order addressed as if it were on the verge of extinction, is another true symbol. The truth of eternal life, in Kafka's officer's case, is not revealed except in his naked self-sacrifice, all the impressive epaulets and refined ladies' handkerchiefs of culture stripped off. Yet, as seen by us explorers, in the officer's nakedness and suffering in the machine is death as everything except an illuminative act.

Kafka's officer may be a member of Freud's fatally cultivated minority; in both we may see the end of that tradition of giving up all those attachments that give excusing reasons for living. Authority in a desacralized world belongs to a human type very different from that Plato made so frighteningly explicit in the *Phaedo* (64a–67d). There is an order still sacred; the authoritative guides are those who devote themselves as they should to the pursuit of wisdom and who have no other goal than to die and remain dead. No less ambiguously than Kafka, Freud resisted the double imagery of nakedness and death as symbols of spiritual salvation. The traditional way, upward in sacred order, of soul separated from body, was completely blocked to him. In negational symbolism, soul reappears to baffle the symbolists themselves, who here staked their genius on the wager that "soul" belongs to the language of a dead culture. Yet, in Death, soul forced itself upon Freud, as an "instinct." Freud should have written of "soul instinct." Only so, by recognitions of soul, timeless in sacred order, can modern symbolists acknowledge the illuminative veto in their own vision.

Relentless in its intellectualizings, modernist authority conceals its resistances to sacred order in torrents of words. Sublimation without soul, as literary achievement, is a polite word for graphomania. Even Freud's bafflements are excessively articulate. Hundreds of thousands of words, in print, all to fulfill the function of modern criticism: to block the downward, or backward, path of the carnal self—since there is no other. But what more can words ever do, if they do not first block the "backward path," the way down, of *soul/self* in sacred order? Freud is as unequivocal as he is confused about the associative word modes of modern repression. "The backward path that leads to complete satisfaction is as a rule obstructed by the resistances which maintain the repressions";[29] so Freud, all unwilling, celebrated sacred order maintained by intellect.

Authority on the "backward path," transgressive movements, now celebrated in our culture as progressive, result no less from the "efforts of Eros taken in conjunction with the results of repression,"[30] than any movement upward. The erotic will not be divorced from the repressive. That is why sublimation has nothing to do with what is sublime. Movements downward may be as sublimated as movements upward in sacred order. Transgressive authority, lowering movements in sacred order, is not the less authoritative for its transgressiveness. In the vertical of possibility, complex relations of command and obedience, at once illuminative and operative in their enactments of sacred order, choice is always the same: obedience or disobedience. Authority is a word describing this self-same choice. Again the great and ancient negation is sounded, mistaking life for death. "The dominating tendency of mortal life, and perhaps of nervous life in general, is the effort to reduce, to keep constant or to remove internal tension due to stimuli." It is this "compulsion to repeat," Freud's indefeasible idea of sacred order, that "first puts us on the track of the death instincts."

Precisely here, on the track of the death instincts, Freud, were he nerved enough to follow it, would have found his solution to the crucial problem of repression. Death instinct and repression are, I suggest, complementary abstractions, negational returns of soul to self; and of self to sacred order.

What is interdictory is concealed in a barrage of negations, as a "tendency which finds expression in the pleasure principle" and, at the same time, gives "one of our strongest reasons for believing in the existence of death instincts."[31] At the height of the interdictory in sacred order

> there is an unborn, not become, not made, uncompounded, and were it not . . . for this unborn, not become, not made, uncompounded, no escape could be shown here for what is born, has become, is made, is compounded. But because there is . . . an unborn, not become, not made, uncompounded, therefore an escape can be shown for what is born, has become, is made, is compounded.[32]

Confronting the supremely directive *Not*, in its movements, soul, in modernity, has been lost in such abstractions as death instinct and repression. It follows that the modern eye has trouble seeing the transgressive predicate of aggression. Critical intellect, the aggression with which we are most in love, confuses our illuminative acts of faith. Sacred order becomes an unacknowledged mystery, compounded, beyond our knowledge, except by indirections, of instincts and their repressions.

Of two minds in his theory of authority, Freud was anything but the great emancipator of our pleasures that, earlier in his century, he was made out to be. Rather, he suspected the popular taste for pleasure must end in even more popular enactments of pain. "The pleasure principle seems actually to serve the death instincts." What is interdictory "keeps watch upon stimuli from without [and] is more especially on guard against increases of stimulation from within, which would make the task of living more difficult."[33] Before the paradox that our lives obey the "death instinct," and that this obedience makes life endurable, Freud could do nothing more than could

Nietzsche with his earlier version of that same paradox: "eternal recur-rence." Neither could accept, except negationally, the messiness of everyday life in sacred order. As the abstraction beyond death and repression, the compulsion to repeat, in Freud's case, had its parallel in the grandiose futility of Nietzsche's vision of life as eternal recurrence, by which he vetoed his vision of life as will to power. Such a rare pursuit of wisdom would teach us the practice, in various disciplines of announcing the "reality principle," of what used to be called a "spiritual" discipline.

The first articulation of a spiritual discipline, which occurs in children even before they do anything right, let alone wrong, Freud recognized in the "sense of guilt." To render their sense of guilt a spiritual discipline, humans perform acts the "danger" of which Kierkegaard recognized more clearly than did either Freud or Nietzsche. Kierkegaard recognized this "danger" as our most "decisive action,"[34] some will to power that cancels itself in our obedience to received commands in a sacred order that will not change even in response to the implicit flattery of decisions in its favor. What does the modern mind now call this illuminative act, the decision that is faith, even in the case of Kierkegaard himself? Something, I fear, very like a neurosis; faith is understood, by inversion, as melancholy. Those Danes, Prince Ham-let and Dr. Kierkegaard, might have been amused and instructed by our sad way with any act approaching the condition of faith. Our religions are far and away too solemn.

Faith: The Rebus of Culture as the Death Instinct

"What is now holding sway in the super-ego is . . . a pure culture of the death instinct."[35] It is in relation to death, Freud's second god-term, that the superego "displays its independence of the conscious ego." On the other side, it displays "its intimate relations with the unconscious id."[36] Yet there is always an historical element in the superego. Freud reminds us of the importance to the unconscious superego of preconscious verbal residues in the ego, of word presentations. The "*culture* of the death instinct" in the superego cannot "disclaim its origin from things heard"—those "things heard" in past generations remain "accessible to consciousness by way of . . . concepts, abstractions."[37] Here Freud's own abstracted understanding of our lives in sacred order is misleading; spiritual discipline, the self entire, made up as it is of apperceptions in sacred order, must be made of responses that are not less visual than auditory, not less sensual than they are intellec-tual, not less dreaming than waking, not less physical than psychical. Faith is a protective ego shield of close and personal readings in sacred order, apperceiving its commands, against the otherwise destructive illusions of autonomy entertained by ego. All abstractions, including Freud's that con-ceal commanding edifications in sacred order are cleverities by which the sense of guilt is falsified in obediences to lowering motifs or true disobediences. False guilt is a special condition of modern life, one in which the direction of our obediences suffers the dubious pleasure of inversion.

What mind denies, body may still affirm. So far in its spiritual discipline as it can perform a decisive act, every ego is "first and foremost a bodyego."[38] Faith, as an illuminative act, is always the sense of guilt embodied. Everything we learn can be truly learnt only upon our bodies. That is how faith becomes urgently important and yet never pompous. There is no other way. Kafka's officer can rightly say, proleptic of his own and every other illuminative act of faith, "guilt is never to be doubted." Our responsibility, for our shifting positions in sacred order, can never be doubted. Our responsibility, the certainty and inevitability of the sense of guilt, haunts modern culture, because it is inexplicable except as the prolepsis of faith. Faith denied, the sense of guilt, before any deed, discovered over again by psychoanalysis, remains inexplicable. As responsibility is denied, transgressions are celebrated as the enactment of that denial; here is enlightenment, indeed.

In superego we see the ghost of sacred order. It haunts our profane moral modernity no less than aggression, the ghost of transgression, haunts our politics. By so punitive a substitution of self-hate for self-love as superego,[39] the sanctuary of modernist moralizing and religionizing becomes a kind of prison. This modernist displacement of what is interdictory, remissive and transgressive entirely from sacred order into psychical is itself a neurotic cleverity, a symptom of what it purports otherwise to deny. The psychological reduction of the authoritative past, into a problem to be resolved therapeutically in the present, is yet another way to see authority engaged in its own lowering. This lowering religiosity is a second kind of death, for all kinds of faith.

In eternal truth, it is to no simple obedience that, in sacred order, we are commanded. Simplicity, some "simple cannot," is the rarest cultural achievement, the result of the most complex indirections in sacred order. "Honor thy superiors," for example, demands that we know what honor is, and what is superior. More certainly than to obedience, we are commanded to responsibility. Responsibility is inoperative without the illuminative sense of guilt. In every complex order of the commanding sacred, our necessary responsibility is to shift for ourselves. Everything we think and do, we are; there is nothing irresponsible about life in sacred order. Freud was preeminently sensible of sacred order when he remarked our responsibility even for our dreams.

Neuroses, which are bad faiths, develop whenever humans can no longer accept their responsibilities, not least because they have been falsely enlightened by doctrines of irresponsibility. Those doctrines parody sacred order, by asseverating some "system" by which we are left no choices except lowering ones; that is, if lowerings had not been declared obsolete fictions.

Raisings and lowerings, the very experience of being, preclude the cult of experience. Verticality unrecognized, all experience is a swindle—and not even a swindle, not even sound and fury, not even signifying nothing; for that last signifying is, at least, a sign of despair. Nothing, non-being, the "death instinct," is a sign of despair. As the "aim" of life, death signals Freud's negational theology, which was concealed from him as a meta-psychology. From that negational theology, we can infer modern morality,[40] as another expression of the characteristically radical dualism of modernity. Our dualism keeps separate what is together: spiritual and physical, mind and body, taste and truth, experience and location in sacred order. Freud's characteristically radical dualism keeps separate what is combined in the experience of the world: the moral and non-moral.

To say "id . . . is totally non-moral"[41] turns the blood of transgressive acts into the wine of remissive ones. Split off from "the pure culture of the death instinct," the eternal "non-moral" becomes illuminative in the remissive mode—as Freud evidently liked to have it, despite his belief that we are responsible for ourselves even in our dreams. Radical dualism levels sacred order, by seeing everything in it from the bottom up and nothing from the top down. Interdicts appear only as splittings of what is transgressive into abhorrences and idealizations; by dubbing transgressions "id" they are natu-ralized, if not civilized.

Our experience, as moderns, has been confused by our enlightenments as radical dualists. Yet our guiding dualism, Freud's, must affirm the fact that the predicate of authority resides in the unsaid, the unheard, the unseen—in the repressive, which is the inversion of everything we once knew about a god we believed to be above everything that it was possible for man to think about. Repression is to truth as god is to mind. Authority cannot be stipu-lated in institutions that can satisfy our ultimate and unfulfillable will to knowledge as power: so to take over all authority, and so become responsi-ble to nothing superior to our own rationalizing will, is transgressive. Yet this will supplies the animus of critical intellect.

Serving the will to knowledge as power, critical intellect is powerful in its remissions. Nothing is more remissive than to hold what is interdictory in culture responsible for the creation of what is transgressive. Evil is there in the world. To deny that fact, in part by charging superego is hypermoral, and "as cruel as only the id can be,"[42] supplies modern ego its power-knowing cleverities. Now a famous Freudian paradox can be read in a different light. How "remarkable," indeed, "that the more a man checks his aggressiveness toward the exterior the more severe—that is aggressive—he becomes in his ego ideal."[43] Here is that identification with the aggressor, that godlike cunning of the ego's futile striving to be good when the good is so beastly to him. In Freudian unmaskings of idealization, of punishment needed as if it were the reward of virtue, modernist movements of deidealization, chiefly in the liberal arts, took on their cleverest rationalization of the prevalent leveling movement against sacred order. What is lowering deals its merciful judgments upon whatever was once above it, as if what is low, raised, were nothing but some culturally valued fiction of itself made acceptable. Modernist morality has reached its most disarming and Freudian paradox: the more a man succeeds in controlling his aggressions, the more intense becomes the inclination of his ideal to aggressiveness against its generating self; what characteristically modern cunning. By such critical inversion, whatever is interdictory became the parent of everything transgressive and, moreover, everything transgressive the parent of everything interdictory. In one illuminatively remissive act after another, critical intellect asks of the sacred Not: "Why not?"

What parental authority is not suspect, nowadays? A litany of "Nots" may survive, but all in quotation marks, for liberating use only; else, what would be the pleasure of understanding the "harshly restraining, cruelly prohibiting quality," of "even ordinary normal morality"? As for that old-time religion, which none of us can recover, it is from its cruelly prohibiting quality that "the conception arises of a higher being who deals out punishment inexorably."[44] Kafka's treatment of this higher being, as the creator of our inherited order, itself an obsolescent punishment colony, both to its last officer and to its evasive explorer, puts the need for punishment at the center of authority. That need for punishment is a negational version of understanding in sacred order. Such understanding must remain uncommunicable to its critics—if, indeed, not also to its last officer, despite the fact that he acts out, in his nakedness and death, the ancient mode of that understanding.[45]

In our penal colony, at the end of its existence as sacred order, the very nature of spiritual discipline is no longer understood, perhaps not even by its last officer. Reordered abstractly, as in modern sociological thought, all individuals reduce to whatever they have in common, their class or some other abstract sameness. Regarded in sacred order, that sameness does not exist at all. Strictly speaking, each shifting for himself in the vertical of authority, no one has anything in common with anyone else. What seems to be common, among God's children, becomes in fact uncommon in the individualities of their responsive address to sacred order, from wherever they are, at any given moment, inside it. As all of us, in our bodies, have our own special constitution, which a doctor must examine in its uncommon particular, so the mind of each is so distinct from all other minds that each may be said to live as it must die—alone. How well Newman knew, in his

Grammar of Assent, that we are all ourselves alone, in our identity, in incommunicability, in personality. The mystery of authority so communicates to each that every other must feel the force, if not the understanding, of that communication. My paraphrase of Newman on the range of that "illative sense" without which authority does not communicate, as from one to another, should end here and direct quotation begin: "There is something deeper in our differences than the accident of external circumstances." For "objective truth . . . we need the interposition of a Power, greater than human teaching and human argument, to make our beliefs true and our minds one."[46]

The ultimate test of authority is its vitality. It proves itself by exercising itself, in one direction or another, interdictory or transgressive. Remissive authority, the characteristic modern kind, wants a vitality of its own; it is transitional, in one direction or the other, subserving or subverting the interdicts. That vitality wanting, we cannot be surprised that the master mind of our remissiveness, Freud, imagined the primacy of possibility as sexual energy. Reverse the ordination of energy, see it from the bottom up, as desexualization, rather than from the top down, as obedience, and "sublimation" follows; for this reason, I have read sublimation as the antisacral equivalent of obedience to the repressive imperative. As sublimations, cultural achievements reduce sacred order to sexual energy raised somehow to a condition in which it becomes something wholly other than itself. In fact, "sublimation" is the most genteel religion without god, humanism deified, that modernism has yet contrived.

Was Jesus sublimating? Not without his completion and perfection in obedience to a superior will: "Thy will be done." Was Hitler sublimating? Is the art of Picasso desexualized? If we concede the artist as a special case of cultural achievement without desexualization, then what of the modernist aesthetic in its concentration precisely on sexuality? I have said that the cultural value of sublimation can be as much a lowering as a raising act. However we tinker with the mechanism of sublimation, it cannot work, I think. And after sublimation, what?

> After sublimation the erotic component no longer has the power to bind the whole of the destructiveness that was combined with it, and this is released in the form on an inclination to aggression and destruction. This defusion would be the source of the general character of harshness and cruelty exhibited by the ideal—its dictatorial "Thou shalt."[47]

Having made its own historic contribution to the destruction of our mindful obediences in sacred order, the dictatorial No, "thou shalt not," has been sublimated into the democratic Yes, "I will." The reverse of desexualization takes place. Where once, in Freud's obsolete vision of it, aggression "extended beyond the id to the super ego," and "increases its severity towards the innocent ego,"[48] now, in modernity, severity itself becomes sexualized. On the basest level, that severity can be seen sexualized in such a film as *The Last Tango in Paris*. On an incomparably higher level, we can literally read the sexualization of modernist culture in the remorseless last forty pages of Joyce's *Ulysses*. There, the true meaning of the sublimating yes practically suffocates us in its embrace. Joyce has the heart of modernist sublimating sexuality going like mad as the climax of his novel: "Yes I said yes I will yes."

Against that yes, so repeatedly urged as sublimation, the received and im-memorial Shalt Nots proved to be playthings, toys of re-educated morality, here yesterday for discard tomorrow. But the Nots have a history that is more than repetitional; they test us in their repetitions. Superior ego has no choice but to draw "upon the experiences of past ages stored in the id." This strength of repetition in the ego may derive from reviving shapes of former egos. "Resurrection" makes its fleeting ghost of an appearance in Freudian theory as these "reviving shapes of former egos."[49] This way only true superego comes into being. This true way recalls the fact that there is a piety of mind, however little that piety is recognized nowadays. It is piety of mind, superior to its critical powers, that marches out to the progressive conquest of id.[50] Critical intellect, without its pieties, cannot conquer its own imagined primacy of possibility. Precisely in its abstraction, ego idealism, Freud's supposed "reaction-formation *against* the instinctual process of the id,"[51] we are given a glimpse of impotent gods in their mythic modern dress. These gods are trimmers of a familiar sort. Politic ego

> disguises the id's conflicts with reality and, if possible, its conflicts with the super-ego, too. In its position midway between id and reality, it only too often yields to the temptation to become sycophantic, opportunist and lying, like a politician who sees the truth but wants to keep his place in popular favor.[52]

"Popular favor" is to social order as "primacy of possibility" is to sacred; both may be achieved only by a systemic mendacity of critical intellect in search of its self-justifying abstractions. In that specially *revealing/conceal-ing* passage, where Freud's death instinct is called "an abstract concept with a negative content for which no unconscious correlate can be found,"[53] the negational truth that every fear is ultimately fear of death is stated only to be denied. As a negational theorist, Freud properly says that such a "high-sounding phrase . . . has hardly any meaning, and at any rate cannot be justified." Yet Freud also says that in the fear of death "the ego gives itself up" to what used to be called final "judgment,"[54] or spiritual salvation.

Fears of death are linked by Freud with an anxiety to please the punitive superego. Here, in the great canon of our century, as in Kafka's penal colony, we see a typical failure to grasp the object of an illuminative act. Self surrenders its identity but only to the superior identity from which it derives its own. This is translated into: "the ego relinquish[es] its narcissistic libidinal cathexis in a very large amount." That to which the ego relinquishes itself is unidentified, except negationally as death. All others denied, this aspect of the sacred must appear like a revenant to a self so doubtful about sacred order that it would protect against precisely its own surrender to the sacred. Hamlet is such a figure of anxiety, threatened by the sacred even as he would obey its command to remember that he must live, or die, obedient to it. Hamlet's anxiety signals his primal doubt in sacred order. Were I his therapist, I would reckon that that university man has been rather too long and hard at his studies. Hamlet has come home from university with a bad case of *contemptus mundi*, which can only confirm everything that is rotten in Denmark. From his primal doubt about everything, Hamlet tries escape into bad faith, a pseudodecisive act of putting his world right, as if vengeance would become operative if only it were illuminative. Hamlet has confused, in an impossible and destructive way, the question of his parents with the parent question that he must face alone, though not he alone has faced it. Claudius makes a politic effort to answer the parent question of authority, in his remarks on the death of fathers. Not less a political man than King Claudius, Prince Hamlet does not understand that in matters of authority, as in country matters, winning is one thing, understanding another. This prince has confused winning with understanding, operative acts with illuminative.

There is nothing to be learned from politics except who won and who lost; no more is there anything to be learned from society, except who is in and who is out. The confusion of performance with insight makes professors turbulent and intellectuals specially subject either to the seductions of power or to what is almost as bad—graphomania. This confusion is so widespread that Freud can easily conflate obedience in the illuminative mode with death in the operative. It is the oldest confusion: of faith and power. Kafka's officer in the penal colony, and Shakespeare's prince, in Denmark, in their confusion of faith and power, decisive action and winning, see themselves in what is called, nowadays, a "no-win situation"; they feel "deserted by all protecting forces." Freud reads this desertion from sacred order in purely political terms, as punitive superego demanding ego sacrifice itself to its protecting, and therefore sovereign, forces.

> The ego gives itself up because it feels itself hated and persecuted by the super-ego, instead of being loved. To the ego, therefore, living means the same as being loved—being loved by the super-ego, which here again appears as the representative of the id. The super-ego *fulfills the same*

function of protecting and saving that was fulfilled *in earlier days* [my italics] by the father and later by Providence or Destiny. . . . Deserted by all protecting forces, [ego] lets itself die.[55]

This abstraction cannot but be inexact when applied to immortal characters. Hamlet is seeking vengeance. The officer is seeking obedience to his old commandant. If both may be said to let themselves die, it is in desperately illuminative acts, to show themselves that they have not deserted forces that demand the obedience even of those desperate acts.

The modernist mind cannot think of self-surrender in anything except terms of defeat. It has deserted all knowledge that does not advance its own power to break any rule that inhibits power. That "guilt is never to be doubted"[56] announces that grace is always to be doubted. Kafka's officer and Hamlet's prince wait as long as they can before they give up the struggle against primal doubt in a self-destruction that becomes, as a surrogate of faith, performed in order to produce a concluding performance. On the gravestone of authority, Kafka inscribed, "in very small letters," the full mendacity of a culture that gives birth only to one death of authority after another. The last sentence on the gravestone of the old commandant runs: "Have faith and wait!"[57] Never have I read a sentence so inseparably compounded of despair and irony. The truest expression of the officer's faith is that he waited no longer. The truest expression of the officer's faithlessness is that he waited so long.

Worse: the nakedness and death of the officer suggest nothing to the explorer (not to mention the author and his readers) except the sincerity or authenticity of the officer. Poor, sincere old fool. There is nothing we can see through in his eyes to suggest that his total sacrifice of everything to the command of his *immediate and ultimate* Superior, to be just, is anything more than plain self-murder. Indeed, the explorer understands just enough to continue, as before, in his office. That office is to keep anyone, by force if necessary, from "attempting the leap"[58] of faith, which must always appear as a sacrifice of everything self-willed. That sacrifice of everything to god has about it the ancient character of a true holocaust. Modernity knows of holocausts only as meaningless deaths. The most horrible aspect of modern holocausts is that they are sacrifices of everything to nothing.

Shifting Responses to Sacred Order; The Unrepressed Repressive Re-enacted

So far as there is a crisis of authority, it is complicit in the efforts of our explorer classes, those ever on the move, as from lifestyle to lifestyle, virtuoso order hoppers, to discourage leaps of faith. Nor would Freud, in the adamancy of his rebellion against sacred order, countenance ideological parodies of leaps, such as Marxism. Yet Freudian theory, like Durkheimian, has served to diffuse parodies of faith, so far as it would see authority lower itself by finding in itself nothing more than residues of primitive *taboo*, or, at best, interdicts.[59] It is in this particular that Freud's internal surrogate for what is interdictory, superego, implies the completest leveling of authority. Psychology is to the levelling of authority as publicity is to charisma. Imagine everyone in modernity intimately famous for five minutes and you have experienced the grace of our new god. Yet Freud, for one, had the grace to be unable even to dream of a world deprived of its truthful distancing and obscurities. Mind's eye cannot see clearly. Whether in its upward movements, or down, the obscure truth of authority is never lost; its complex, shifting balances, movements upward and down, never end. A veridical of vital indirections—interdictory, remissive, transgressive—guides us always and everywhere, whether we can follow, in something other than negational ways, those indirections or not.

Repressive commands, the sacred in its stipulations as culture, form normally around interdictory motifs and their remissions—what is not to be done, yet done. By their efforts to rationalize away the interdicts as merely obsolete "taboos," suitable to earlier, less enlightened states of social evolution, the enlightened in American culture have attacked, largely unaware of what they are doing, the fundamental form of culture in any possible content. Huizinga hints at the secret truth of this cultural suicide when he commented on that

> early stage of social organization [when] obligation expands into conventions, rules of conduct and cults, in the form of *taboos*. In wide circles the popularisation of the word *taboo* has led to an undervaluation of the ethical element of the so-called primitive cultures, not to say anything of that body of sociological thought which with truly modern simplicity disposes of everything called morality, law, or piety, as just so many *taboos*.[60]

The suicide of a culture can be seen in its levelling of differently valued facts. The contents of experience come nearer and nearer to their ultimate and original condition of meaninglessness. Critical intellect can teach nothing except one critique of "meaning" after another. Then our obligations expand no longer into conventions of commands and obediences as into conventions of remissive explanations that put in doubt the very idea of obligation. Authority levelled is authority destroyed. An authority that can brook its own lowering must be transgressive. The predicate of transgression is remission. Our remissive teaching elites have made a piety of endless criticism. The more obligation expands into convention, limiting the range of action otherwise open to human "impulse"—"impulse" being secondary to "habit," as Dewey rightly argued, not prior to it—the higher a culture. Low culture is the doing, more or less openly and in the wrong time space, of what is not to be done. It is high culture that is under siege in American society. This siege has taken the form of a fusillade of critical lowerings, a critique of all raisings, sacred order acknowledged only in the identification of culture with endless criticism. This endless criticism is of neither the "Left" nor "Right"; rather, it is a nothingness that can be both radical and reactionary at the same time. Nihilism stood at the door of European culture in the late nineteenth century. In America, as the successor to European culture, the door has been opened.

Behind its closed doors, high culture develops in expressive limits upon the primacy of possibility. If, at the commanding heights of every culture are its interdicts, then the more interdictory a symbolic, the more is "not done," if that symbolic is "true"—that is, if it has descended deeply enough into self and society. To do nothing lowering would be the highest cultural achievement of all. Some ancients called this "nothing doing" the "contemplative life." Aristotle came close to this meaning, when he declared leisure the first principle of action.[61] Prepared in contemplative leisure, the interdicts can challenge the primacy of possible acts even in the world of its technological facility.

Modern technology gives the primacy of possibility an immediacy not dreamt of in the magic universe that is its true ancestor. Modern therapy will soon have nothing of the authoritative past left to interiorize except the panic and emptiness of the cult of experience. The doubly strange thing about this cult is that our experiences teach us nothing and therefore none appears worth giving up. Every experience being, in modernity, worth having, an unprecedented cultivation of vulgarity has set in. The culture of panic and emptiness is indistinguishable from one in which idealizations are admitted only as constructs, never as realities beyond our will to construct.

Balancing this endlessly lowering effect of culture as experience, there is the blind spot in every vision that permits what is envisioned. The veto complicit in every vision warrants the manifold hierarchies in which we live. These hierarchies will not be rationalized. To say that it is against God to kill animals, depends upon the acceptance of animals within the manifold hierarchies that are sacred order. Saint Francis pitied fire. Blake thought of a white cloud as sacred. Thomas More thought animals were made for innocence. What, then, is beneath sacred order?

There is always something with which, in its identity, we cannot identify. I may feel regret at throwing away an old tie. But what of Gregor Samsa, who awoke one morning to find himself transformed into a gigantic insect? A man cannot maintain sympathy with himself as such a body ego. Gregor's decision to disappear expressed at once his act of faith that there are sacred orders for insects as for humans and that he was a member of neither. "The Metamorphosis" is Kafka's story of such a lowering in sacred order that only the death of so lowered a body ego can raise its sibling, the sister body ego, into full life.

Kafka's story of a lowering is a terror to read, worse than any horror film; indeed, that genre depends upon our terror at being lowered, or at being attacked by lower creatures, even if they descend from above. But, as modern culture is levelled down, our lowering acts are more and more experienced as the possibility of unlimited pleasure. Plato understood the insolence of that kind of possibility.

> The goddess of limit, my dear Philebus, seeing insolence and all manner of wickedness breaking loose from all limit in point of pleasures and self-indulgence, established the limit of law and order, of limited being; and you say this restraint was the death of pleasure: I say it was the saving of it. [62]

The death of pleasure is no small cultural achievement; it may be the most powerful, though not the highest, of modernist cultural achievements. As Trilling noted, in "The Fate of Pleasure," [63] modern spirituality has long rejected, as repressive or specious goods, those restraints and refinements established by the Platonic goddess of limit or the Judaic God of commandment. Instead, the heart of everything authoritative was to be sought in the cultivation of lowering violence, in pain. The destruction of what is interdictory, regarded in a variety of specious goods—or as "bourgeois," or "repressive"—is "surely one of the chief literary enterprizes of our age." Modern spirituality proposes a return to the ethos of holy fools; to madness as the expression of faith; to a perverse fundamentalism of "insistence upon the sordid and the disgusting" [64] rather than upon the noble and the pleasing. We can see this perverse fundamentalism, this insistence upon truth as the experience of what is lowering, captivate the liberal imagination. The negational work of the prophets of modernity, in search of the sacred in its transgressive modes, has triumphed in the tremendous variety of demoralizations, of lowerings, marketed as "lifestyles," in contemporary culture. Transgressive spirituality for mass consumption makes Freud as much a figure of the past as his immediate predecessor, Nietzsche. As practiced by the remissive parental generations of modern social order, by our leaders in "lifestyles" and lowering conduct, the affects of transgression, identifications down the unalterable order of culture, are constituted by less limited and more self-expressive being. The ethic of honesty is now played out, like a game, against our cunning uses of that ethic. Inversely moralizing revolts against the eternal vertical of existence, its interdicts unalterably in place, once played out as tragedy by King Oedipus, have been transformed into the democratic comedy of the Oedipus complex. The parent question, asked of humanity in every variety of its universal experience of existence in sacred order—"Am I thy Master, or art Thou Mine?"—was persuasively disguised by Freud, as therapist, but not as metapsychologist, in the question of parents. It is always surprising when parental authority is caught out by transgressive spirituality, as if that were something youthful. What is youthful, to the point of being infantile, is the denial of spirituality, not celebrations of its downward motions. The death of Satan, that tragedy of the Western imagination, has been succeeded by an aesthetic that admits no evil. In the culture of the therapeutic, there are neither raisings nor lowerings. Everything is on the level. So honest, we live in a world of "comic ugliness or a lustred nothingness."[65] Sacred order has become nothingness lustred, studied nostalgias, for that "place in which to be is not enough to be."[66]

This modernist tradition, of spirituality like a tongue touching a cavity, will always have its risible aspect. The pleasure of our lowerings can appear comic no less than the pain of our raisings can appear false. Something rotten is always there for those with a nose twitching for it.[67] We can always be joked out of our straightforward obediences, from which the true sense of guilt derives.

As an example of man as joker, pretend with me a moment to Hamlet as the case history of a student who studied philosophy too long in a German university. In German, the word *sein* stands not only for *to be*, but also for the possessive pronoun *his*. Hamlet's problem, all but self-understood, but not, that he belongs to nothing and no one, certainly not to the memory of his father, must turn, upon a therapeutic reading, into a question about his questionable attitude toward his parents. The tragedy of a transgressive Hamlet cannot be played, in the Ernest Jones-Laurence Olivier version, as a family problem; that would make it a role fit for Woody Allen, spreading sad cheer rather than deadly evil round him.

Hamlet is a tragic hero because it is he, more deeply than either his transgressive uncle or mother in theirs, who doubts authority in its sacred order. Suffering his case of primal doubt about it, testing sacred order as if against his own will, Hamlet knows his rebellion must fail as surely as none can be "the indifferent children of the earth."[68] The permanent crisis of authority, and the tragic hero caught in that crisis, has now been democratized. Oedipus was neither intellectual nor democrat; nor joker. It is Hamlet who should have got himself to a monastery. His crucial problem is more spiritual than sexual. Because the No seems to him, as it has to every other rebel against it, mortal, Hamlet finds his world-rejections, as they are, no less suspect than the acceptances made by others. Nothing can satisfy his sense of justice. The famous "dream of evil" extinguishes all "noble substance."[69]

Freud might have more accurately named the nuclear complex after Hamlet instead of Oedipus. In his blindness, Oedipus never ceases to blame the gods. Still, he accepts the reality of sacred order. Hamlet accepts nothing of the sort. Though both are asked the parent question under the concealment of questioning their parents, Hamlet seems to me the more fanatical questioner; his is nearer that modern fanaticism that expresses extreme skepticism in the most destructively violent manner. It is from Hamlet that veritable contagion of what is transgressive spreads, to take in even Ophelia.

The rebellion characteristic of modernist fanatics, against the subtleties and indirections of sacred order, can never be doubted. That rebellion is no matter of crude certainties. It is primal doubt, not certainty, that has led to the present monstrous compound of fanaticism and unbelief, as in Nazism and Marxism. This faithless fanaticism, in our politicized experience of it, gives the lie to the notion that authority is whatever legitimates power. The most elementary fact of the Nazi regime was that it recognized no authority superior to its own; nor does any Communist regime recognize an authority superior to winning and keeping power, despite the Marxist rhetoric of a class that, when triumphant in the class war, will abolish all winnings including its own. Somewhere in the Zurich of the next social order, its next officer walks and talks away the time until he succeeds and brings with him his own capital of the spirit, to invest in his own paradise of winning meanings. So Weber imagined, in his ideal typology, the modern capitalist, son of a Calvinist father. But in the Weberian typology, as in the Marxist, the capitalist must be the last officer of a sacred order. After all, Marx celebrated the bourgeoisie as the most revolutionary class, abolitionists of everything sacred. In the capitalist and rationalist "as if," that last officer strips his paradise of winning meanings. Rather, "meaning" itself becomes a critical glass-bead game, the intellectual form of "legitimation." Engaged in such gamesmanship, upon which their offices depend, the officers of our radically desacralized reality, one in which every construct deserves its deconstruction, win their right, as authors, to invent our next winning "meaning," by which even the weakest noodles can make their critical refusals of sacred order. In such a culture, the final solution of the criticism problem can happen: the primacy of possibility will be treated as if it were a reality. In such a "reality," asceticisms would be prescribed as needed; the therapeutic need exclude nothing from his repertoire of roles—including "sainthood" and "martyrdom." Even Kierkegaardian "decision" would become an endless performance, not excluding life-and-death performances.

The world as hospital would be transformed into the world as hospital-theater.

How to describe the anticritical critic? I am reminded of his predeceasor, the artful dodger turned artist, as once described by the Abbe Galiani:

> Imagine an artist whom the police have commissioned to paint in large letters on a wall: "It is forbidden to commit any nuisance here under penalty of a fine or corporal punishment." The painter gets to work, but in the midst of his work he feels the call. Down he climbs and, while breaking the law, admires the beauty of his own inscription.

The artistry of a therapeutic culture heroically remissive has been easily imagined since at least the late nineteenth century. Empathy, *feeling*, is in widest supply. Dr. Johnson was well ahead of the modernist game when he was hard-headed enough to make his famous remark:

> If Baretti should be hanged, none of his friends will eat a slice of plum pudding the less. . . . You will find these very feeling people are not very ready to do you good. They *pay* you by *feeling*.

And, if they go beyond the payment of feeling, and would volunteer to be hanged in your stead, or at least go to prison, you will find these very activists are self-consciously making a fine spectacle for themselves—rather like the character played by Woody Allen in *The Front*. That character is seen off to prison on camera, with feeling people paying him off with "Free Howard Klein" placards jerking up and down—all on camera. The secret is now open. It is publicity, not relentlessly critical intellect, that will bend the Higher Powers. The "aesthetic yes" of the early modern artist, as in Joyce or, earlier, in Nietzsche, in which suffering is experienced as a pleasure,[70] has become no less obsolete than the spirituality of knowing oneself. To the modernist mind, "know thyself" is the greatest public relations slogan ever devised.

The power of publicity as therapy may be inferred from the famous little "just suppose" story Freud once told.

> Suppose . . . a number of ladies and gentlemen in good society have planned to have a picnic one day at an inn in the country. The ladies have arranged among themselves that if one of them wants to relieve a natural need she will announce that she is going to pick flowers. Some malicious person, however, has got wind of this secret and had printed on the programme which is sent round to the whole party: "Ladies who wish to retire are requested to announce that they are going to pick flowers."[71]

As I have implied elsewhere[72] in remarking on Freud's easy target practice, malice is no basis for the ethic of honesty. The artfulness of those ladies was without malice. As a result of his malicious action, Freud's story against himself continued:

> No lady will think of availing herself of this flowery pretext, and, in the same way, other similar formulas, which may be freshly agreed upon, will be seriously compromised. What will be the result? The ladies will admit their natural needs without shame and none of the men will object.[73]

That cant phrase, "natural needs," begs the question of how easily and elaborately all such "needs" must go well beyond anything that can be called the "call" of nature. To be "without shame" is scarcely possible in the sacred order from which every culture derives, for that condition would admit nothing as transgressive, that is, as shameful before the blind eye of whatever god's body may be in that culture.

High culture is a flowering of pretexts; shame follows upon not abiding by them. In the *Laws,* Plato understood these matters differently and perhaps better than Freud. Only through its concealments can the body express itself beautifully in a profane world. The nude belongs in the world of the sacred.[74] These manners of reticence express that divine fear, commonly experienced in reverence and shame before the primacy of possibility, which less religious minds than Plato's, including Freud's, ascribe to a fastidiousness and taste so powerfully ordaining that it acquires the character of religiosity.

Guided, as it must be, by just and noble fear of the sheer movement humans can achieve in the vertical of possibility, a true officer class in that order will not be too embarrassed to take up arms at the approach of an insolence of lowerings that publicizes its movement as a "liberation."[75] In either case, raising or lowering, authority, in its moral range, is always present and invariably presides over our lives; this remains so, even in the modernist conceit of identifying downward, as if that downward identification were somehow anti-authoritarian.

Notes

1. George Bernard Shaw, *The Complete Plays* (New York: Dodd, Mead, 1971), p. 80.

2. But see *Measure for Measure,* II, ii, 118.

3. Sigmund Freud, "Repression," in *The Complete Psychological Works of Sigmund Freud, Standard Edition* (London: Hogarth Press, 1953–), XIV, 148.

4. Freud, "The Ego and the Id," in *Standard Edition,* XIX, 18.

5. Ibid.

6. In Freud's negational symbolic, the symbol is what it represents. So instinct and its vicissitudes represent the primacy of possibility. Secondary imaginative processes suffer complete inversion. What is primacy becomes secondary and vice versa. On Freud's inversive

inability to lay down, in his theory of repression, a general rule of a little more or less in sacred order, those necessary degrees of distortion and remoteness by which self, in its artfulness, is constituted as our continuous address in sacred order, to it: See Freud, "Repression," p. 150 *et pass*. The papers of 1915 are specially important in working through Freud's negational recognitions of sacred order. See Freud, "Repression," pp. 117–307.

7. Even in the *Standard Edition*, Freud was not entirely well served by his English translators. I have always considered that "unconscious," so far as it renders *unbewusst*, conceals more than it reveals.

8. Samuel Taylor Coleridge, *Biographia Literaria* (London: G. Bell, 1905), p. 144. I cannot probe, here, the relations between Coleridgean primary and secondary imagination and Freudian conscious and unconscious. Coleridge's Chap. 13 will be familiar to my readers.

9. Freud, *Standard Edition*, XVIII, 29.

10. Ibid., p. 29.

11. Ibid.

12. Ibid. p. 30.

13. Ibid.

14. Ibid., pp. 30–31.

15. Ibid.

16. Ibid., p. 33.

17. Ibid., p. 35.

18. Ibid.; Freud's italics.

19. Ibid.; Freud's italics.

20. Ibid.; Freud's italics.

21. Ibid., p. 39.

22. Ibid., p. 40.

23. Ibid., p. 42.

24. Ibid., p. 44.

25. Ibid.

26. Ibid., p. 50. I shall deal directly and briefly with sublimation later in this essay; that demigod term seems to me a polite negation of obediences in sacred order. (See pp. 236–237, 242–243.

27. Ibid., p. 42; my italics.

28. Ibid.; my italics.

29. Ibid.

30. Ibid., p. 43.

31. Ibid., p. 36.

32. Edward Conze, *Buddhist Texts through the Ages* (Oxford: B. Cassirer, 1954), p. 95.

33. Freud, *Standard Edition*, XVIII, 63.

34. See, on the parallel of spiritual life as it is being "watched over by the danger of death," and the "danger of [an individual's] decisive action," Søren Kierkegaard's *The Present Age* (New York: Harper Torchbooks, 1962), p. 37.

35. Freud, *Standard Edition*, XIX, 53.

36. Ibid., p. 52.

37. Ibid.; my italics.

38. Ibid., p. 27.

39. Ibid., p. 53.

40. Ibid., p. 54.

41. Ibid.

42. Ibid.

43. Ibid.

44. Ibid.

45. Franz Kafka, "In the Penal Colony," in *The Complete Stories* (New York: Schocken Books, 1972), pp. 140–167.

46. John Henry Cardinal Newman, *An Essay in Aid of A Grammar of Assent* (New York: Image Books, 1958), p. 293 (1st ed.; 1870).

47. Freud, *Standard Edition,* XIX, 54–55.

48. Ibid., p. 55.

49. Ibid., p. 38.

50. Ibid., p. 56.

51. Ibid., p. 56; my italics.

52. Ibid.

53. Ibid., p. 58.

54. Ibid.

55. Ibid.

56. Kafka, "In the Penal Colony," p. 145.

57. Ibid., p. 167.

58. Ibid.

59. See Émile Durkheim, *The Elementary Forms of Religious Life,* tr. J. W. Swain (Glencoe, Ill.: Free Press, n.d.), pp. 299–307 *et pass.* Freud likens "a general taboo" to "a Papal Interdict." These "prohibitions are mainly directed against liberty of enjoyment" (Freud, *Standard Edition,* XIII, 21).

60. Johan Huizinga, *In the Shadow of Tomorrow,* tr. J. H. Huizinga from the Dutch (New York: W. W. Norton & Co., 1936), pp. 44–45.

61. See *Politics,* VIII.

62. *Philebus,* 26c. Some praise of the political meaning of "law and order" seems in order here. The monarchical principle is the best political expression of law and order wherever a heterogenous association of people have nothing else necessarily in common except submission to one sovereign power. A king rules according to law; that is his fundamental distinction. Despots, tyrants, modern totalitarian rulers—none of them rule according to law, which is nothing if not a stipulation of the interdictory.

63. Lionel Trilling, *Beyond Culture* (New York: Harcourt, Brace, Jovanovich, 1963), pp. 57–87.

64. Ibid., p. 76.

65. Wallace Stevens, "Esthétique du Mal," in *Collected Poems* (New York: Alfred A. Knopf, 1976), pp. 313–326.

66. Ibid.

67. Hamlet knows and does not know, that those who will "nose" the body of Polonius, should it not soon be found, will also nose his own deed. 4.3.34–39. Hamlet's act is itself lowering, however cleverly he talks about it. After Hamlet, there have been veritable armies of young men who have declared, specially in the most warring moments of their lives, specially if they are caught into a war, that: "I don't know what to think. . . . The world's rotten" (Ford Maddox Ford, "No More Parades," in *Parades End* [New York, Alfred A. Knopf, 1961], p. 304). In Hamlet, above all other addresses to sacred order, the question is raised, in Tietjen's truest last words, whether "the game is worth more than the player" (Ford, "No More Parades," p. 305). God intended Prince Hamlet for Intelligence, as He intended animals for Innocence, and "not for the footslogging department," where real wars are always fought (ibid., p. 307). The intellectualizing, and consequent abstraction, of the Western imagination spells the real tragedy of Western culture.

68. Hamlet, II, ii, 231.

69. Ibid., I, iv, 36.

70. Friedrich Nietzsche, *The Will to Power,* no. 852, "The Tragic Artist," tr. Walter Kaufmann and R. J. Hollingdale (New York: Vintage, 1968), p. 450. "It is the *heroic* spirits who say yes to themselves in tragic cruelty; they are hard enough to experience suffering as a *pleasure.*"

71. Cf. Philip Rieff, *Freud: The Mind of the Moralist* (New York: Doubleday Anchor, 1961), pp. 316–317.

72. Ibid.

73. Freud, *Standard Edition,* XI, 49. Cf. Garry Watson, "The Impossible Culture . . . ," *The Compass* (Winter 1979), p. 52.

74. Cf. Titian's "Sacred and Profane Love." "God creates out of nothing, but here, if I dare say so, He does more by clothing an instinct with the beauty of love, so that the lovers see only the beauty and are unaware of the instinct. Who would dare to do that? The ideal beauty is the veiled beauty and . . . the sea by its half-transparency tempts only half so strongly as the . . . wife through the veil of modesty." Søren Kierkegaard, *Stages on Life's Way* (New York: Schocken, 1967), pp. 125–126.

75. Cf. *Laws,* 671d.